D1478405

NSFW

NSFW

Sex, Humor, and Risk in Social Media

Susanna Paasonen, Kylie Jarrett, and Ben Light

The MIT Press
Cambridge, Massachusetts
London, England

© 2019 Massachusetts Institute of Technology

All rights reserved. No part of this book may be reproduced in any form by any electronic or mechanical means (including photocopying, recording, or information storage and retrieval) without permission in writing from the publisher.

This book was set in Stone Serif and Stone Sans by Jen Jackowitz. Printed and bound in the United States of America.

Library of Congress Cataloging-in-Publication Data is available.

Names: Paasonen, Susanna, 1975- author. | Jarrett, Kylie, author. | Light, Ben, author.
Title: NSFW : sex, humor, and risk in social media / Susanna Paasonen, Kylie Jarrett, and Ben Light.
Other titles: #Not safe for work
Description: Cambridge, MA : The MIT Press, 2019. | Includes bibliographical references and index.
Identifiers: LCCN 2019001446 | ISBN 9780262043052 (hardcover : alk. paper)
Subjects: LCSH: Computer sex.
Classification: LCC HQ23 .P33 2019 | DDC 306.70285--dc23 LC record available at https://lccn.loc.gov/2019001446

10 9 8 7 6 5 4 3 2 1

Contents

Acknowledgments

We would like to thank the scholarly community of the Association of Internet Researchers both for bringing the authors together a decade or so ago and for facilitating dialogues on the topic of this book over the years. In particular, we would like to thank Nathan Rambukkana, Jenny Sundén, and Katrin Tiidenberg for contributing to our NSFW panel at the 2017 Association of Internet Researchers conference in Tartu, Estonia, and the audience of that particular session—including, but not limited to, Crystal Abidin, Tarleton Gillespie, and Michael Petit—for their comments and suggestions. Part of the initial planning of this book was made possible by Susanna's 2015–2016 sabbatical grant from the Jenny and Antti Wihuri Foundation, which also made it possible to discuss the early stages of the project with the Microsoft Research New England's Social Media Collective in the spring of 2016.

We would like to dedicate this book to Britney Spears, whose live performance of *Work Bitch* in Las Vegas, October 28, 2015, culminated the writing retreat during which we coined our book prospectus.

1   Introduction: NSFW as Warning and Invitation

The Internet slang term and social media tag NSFW—"Not Safe/Suitable for Work"—is widely used in Anglophone contexts (and beyond) to organize and regulate sexual content and pornographic imagery, often in connection with humor. The online information resource Know Your Meme has tracked the emergence of NSFW to the social news aggregator site Fark in the year 2000. On Fark, the disclaimer "Not safe for work. Not safe period" first accompanied a link to the Stile Project, a site famous for its galleries of gross-out imagery, shock porn, and explicit violence. The term was gradually adopted on Usenet, and, by 2005, websites were dedicated to NSFW content (Know Your Meme 2013). As a classifier, NSFW resonated among newsgroup users before becoming applied by commercial platforms and growing ubiquitous within social media as both a warning and a lure.

Coined before the rise of Web 2.0 and the era of personal portable devices, the tag points to content not assumed safe for consumption, or indeed production, in workplaces and in the context of work, independent of what these may be. At the heart of NSFW lies the notion of unsafety connected to the risk of losing one's job or social status, yet, as we argue in the chapters to follow, it also extends to an unspecified sense of risk in connection with sexually explicit media content and sexual communication more generally. Unlike media content markers such as "sexually explicit content," NSFW does not identify the representational properties of the images, posts, or video files to which it is primarily applied. Rather, the tag marks sexuality, pornography, and a range of bodily displays as lacking in safety in a markedly abstract, and hence obscure, vein. A similar decontextualized application of the notions of safety and risk where these are reduced to properties of specific media content is evident, for example, in Google's SafeSearch mode, which seeks to exclude sexually explicit hits. This practice of conflating safety with the filtering of sexual content both builds on and bolsters an understanding of sex and sexuality as inherently risky, potentially harmful, and best hidden away and left unmentioned. Our interests lie in unpacking the logics within which this conflation occurs and in offering alternative ways of understanding the distribution of safety and risk connected to social media.

As we shall show, given the tag's virtually exclusive uses in the context of sex, other forms of content that for good reasons can be deemed risky or problematic—such as those connected to sexist harassment and racial violence—readily fall outside its reach (see also Tiidenberg, n.d.). This is striking, given that these forms of communication are considered unsafe at/ for work in the sense of being addressed by specific harassment and equal opportunity policies. Meanwhile, excessively violent content is occasionally, albeit much less routinely, tagged and bracketed out with the related term NSFL, "Not Safe for Life," on platforms such as Reddit (Massanari 2015, 132). The limitations of what falls under the rubric of NSFW media then raise particular questions about the kinds of cultural work being done by this labeling.

Despite, or perhaps precisely because of, its connotations of risk, NSFW is also intimately tied in with humor and the quest for diversion, amusement, and titillation. Like the Stile Project, the tag of NSFW appeals as much as it averts, and it titillates as much as it repulses. In the economy of links, shares, likes, and mentions that drive social media, NSFW content is both risky in the disapproval and flagging it may evoke and highly lucrative in the eyeballs that it captures and the affective quavers it manages to evoke. Presenting content marked out as risqué, the NSFW tag seeks to generate instant attention value. Furthermore, as Katrin Tiidenberg (n.d.) notes, "the choice to heed to the tag—to obscure or ignore—is *temporary*. It's not rejection, but postponement. Warning becomes a *promise*; apprehension morphs into excitement." That is, if certain content is not considered suitable for viewing at work, it can be viewed during a break, on a personal device, or after working hours and thus can be treated as something to look forward to.

Underpinning these considerations is the broader sense that work can be made unsafe when it intersects with social media. NSFW, in its association with data flows tapping into the dynamics of attention and attraction, contributes to that which Jodi Dean (2009, 26, 2010) defines as communicative capitalism. The excessive flow of posts and messages in networked digital systems creates potential risks of unwanted exposure and reputation management, just as it allows for the expansion of sexual expression, political commentary, and humorous exchanges. The rapid diffusion of Internet-enabled mobile devices and the penetration of the workplace with both personal and occupational information mean that these diffuse data flows have become deeply entangled with what we do at work and how we do it. Organizations and individuals aim to manage the tensions that this intersection produces, and especially those that occur when personal communicative styles and contents meet the more controlled spaces of work. At the same time, social media can allow for greater agency, and indeed safety, through the horizontal communication channels evading organizational control that it provides for coworkers and colleagues. Consequently, the marker NSFW not only highlights particular kinds of social media content but also draws our attention to the interconnections of sex, humor, and risk within labor environments.

Through an exposition of its interpretive flexibility and agency, in this book we set out to do three key things with the social media tag NSFW:

First, we track the tag's different uses and functions in contemporary social media and analyze its role in drawing boundaries of acceptability.

Second, we consider how the NSFW tag seeks to invite certain kinds of encounters with online content.

Third, we propose additional meaning for NSFW by taking the term literally and using it as a framing device to explore the changing contours of risk, safety, and work in a landscape shaped by digital media and networked communications.

In mapping and conceptualizing NSFW, we chart its different roles in platform politics and in practices of social media governance. With notable exceptions such as the Chinese Tencent QQ (est. 1999), Baidu Tieba (est. 2003), Qzone (est. 2005), Sina Weibo (est. 2009), and WeChat (est. 2011), or the Russian VKontakte (est. 2006), the most broadly used social media and instant messaging services all originate from, and remain based in, the United States. For reasons of clarity and pragmatism, this book focuses on U.S.-based, internationally operating platforms. As these social media services have been rendered available in, or are used for communication in, a range of languages, the notion of NSFW has gained cross-linguistic under-standability even in contexts where its uses remain limited to the platforms in question. That is, NSFW makes sense on Reddit and Facebook, indepen-dent of the language of communication, but may not necessarily resonate beyond them in languages other than English.

In what follows, we examine early Web history, prototrolling practices, and nonmobile computer cultures in order to chart the continuities and transformations that NSFW, as contextual metadata, involves. Through this, we demonstrate how the meanings of the tag have become stabilized since the early 2000s in practices of work and play alike, and how online sexual content has been managed and governed at different points in time. This does not involve a chronological approach either across this volume or within its individual chapters. Moving back and forth between the contem-porary moment and the past, we ground recent developments in order to avoid the kind of historical myopia that easily looms close when examining the so-called new media and its emergent trends. In the following sections we briefly expand on each of the three key themes and contributions of *Not Safe for Work*.

The Classification and Boundary Work of NSFW

NSFW is first and foremost engaged with as metadata to classify online con-tent, to flag and filter it out, to orient user attention, to aid searchability, and to profile sites as brands that offer particular kinds of content. These practices build on, and feed, assumptions concerning the role and position of sexuality, safety, and risk in communicative practices. While NSFW clas-sifies media on the basis of its imagined suitability for the contexts of work, classification and rating systems to demarcate content deemed appropri-ate for different audiences have historically been based on age. Age limit, parental guidance, and advisory notifications have long worked to separate materials suitable for adults from that which should be consumed by chil-dren for the reason that some media content may be harmful to their devel-opment. Established in 1912, The British Board of Film Censors (currently The British Board of Film Classification) set in place the film categories of U–Universal, A–Adult, and, in 1932, H–Horrific. The X rating was first intro-duced in 1951 to mark content suitable for those aged 16 and over and, since 1970, for those above 18. In the United States, the four-tier Motion Picture

Association of America rating system was introduced in 1968 as the film industry's system of self-regulation. Divided into G for general audiences, PG for parental guidance, R for restricted, and X for adults only, the system was centrally concerned with displays of nudity, sexuality, and violence.

The introduction of the X rating to indicate the presence of gratuitous or excessive degrees of sex and violence soon led to the distribution of print advertisements and trailers for films thus classified, as well as to these films being barred from network television (Friedman 1973). Ratings limit potential audiences in ways that can, in the case of "adults only" ratings like X or the currently used NC-17, be financially disadvantageous. At the same time, adult ratings involve a considerable degree of allure, affording media products a scent of forbidden fruit. Porn producers and distributors soon appropriated the X rating and embraced it by devising their own hyperbolic marker of "XXX." XXX was, from the beginning, an advertising ploy promising truly explicit action for a firmly adult audience, yet one that gradually grew synonymous with hardcore pornography (Yang and Linz 1990, 28). By the year 2008 when the fashion brand Diesel marked its thirtieth anniversary with the video "SFW XXX," the humor involved in combining the marker "XXX" with the much newer notion "Safe for Work" was recognizable enough to help the video toward some of its intended viral circulation. Consisting of 1980s hardcore porn clips covered with nonexplicit animated effects that turned oral sex into voracious corn eating and penetrative sex into horseback riding, the promotional clip poked fun at the excessive gestures of vintage video porn. With its flirtation with the visually trashy and the culturally low, the video contributed to edgy brand building and invited sharing well beyond Diesel's factual clientele.

The term NSFW involves similar affective dynamics of risk and attraction, warning and promise, to those connected with the X rating, or the more informal marker of XXX. As Tarleton Gillespie (2013) points out, this "checkpoint" approach for dealing with so-called inappropriate media content is akin to strategies such as "putting the X-rated movies in the back room at the video store, putting the magazines on the shelf behind the counter, wrapped in brown paper, scheduling the softcore stuff on Cinemax after bedtime, or scrambling the adult cable channel." In this sense, NSFW marks out the boundaries of permissible sexual content in services that mainly define their community standards according to morally conservative, corporate definitions of appropriate media content.

It is possible for platforms, for instance, to limit the searchability of content tagged as NSFW even when they allow users to share and access it (see also chapter 2). The previously Yahoo!-owned microblogging platform Tumblr (est. 2007, currently owned by a subsidiary of Verizon) was long known for the presence of diverse sexual cultures and pornographic and NSFW blogs (see chapter 4), yet created new accounts in "safe mode" by default. Even if users turned the setting off, sexual content did not appear in search results unless they also clicked on a small lock symbol embedded in the interface. In December 2018, Tumblr changed its content policy, forbidding all adult content, and removed blogs not compatible with the new community standards. For its part, Twitter, discussed in more detail in the following chapter, makes use of the somewhat euphemistic category of "sensitive" content as that which users may opt for either seeing or not. Tim Highfield (2016, 23) notes, "A framing like NSFW attempts to balance what is and is not 'accepted' in society and on platforms, acknowledging its inappropriateness for conservative environments but still sharing the content." As the example of Tumblr nevertheless illustrates, social media platforms increasingly simply exclude nudity and pornography from their service, leaving NSFW to connote sexually suggestive, rather than explicit, content.

Social media content is largely categorized, curated, filtered, flagged, organized, and screened by users and/or algorithms but also with interventions from volunteer and professional moderators. All this leads to instability in how, and with what kinds of motives, things get tagged and flagged, and how the ensuing boundaries of acceptability are being drawn (see also Gillespie 2013).

NSFW as an Engagement Device

Our second point is that NSFW acts as an engager. Via its explicit references to safety and work, NSFW creates engagements by playfully drawing on, and constructing, divisions and juxtapositions between the practices and spaces of labor and leisure, things considered professional and personal, public and private. Yet these spaces, contexts, and activities, blurred as they always have been, have grown ever more difficult to pry apart from one another. Work tasks are managed and escaped from on the same device as people move between different screens, applications, windows, and user accounts for purposes both occupational and decidedly not. And as people befriend and follow their colleagues, acquaintances, intimate friends, and virtual strangers on social media, the intended audiences for posts become blurred. Contexts collapse, occasionally in awkward ways—and not least so when it comes to sexual content (Collins 2013; Duguay 2016; Marwick and boyd 2011). A post perceived as plain funny by some can be highly offensive to others while even allusions to one's sexual preferences, likes, and routines can evoke friction and discrimination at the workplace or breach regulations and policies related to equality or harassment. The marker NSFW is one solution for managing the circulation of edgy humor and sexual content in this context by orienting the reader to ways of approaching it.

Like contextual metadata more generally, the tag NSFW connects images, posts, texts, links, and videos under a category, makes them searchable, and builds expectations as to their content. Tags are "multiple, open-ended, and contingent phenomena" (Rambukkana 2015b, 5) speaking to assumed audiences, both drawing from and building assumptions about values. For instance, the current applications of NSFW on image-based social media services such as Instagram and Pinterest have little connection with the term's initial uses in the context of the Stile Project's extreme gross-out and shock content (see Paasonen 2011, 226–230). Since both of these image-sharing services firmly exclude pornography and violence, the marker NSFW is used to mark out selfies involving degrees of undress and sexual flirtation, drawings and paintings featuring degrees of nudity or sex, as well as pictures of donut holes, flowers, and handbags seen as playfully humorous in their sexually suggestiveness. Such playful, flexible, and context-bound applications of NSFW speak of the tag's default familiarity, as well as its malleability in orienting attention and creating expectation.

With its conflation of sex and risk, the tag NSFW comes with specific affective stickiness of anticipation and apprehension, illustrating how "neo-conservative values frame and monitor interaction and the objects and ideas around which interaction takes place" (Payne 2014, 4). Whether this be in the form of a Twitter hashtag, an e-mail header in an exchange between friends, or a definition of a genre of WordPress blog identified as "mature," NSFW works as a barrier against inappropriate communication while also proclaiming its own juiciness as a form of advertisement, capturing user attention and fueling the flows of data upon which the contemporary social media economy relies. The tag protects the sender from losses in status or censure that might otherwise result from breaches of social convention. It also protects the communication from negative, challenging, or toxic intensities such as those associated with trolls, haters, or flamers by framing content as humorous or risqué.

NSFW as a Framing Device

The third point of this book is to engage NSFW as a mechanism for understanding the conditions of work as they interact with digital media technologies. We suggest that, as a framing device, NSFW allows for critical analyses of the governance of sexuality on social media; the affective ecologies connected to titillation, humor, and risk; the political economy of social media; as well as occupational and workplace safety in a context where these spaces are both physical and of the more virtual kind.

Here, our analysis broadens into the regulation of online content in contexts of work, as well as into the different ways in which labor that is shaped by social media is undercut by risks of unsafety. Setting NSFW in the broader context of online economies, we address the different forms of work that go into the creation and management of content—from commercial content filtering to the transformations in the work of online pornography as an expansive part of the information technology (IT) sector—and explore instances where digital labor itself turns unsafe through harassment when privacy and personal security are compromised. This line of inquiry expands into analysis of the political economy of digital labor in a framework where social hierarchies and divides limit agencies and careers in explicit, occasionally violent ways.

That the social media environment is unable to be contained to times of leisure or play also means that NSFW content has a wide social—as well as economic—impact in the realm of labor, from the nonpaid, voluntary work of social media users to the poorly compensated, heavy service of outsourced commercial content moderators; the gig economy of porn and online sex work; the precarious, yet lucrative, careers of social media influencers; the IT professions connected to porn aggregators sites, clickbaits, and other online platforms; as well as the range of work that algorithms perform. Making use of NSFW as a framing device to unpack these interconnections, we illustrate the complexity of the notion of safety connected to work in the context of social media as one concerning bodily integrity and violations thereof; moral and symbolic breaches of proper demeanor;

the circulation and intensity of online hate; and the risks and insecurities connected to income, careers, and reputation. Such a contextual take on social media safety, while crucial, is all too easily overshadowed by a straightforward focus on the accessibility, consumption, and qualities of online content.

The role of social media at work is far from being clear-cut or limited to the negative. Engagements with social media technologies may just as well render workplace environments more desirable, pleasurable, and manageable. This book explores the various ways in which both control and agency, as key components of occupational safety, emerge and take shape with social media. We also examine how the playfulness, desires, and frissons associated with the sharing of NSFW content are, in themselves, a vital part of the contemporary occupational realm. Factoring in the libidinal economy of social media and workplaces by looking at risqué humor and people's negotiation of sexual relationships via hookup apps and dick pics, we set out to complicate understandings of the cultural and economic functions of NSFW content in occupational contexts.

Throughout our analysis of these various dimensions of NSFW media, we show that safety has, in myriad ways, become a euphemism for the policy of filtering out or limiting access to sexual content online. We further argue that this involves a sloppy conceptual conflation of safety with sexual nonexplicitness and, by extension, of riskiness with sex. At the same time, sexual content—from pornography to hookup apps and naked selfies—remains notably popular, ubiquitous, and even magnetic in its appeal among users of all kinds. We therefore argue for the importance of questioning the default, even exclusive association of risk with sexual content and the linking of unsafety with sexuality, as implied by the normative uses of the NSFW tag. In doing so, we make a case for shifting considerations of safety from the visibility or invisibility of nudity or the accessibility of sexually explicit content to more complex and critical considerations of consent, labor, governance, and pleasure connected to social media.

Outline: From Hashtags to Harassment

Taking the tag NSFW as a key focus and a broader framing device, this book investigates how sexuality and labor are articulated and managed with social media. We examine the different applications of NSFW on platforms such as Twitter, Facebook, Reddit, Tumblr, Instagram, and Pinterest and inquire after the boundaries of NSFW and "Safe for Work" (SFW) in contexts ranging from social media coverage of porn sites' publicity stunts to sexual humor at the workplace, and the multiple applications of user-generated dick pics as a form of vernacular NSFW content. But we also extend the focus beyond the tag itself by deploying the term's phrasing literally to explore the interconnections of work and safety in networked media. In doing this, we engage with debates on work, labor, and social media and connect them with the equally pertinent examinations of sexually explicit content, privacy, and safety online through a range of empirically grounded examples. We ask what is meant by both work and safety when tagging things NSFW and what needs to be learned from such acts of boundary maintenance.

We start with a contextual analysis of the tag and hashtag NSFW and acts of regulation and filtering in social media services. Chapter 2 provides a historical overview of the development and diverse role of tags, hashtags, and other digital content moderating techniques before zooming in on the functions of #NSFW on social media. The chapter involves a multimethod exploration ranging from Twitter data analysis to the study of social media services' community standards and terms of use, and an inquiry into the multiple ways in which NSFW is deployed as a tool for governance. Focusing on practices of tagging and flagging, the chapter provides a highly concrete take on NSFW, its role and overall presence.

In chapter 3, we move to address pornography, the key media genre and content category to be tagged as NSFW and which is occasionally conflated with the term itself. Online pornography is both ubiquitous in its popularity and constantly screened off from social media. The chapter focuses on these contradictory pulls, exploring the brand-building efforts and SFW publicity stunts of the key porn video aggregator site, Pornhub, as well as the uses of social media in the management of porn celebrity in what has quintessentially grown into a gig economy. Further examining the business and labor of contemporary online pornography, we address its increased dependency on the technical backbone of aggregator sites. In this context, the labor of porn extends to running servers and the design of information architecture as much as it does the production of pornographic content as such, leading to the questions of how the labor of porn is being redefined from risky to safe, where its risks may lie, and how the work of porn is performed by algorithms, as well as how the cultural role and position of pornography may be shifting as it intersects with digital technologies.

Building upon chapter 3's concern with what is often seen as troublesome matter and how it may be rendered safe, visible, or invisible, chapter 4 focuses on user-generated NSFW content in the framework of social media's visual attention economy. Starting with a discussion of sexually explicit viral gross-out humor and its displays of male bodies, we explore the gendered dynamics of shame, humor, and desire connected to the circulation of naked selfies in networked exchanges. The chapter's main focus is on the multiple uses, functions, and interpretations of a particular form of user-generated content—the dick pic. We ask how dick pics emerge as objects of aversion and attraction; as instruments of communication, self-representation, and hooking up; and as figures of violence, humor, harassment, and sexual desire in contexts both heterosexual and not. Expanding our analysis from considerations of dick pics as unsolicited tools for sexual harassment, we address Tumblr's dick pic galleries preceding the platform's current content policy and the presence of the visualized penis in hookup cultures of men who have sex with men. Emphasizing the diverse applications and functions of the dick pic, the chapter argues for shifting analytical focus from the fact of representational sexual explicitness to issues of consent, desire, agency, and social power in considerations of risk and safety in the context of social media.

In chapter 5, we extend the discussion of humor and sexual content into a workplace context. We examine the role of sex at work, and notions of safety and risk associated with this, before paying more detailed attention to the deployment of humor, particularly that of the risqué kind, in the workplace, considering its multiple purposes in terms of enabling productivity, participation, resistance, and the maintenance of hierarchies. We connect this line of inquiry to a consideration of the parameters of safety and risk involved in meeting sexual partners at work. Throughout, we explore the processes, structures, and political economy of making people safe for work through the regulation of sexual media content. More specifically, we attend to the deployment of policies that seek to block and regulate social media use at spaces of work and which, contradictorily, allow for the surveillance of current and potential employees. Tied to this, we investigate the dirty work of NSFW via an analysis of the labor of commercial content moderators whose task it is to keep social media safe. Here, creating SFW conditions comprises an occupation. Following this, we consider the role of networked media in the context of sex work, an occupation decidedly enmeshed with questions of safety and risk. Overall, this chapter argues for the need to acknowledge diversity in occupational contexts and what this means for notions of risk and safety in relation to social media. We equally argue for the need to pay attention to issues of consent, reciprocity, and pleasure over blanket prescriptions of sexual abstinence and the erasure of sexual media content.

While chapter 5 focuses largely on physical workplaces, chapter 6 asks how the notions of safety, risk, and loss are articulated in relation to online harassment connected to careers managed with social media. We explore forms of digital labor that have turned unsafe. Focusing on instances of sexist and misogynistic harassment in particular, we address their ties to the logics of online geek culture, the cultural economy of the tech industry, and its wider political economy. In doing so, we frame the operations and risks of toxic masculinity as an issue of labor and socioeconomics. This involves an understanding of trolling, bullying, and harassment as forms of attention capture and as tools of governance that support and accelerate inequalities connected to gender, ethnicity, race, and sexuality. The complexity of what it actually is that makes work unsafe explored in this chapter highlights how reductive and simplistic it is to emphasize and control only social media's sexual content.

Combined, these strands of investigation, which are brought together in the concluding chapter 7, map out the multiple meanings and forms of NSFW, the appeal and risks of circulating sexual content and "on the edge" humor online, as well as the boundaries of professionalism and privacy that these entail. Our book builds on a range of media research methods generating empirical evidence about the sociotechnical assemblages of social media. These are underpinned by the strategic deployment of a science and technology studies–informed relational ontology that points to key moments of human and nonhuman agency in the workplaces of media industries and in the maintenance of communicative boundaries. It is in the context of the growth of attention to the nonhuman that this work is situated.

Our exploration of NSFW combines big data analysis with the multimodal analysis of specific social media materials from individual tweets to animated GIFs, Facebook posts, Pinterest boards, clickbait headlines, hookup apps, social media services' terms of use, and people's accounts of workplace regulation connected to online content, as well as media coverage of NSFW incidents in social media. Rather than focusing on any singular platform or user culture, our interest lies in the broader logics of NSFW within the attention economy of social media, its logics, routines of governance, control, and resistance. In conducting these analyses, we draw on a diverse palette of affect theory, feminist and queer theory, labor studies, cultural studies, porn studies, and a breadth of engagement with the field of Internet research both past and present.

Coined in 2000, NSFW became a legal adult in traditional, age-based media regulation terms at the time of finishing this book in 2018. NSFW continues to operate in the midst of a highly contradictory online culture that is, in the framework of social media and the broader uptake of Internet-enabled applications and devices, becoming increasingly governed and regulated. Counter to the continuing imperative of weeding out nudity and sexuality from social media in the name of unspecified user safety, toward which diverse content policies and filtering practices have been deployed, we argue for the value of things labeled NSFW—and indeed for the value of users being NSFW. Sexual cultures, desires, expressions, and identifications matter on levels both collective and social, and in ways irreducible to the profit mechanisms of pornography or the deployment of dick pics in campaigns of gendered harassment. Applied to all kinds of sexual images and formations, the tag NSFW flattens crucial differences between them under the opaque blanket of offensiveness, riskiness, and unsafety that it connotes. It nevertheless remains crucial to resist categorical effacement of sexually suggestive and explicit content if we are to envision social media ecologies capable of accommodating sexuality as a field of pleasure, communication, occupation, and world making.

Not Safe for Work builds on the argument that sex is not the problem in how platforms, exchanges, or careers grow unsafe. Rather, the notion of safety needs to be considered contextually as inseparable from consent within social media exchanges—be these ones connected to occupational practices, hookup encounters, or something entirely different. Sex may well be that which drives the motions and interests of people in online exchanges. Its default framing through notions of risk and unsafety both undermines the centrality of sexuality in people's lives and helps to hide from view the operations of power and practices of governance that affect these lives. Our critical analysis of the social media tag NSFW is a means of challenging these assumptions.

2   What's with the Tag?

NSFW is used both as tag and hashtag in combination with other metadata as a means to identify, mark, and possibly filter out social media content. It plays a key role in thread functionality where various nonhuman actors help to guide what is considered NSFW, SFW, and NSFL on the platform in question. This chapter examines the applications of the marker NSFW from Facebook to Twitter, Pinterest, Reddit, Instagram, Tumblr, and eBay, addressing their interconnectedness and multiplicity. This involves analyzing social media data both big and small, including community standards and terms of use governing the ascription of appropriateness to content. In order to understand the general logic of social media tags, and hashtags in particular, we map the emergence of tagging and governance practices in both social media and pre-Web online exchanges. Looking both backward and sideways, this chapter explores the shaping influences that have given rise to a tag like NSFW and its multiple applications across social media.

In this chapter, we also begin to trouble the links between sex, sexuality, naked bodies, and the assumption of unsafety that forms one of the key themes of this book. By exploring how NSFW specifically, and tagging and flagging more generally, work as mechanisms of governance, we can see their role in organizing connections between particular fragments of content and in managing relations between users, as well as identifying their more ideological functions. In particular, we place the hashtag's emergence in the context of increasingly corporate taxonomic organization that raises questions about the agendas that such tagging may serve. We begin by locating NSFW in the broader ecology of hashtags on and off Twitter.

The Functions of Hashtags

The use of the hash symbol combined with metadata about online content is usually traced to digital media consultant Chris Messina (2007) and his suggestion for its adoption on Twitter (Cohen and Kenny 2015; Gannes 2010). On August 23, 2007, he proposed that Twitter's users adopt the hash symbol—or pound symbol as it was called at the time—to create groups (see figure 2.1).

However, both tagging combined with metadata and the use of metadata without tags have been features of online communication long before the existence of Twitter and the popularization of the hash symbol prefix: hashtag signs were used in Internet Relay Chat (IRC) as early as 1998 to identify and mark out different channels (Gannes 2010; Rambukkana 2015a, 30). Adding metatextual features to aid navigation, filtering, or search takes and has taken various forms across the variety of digital media platforms. As such, tags and hashtags belong to a much broader metatextual ecology also encompassing keywords, categories, and breadcrumbs. Tags of various kinds are used to link messages, posts, names, and terms into longer meaning chains, but they also function as management tools within diverse social relationships and networks.

Even more importantly, tags are performative in how they give rise to configurations of images, social media updates, tweets, links, and users—to networks of actors both human and not. In some instances, tags configure

Figure 2.1
Chris Messina's 2007 tweet introducing the hashtag symbol.

communities by articulating their values, rules, and boundaries. At other times, no shared values and interests are to be identified. Writing on Twitter, Axel Bruns and Jean Burgess (2015, 20) point out that "at their simplest, hashtags are merely a search-based mechanism for collating all tweets sharing a specific textual attribute, without any implication that individual messages are responding to one another." Contingency of use, purpose, and effect is therefore central to the uses of hashtags. As Nathan Rambukkana (2015b, 5) notes, hashtags can be used to articulate "advertising campaigns, political platforms, social movements, smear campaigns, activist protests, harassment crusades, consumer products, and revolutions."

In light of this complexity, and in order to gain a broad, hands-on understanding of the current presence and uses of #NSFW, we collected a Twitter data set of 1,134,846 tweets using it both as hashtag and tag, from February 6 to March 2, 2017, with T-CAT (Borra and Rieder 2014). All tweets collected were then exported to a tab-separated value (TSV) file and processed using a JavaScript (Clausner 2017) to generate two extra data tables—one for mentions, replies, and retweets, and one for tags/hashtags. These files were imported into, and connected within, the Tableau analytics software package and the University of Salford's Big Content Machine (Light et al. 2017). This allowed us to explore which other hashtags the tag NSFW and the hashtag #NSFW were combined with, who used them, who got mentioned in these tweets, and how they were retweeted and mentioned.

This inquiry is, of course, partial in terms of the platform and the people involved: after all, only certain people from certain countries use Twitter. Furthermore, Twitter accounts and the people making them are two different things. Accounts may have single or multiple human users, or they may be operated by nonhuman bots—software applications that run automated or semi-automated tasks such as sending out repetitive tweets that have been estimated to generate a quarter of all Twitter traffic (Bucher 2014). Some users, human or not, can have several accounts and therefore be represented multiple times in any data set. Twitter accounts need not be operated by humans using their "real name" for a variety of reasons, such as the nature of the account they want to run, the nature of content they wish to engage with, the nature of their careers, or the risks faced by speaking publicly about certain matters (see Light 2014). The methods we have deployed also tell little about those Twitter users who have consumed content attached to a tweet but have not signaled this publicly. Such lurking, listening, and reading is a long-lived and extensive social media practice (Crawford 2009; Preece, Nonnecke, and Andrews 2004).

With these caveats in place, the data set we created shows that which is predictable and probably obvious: that NSFW on Twitter, like elsewhere in social media, is used to mark pornographic and sexual content. Figure 2.2 shows that the hashtag #NSFW and the tag NSFW are predominantly attached to pornographic imagery featuring women in a firmly heterosexual framework.

In our data set, it was most often combined with the tags #porn, #xxx, #bubble, #bath, #adult, #sex, #nude, #tits, #teen, #sexy, #naked, #hot, and #boob that consistently gesture toward the field of straight mainstream porn and its commonly used search terms. The high frequency of the tags #bubble and #bath, neither of which have much general currency in pornographic vocabulary, was due to their relentless use by bots during the data collection period. These tweets aimed to lead users to an Indonesian beauty and relationships clickbait site. Notably, the second most popular hashtag is actually the tag NSFW, with no use of the # attached to this term. While this tag may, of course, be combined in tweets that contain other

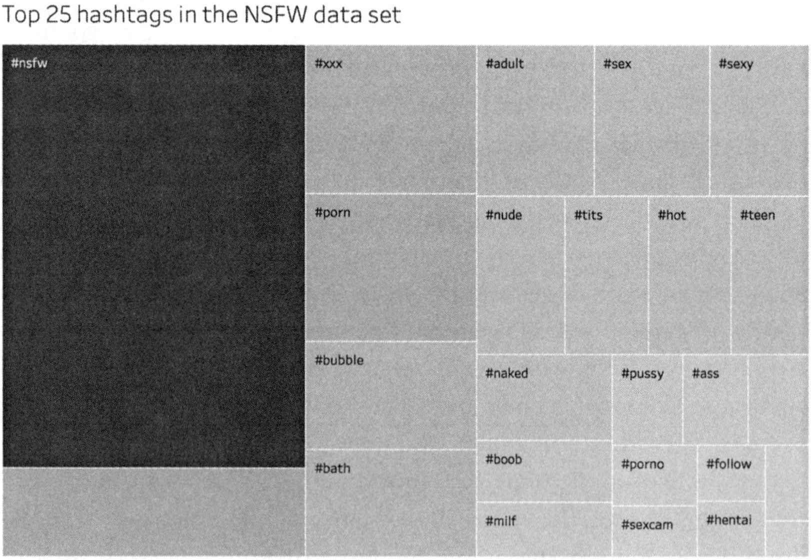

Top 25 hashtags in the NSFW data set

Figure 2.2
Top 25 hashtags in the NSFW data set.

hashtags, the 191,783 uses of the tag are interesting for their lack of the # and its associated functionalities.

Hashtag Publics and NSFW Bots

Although Twitter tries to weed out bots, they are in broad use for the purposes of generating attention and increasing visibility for various content providers. In the context of #NSFW, their presence is simply striking. The ten most active accounts using the hashtag #NSFW in the data set in terms of tweets, retweets, and mentions combined—which comprised 11.5 percent of the overall traffic studied—were mostly bots. Such nonhuman engagements with #NSFW, massive in scale, involve interaction between bots that amp up the visibility of posts and the volume of communication with the aim of reaching the broadest groups of users possible. In most instances, the URLs circulated within the tweets lead to profiles on pay camera sites, one of the few remaining forms of sexually explicit content for which users are ready to pay given the abundance of freely available video clips that has eaten away at the porn industry's profit margins (see chapter 3). Two of the most active ten accounts advertised the rather unknown video aggregator site, Unyporn, with others linking to pay sites such as Xcams, Boldflirts, Webcamporn, and Slutroulette.

#NSFW is, in sum, a popular hashtag among Twitter bots. Meanwhile, porn studios, porn sites, and porn performers promoting their work on Twitter do not extensively make use of the hashtag. Globally leading porn video aggregator sites such as Pornhub and xVideos do not necessarily use any tags in their tweets. For their part, gay and queer pornographies resort to more specific tags when promoting their visibility, from the #Gay, #GayPorn, #GaySex, #GayHot, and #GayHunk deployed by Men.com to the #trans, #transmen, and #community used by the trans male porn star Buck Angel. User accounts focused on sexual subcultures, such as kink role-play in a noncommercial framework, do not always use tags, both because their focus is too defined and obvious for their followers to have much use for them, and because outsider attention aided by metadata is not necessarily welcomed. While the Twitter accounts themselves are routinely labeled NSFW, this broad use does not fully extend to tweeting.

Our data set clearly points out the specificities in how #NSFW gets applied on Twitter. By doing so, it pushes us to consider some of the general terms in which hashtags are discussed in social media literature. As Dhiraj Murthy (2013, 3) notes, on Twitter the hashtag is a simple but effective mechanism for "connecting tweets to larger themes, specific people, and groups" and is "an integral part of Twitter's ability to link conversations of strangers together." Whether an activated hashtag or a static label, a tag can unite texts and, in doing so, enroll its authors and others into a wider conversation. Tagging may thus allow for the formation of communities and publics, both ad hoc and calculated, around a particular theme, topic, or event (Bruns and Burgess 2015, 23–25). Consequently, scholars have been interested in the role that hashtags play in the networked spread and resonance of political news and activist Twitter campaigns. This making of publics, however, is not necessarily the function of all hashtags, as exemplified by the uses of our specific hashtag of interest.

In our data set, #NSFW involves no temporal element connected to a particular event. It is used centrally for identifying the quality and nature of (typically) visual content and/or providing links to content on sites other than Twitter, rather than for assembling people in networks of exchange of any endurance. #NSFW does not so much evoke, sustain, or link together conversations as it marks out, highlights, warns, and advertises sexual content in Twitter exchanges. The hashtag is not efficient or active in the construction of publics: furthermore, in our analysis, the most active user accounts deploying the hashtag are run by bots spewing out automated tweets, mentions, and retweets at more or less regular intervals, often in excessive volume. These bots are "old school" in that automated posting involving high volumes of content generation, together with the random following of user accounts in order to grow the social circle, was characteristic of early social media bots. This also made them easy to identify in comparison to more sophisticated social bots that can make use of Web searches, engage in conversation, and produce semiotically and contextually meaningful responses through natural language–generation algorithms (Ferrara et al. 2016, 99–100). The bots in our data set follow generic patterns in their duplicate tweet structures and content by, for example, sharing a link to the same URL over and over again, using a different image and different mentions but an identical line of hashtags. The advertised content may or may not match the images, mentions, or tags used, the main point being to attract curious clickers.

The account most actively deploying the hashtag #NSFW in the data set was operated by a bot relentlessly sending the same identical tweet linking to a nonexistent YouTube video. Set up in January 2017, the account had, by late March, generated a total of some 154,000 tweets and 154,000 photos and videos but had only seven followers. On May 9, we took a further screen grab (figure 2.3): at that point the profile was doing exactly the same thing, although the bot had now generated 231,000 tweets, photos, and videos and had lost two followers. In other words, the account kept on sending messages with no communicative or social value into a vacuum.

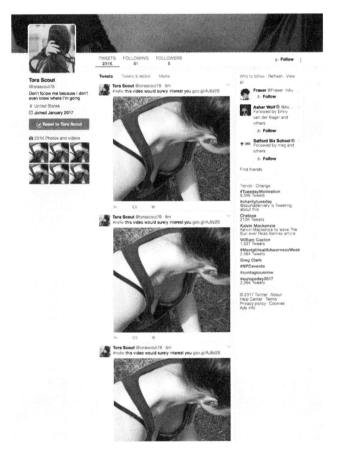

Figure 2.3
Bot-like Twitter account serving only identical duplicate tweets.

While some of the other bots had more impressive groups of followers, the exchanges they engaged in with retweets and mentions were overwhelmingly to accounts run by other bots.

Furthermore, the ratio of tweets, retweets, and mentions in the whole data set was particular in the sense that interactions remained passive and the number of individual user names mentioned or retweeted was notably low. Tweeting comprised 61.5 percent of all activity (697,298 original tweets in total). The 133,402 mentions were only to 27,718 accounts and some mentions kept on repeating in ways suggestive of bot activity. The 389,130 retweets were similarly from only 13,102 accounts, many of them these being retweeting bots programmed to generate traffic. Other interactions, such as likes, remained equally low (figure 2.4).

On the whole, interactions between users—both human and nonhuman—connected to the hashtag #NSFW were repetitive, and the tweeting activities remained notably insular. Most tweets did not spread, and those that did seemed not to have much reach at all. In the light of this specific data set, as a hashtag public, #NSFW would seem to be a failing one.

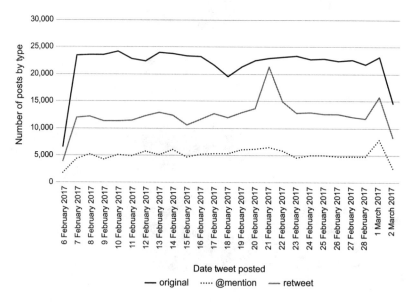

Figure 2.4
Retweets and @mentions of tweets containing NSFW. *Note: n* = 1,134,846.

The somewhat dysfunctional applications of the tag further suggest that it is too general to work either in the promotion of pornographic content or in the maintenance of sexual subcultures and communities. As a general means of content classification, NSFW fails to communicate much nuance and is mostly deployed in connection with other similarly generic, general tags, such as #porn, #xxx, and #sex that, while broadly used by bots and porn studios alike, are equally inefficient as search terms for those looking for particular kinds of image and videos. This is central since, with the emergence of tagging and uses of other contextual metadata, pornographic taste cultures, subgenres, and preferences have grown increasingly articulate since the mid-1990s.

Hashtag Genealogies

By the time of Messina's suggestion to adopt them in tweets, the use of metadata to organize content, to render it searchable, and to create complex meta-texts was already widespread in social media: indeed, the generic qualities of online exchanges were profoundly social in their causes, forms, and effects well before the popularization of the term social media (see also Marlow et al. 2006). Prior to the proliferation of Twitter hashtags, tagging had particular purchase in image-sharing platforms such as Flickr (est. 2004) and porn link sites such as Gigagalleries (est. 2003). Textual description of image content attached by a user, advertiser, or any other party was vital to rendering images findable in the absence of viable image search functions. In the case of pornographic content, the uses of metadata for the purposes of indexing and search gradually resulted in the identification of an unprecedented taxonomy of subgenres, sexual preferences, acts, bodily aesthetics, body parts, locations, toys, props, performance styles, motions, and countries and contexts of origin, allowing for choices between them (Chun 2006, 106; Paasonen 2011, 38). Consequently, metadata worked to tease out inner divisions, categories, and distinctions connected to sexual cultures and fantasies within the broad media genre of pornography. No such nuance comes with the tag NSFW when used in isolation.

Tagging practices serve various other functions in addition to the generation of publics. As descriptive metadata, tags work like keywords in library catalogues, pulling out particular features of a text, making them visible and, subsequently, more salient. Yet tags are not merely functional or neutral in that they equally add, orient, and even subvert meaning. Tagging was a feature of social bookmarking or indexing sites such as Del.icio.us (est. 2003) and CiteULike (est. 2004) where users would bookmark and annotate websites and other online resources. These tags collated content under particular themes or topics for later access but were also shared, allowing others to retrieve or add material to each tag. In their study of Del.icio.us, Scott A. Golder and Bernardo A. Huberman (2006) noted that collaborative tagging had more purposes than facilitating information retrieval. They described seven functions:

1. Identifying the content of the material (what or who it is about)
2. Identifying the nature of the resource (e.g., article, blog, news)
3. Identifying ownership (e.g., name of blogger, authors)
4. Refining categories (e.g., by adding to existing tags)
5. Indicating qualitative aspects of the resource (e.g., humor, scary)
6. Referring to self (the relationship of the material to the tagger)
7. Indicating tasks (e.g., toread, toprint)

Following this schema, #NSFW can be placed in category 1 as the content thus marked tends to involve degrees of explicitness in the depiction of human bodies and their sexual interactions. It can also be identified as belonging to category 5, serving to indicate genre and to set up expectations as to content—given that the genre of pornography remains a key terrain of NSFW. Tagging can also be seen to involve additional functions, such as affective modulation, that are not limited to qualitative aspects of the resource.

Golder and Huberman see a tension between tagging intended for personal use and that serving a social function though. They suggest that the final three types in their taxonomy, including tags like NSFW that note the qualities of content, are intended only for personal use as they indicate a level of meaning specific for that particular person. This clearly does not reflect contemporary applications. What their analysis fails to capture is the sedimentation and diffusion of particular genre tags as the phenomenon of tagging has grown within and between digital media applications and platforms. As social media has penetrated further into everyday lives, generating greater degrees of context collapse—and as the amount of information processed daily through mobile digital media in particular has exploded—being able to identify the generic function of shared content has grown into a crucial skill. This has placed a premium on sharing and normalizing genre categories that have, in process, grown mundane in their broad recognizability. While tagging something as NSFW on a single platform in 2006 may have been interpreted as a personal, subjective act, at the time of writing this book it is also concerned with configuring communicative threads and paths, promoting the content tagged, and increasing its general visibility. At the very least, the normative use of #NSFW as a warning flag similar to more conventional and institutionally formalized content classifications necessarily marks it as other-oriented, social communication.

Nevertheless, Golder and Huberman's taxonomy is still useful in that it emphasizes how #NSFW adds a signifying layer to its anchor images and texts rather than merely serving a warning function. This takes two forms. First, tags provide meta-commentary, adding semantic and contextual information that works alongside the semiotic content of posts to frame and fix their meaning. This function is particularly important for images where informational and contextual content is reduced, allowing for not only findability but comprehensibility. Tags can help convey intended meaning in a context of reduced cues.

Second, particular dimensions of the communication can be amplified by, for example, using or coining tags that are not searchable or that link to other posts. Such tags are intended to underscore some aspects of the post in question. For instance, one of the authors recently posted a Facebook status update proclaiming how happy she was at the insights being generated by her final year undergraduates. This post concluded with #notamarkingmoanforonce. This tag was not intended to render her status update searchable, but to convey meaning to an imagined audience (Litt and Hargittai 2016; cf. Marwick and boyd 2011) made up of many academics who were also likely to be marking papers at the time. Most importantly, it added meaning to the original post. In other words, tags also convey meaning without necessarily functioning as metadata in a technical sense. They are broadly used for humorous, ironic, sarcastic, and critical ends that well exceed, and occasionally conflict with, their functional purposes in aiding searchability. On Twitter and Tumblr, obscure, convoluted, and unique hashtags are used in ways that do not join the posts into larger conversations, or even to any other available content.

Hashtags are thus both text and meta-text (Rambukkana 2015b, 3), and hence essential semiotic elements of the posts in which they are inserted.

It is possible, for instance, to add racist tags such as #WPWW (an acronym for White Power World Wide) to otherwise innocuous posts to frame them as discussions offering further evidence of assaults against white supremacy (Titley 2014). A tag may then be as integral to the meaning of a tweet, e-mail, image post, or status update as its substantive content. This is particularly relevant for Twitter where the hashtag is centralized to the body of the message (Zappavigna 2011) but also applies to online communications more generally. Through this mechanism, adding NSFW with or without the hash symbol in a status update, clickbait headline, or in the header of an e-mail renders it inseparable from the signification of that text and adds a frisson that frames the interpretation of the associated content. A worker receiving a message tagged NSFW is thus not only alerted to the risks involved in exploring its content at work but also given a guide to how such content should be interpreted—the meaning of its content becomes both risqué and potentially risky.

While a racist Twitter hashtag may make the body of the text and the body to which it refers sticky with negative affect—or hate articulated as love for certain populations over others (Ahmed 2004)—bodies tagged as NSFW are inflected with a complex array of intersecting intensities from the visceral pulls of sexual titillation to the conflicting affective ambiguities of gross-out humor. The patterns that such resonances take often follow the contours of embodied identity categories identifiable as gender, age, sexual orientation, or race. Tags stick differently to different bodies in how these are perceived as objects and sources of desire, amusement, resentment, and disgust. Both a warning and an invitation, #NSFW adds a level of expectation that invites fascinated proximities and exclamations of distaste alike, yet without offering much specificity as to the expected pictorial content. In our Twitter data set, for example, #NSFW is used predominantly in connection with images of female bodies promoting commercial straight porn. As the tag sticks to these bodies, they become coded as NSFW in themselves. Meanwhile, some bodies, particularly those marked by their whiteness, maleness, leanness, and straightness, resist semantic stuckness in the ease with which they slide through and across the diverse pigeonholes where embodied identities get pinned.

A tag thus contributes to the definition of its anchor post, image, or update, not least by establishing genre expectations. But it may also place that post in relationship to other content circulating under that same tag within a particular context. The second contribution of tagging to meaning making then lies in the intertextuality fundamental to hypertext where meaning emerges from the relationships made between files as much as it resides in the individual ends of the hyperlink (Landow 2006). This principle is demonstrated in the phenomenon of Rickrolling, in which a user can follow a link supposedly to a news item or work-related document only to end up, through a disguised hyperlink, at the YouTube page playing Rick Astley's *Never Gonna Give You Up* music video. The humor—the very significance and impressiveness of a good Rickroll—cannot be located in the video (despite all its tacky 1980s glory) and certainly not in the anchor file the user had followed, but in their unexpected entwining. In hypertextual environments, meaning emerges from juxtaposition and aggregation. The tag and its capacity to generate and organize relationships between online content join together separate lexia—or blocks of text—into new, unfixed assemblages with their own significance (Landow 2006). Jill Walker (2005) describes the poetic, distributed narratives that emerge when searches for user-generated tags on Flickr juxtapose an often complex array of images. This interpretation of tags as "feral hypertext" (Walker 2005) is particularly apt given the automatic hyperlink qualities of hashtags on Twitter, Instagram, or Tumblr.

That meaning lies in association is particularly important when a tag is used to express solidarity with a political cause or idea such as in #Blacklivesmatter, #Indignados, or #WPWW (see Korn 2015; Rambukkana 2015a). In these instances, the hashtag performs an act of alignment that renders the content inextricably part of a larger discussion of that issue. Hashtags help build "ambient affiliation" (Zappavigna 2011) in that they not only organize relationships between tweets or posts but equally the temporal, emergent, and topic-specific relationships between them (Korn 2015, 135). There is a range of performative qualities to a hashtag that add layers of signification to its associated exchanges even when formal connections are not being activated by technological meanings. The "meaning" of a tweet may lie much more in how it is lumped together with other tweets employing the same hashtags, or in how it is combined with them, than in what its substantive qualities may be. Rendered guilty by association, attaching the hashtag #NSFW alone will instantaneously help to smut up a tweet, independent of what its initial point might have been. This is also how particular bodies come to be stuck together under the NSFW label; the lumping of various naked and othered bodies under the same hashtag enters them into similar circuits of desire and anxiety.

The Social Lives of Hashtags

If a tag adds meaning through association, these meanings are also socially bound and thus shaped by a variety of forces. In the classificatory systems that emerge from the "social tagging systems" (Golder and Huberman 2006; Marlow et al. 2006) of Del.icio.us or Twitter, tags are not predefined nor articulated by any elite gatekeepers. Rather they "rely on shared and emergent social structures and behaviors, as well as related conceptual and linguistic structures of the user community" (Marlow et al. 2006, 31). The shared vocabularies generated by tagging are, effectively, folk taxonomies, or folksonomies (Mathes 2004; Wichowski 2009). Unlike taxonomies, the categories and parameters of which are set by the platform, folksonomies emerge from the efforts and interactions of the users themselves.

If a tag such as NSFW is to be capable of conveying meaning, its language—or the meaning of the acronym at the very least—and the values it represents must obviously be socially legible. In a user-generated system where the options for tagging are effectively infinite, tagging can be routinely inconsistent and confusing. Tag usage, though, must reflect the expected logic of a platform if a user's post, image, or dating profile is to be found in searches, make sense to others, or be appreciated in an appropriate context. Should this fail, the post may attract censure by other users or system administrators. This is particularly crucial with NSFW. Since a user's cultural capital within a platform or his or her capacity to attract adequate attention can be bound to the appropriate and effective use of hashtags as defined by in-group sense making, a premium is placed upon imitation, repetition, and normativity in the marking out of metadata. Consequently, hashtags, like tags more generally, demonstrate a conservative impulse, with social norms fixing definitions over time.

This is evident in the power law distribution exhibited by tagging practices in which the most commonly used tags appear in far greater proportion than less popular ones. In effect, there is a clustering of use among particular terms, followed by a sharp decline in frequency, with the majority of terms forming part of a long tail falling below the median level of popularity. Golder and Huberman (2006) described the fairly rapid convergence upon particular tags on Del.icio.us, producing the stability that allowed the site to serve its social functions. They ascribed the emergence of such consensus to automated systems, such as autocomplete features, that propose or indicate popular tags but also to homogeneity in the site's users in terms of social class or linguistic and educational background This assumption was also made by Marlow et al. (2006), who recognized the congruence between particular Flickr users' tag vocabularies and those of followers. Moreover, such automation in tagging is also regulated. For example, Google's autocomplete function has a report facility, with a supporting policy that advocates for the removal of sexually explicit, hateful, violent, and dangerous predictions (Google Search Help 2018). Tagging practices and cultures display significant levels of calculated and political normativity as humans and nonhumans collectively prioritize and promote certain agendas.

Shared knowledges fundamentally influence tagging behavior, but these insights, and the gains from their effective deployment, can also be easily acquired. Sites such as TagBlender, TagsForLikes, and InstagramTags offer cut-and-paste lists of the most popular tags—such as #love, #instalove, #me, #cute, and #like—that can be inserted in posts in order to amp up the likes and followers associated with them and the status of the account from which they originate. In such instances, the suggested tags are fully independent of the specificities of the images they are added to, drawn as they are from much more abstract, platform specific hierarchies of popularity. Lacking any clearly identifiable semantic or contextual ties, and hence ultimately devoid of meaning, such deployments of trending tags merely aim at increasing the attention directed toward social media content.

Even when used opportunistically, tags can still illustrate the embedded cultural logics and definitions that articulate the values of the particular groups who use them, as well as the interests and motivations of users attracted by specific sorts of content. They may generate, reflect, and reproduce cultural norms in ways that result in degrees of sameness across vast amounts of data. The association of the tag NSFW with sexualized female bodies by the Twitter bots identified in our study both articulates and reproduces the normative association of these figures with a risky sense of desirability. They reflect both a platform and heterosexist social norm in which sex and sexualized female bodies become troubling, yet titillating cultural objects.

NSFW within Diverse Terms of Use

Within this general trend, there are clearly distinct ways of labeling content as risky or unsafe in its sexual suggestiveness in different social media platforms. Twitter users, for example, can decide whether they want to view content marked as "sensitive" (or to mark their own tweets as such) without needing to resort to the hashtag NSFW. Porn studios and porn stars who make broad use of Twitter for promotional and networking purposes may use NSFW to characterize their whole account without using the hashtag in their tweets—for, as pointed out above, it would add little in terms of relevant contextual metadata. Furthermore, our data set shows that users regularly type in NSFW as a tag rather than hashtag and, by doing so, fail to make full use of the hypertextual features that the platforms have to offer. The example of Twitter alone shows how #NSFW belongs to a broader ecology of sorting out and circulating sexually explicit content through automated features—such as the default invisibility of content marked sensitive—and through divergent user practices that are both specific to the platform and vary according to the intended audience.

Platform specificity is key to the social life of hashtags and their embedding in cultures of use. That a shot of a woman in lingerie may be tagged NSFW by a user pinning it to their Pinterest board is because that user comprehends and articulates the classificatory logic specific to that site: the user understands that *this* much nudity equals risqué content according to its rules of conduct. That this same image would pass without warnings on almost any subreddit speaks to the same logic, given the range and diversity of sexual content that the site offers. The differences in these codes are clearly dependent on the different foci, rationale, user base, content policy, and functionalities of the site in question. Here, Pinterest and Reddit represent the opposite in terms of content policy, the former aiming to keep posts as smut-free as possible and the latter allowing for a range of NSFW content.

Reddit (est. 2005), defined in the site title metadata as "the front page of the Internet," combines user discussions with the rating of Web content. Many of the site's numerous subreddits host controversial content, and, in 2014, a notorious celebrity photo hack was shared on the site in an event titled "The Fappening." The very same year, Reddit was a lively hub for Gamergate discussions targeting female game journalists and game developers. In her study, Adrienne Massanari (2015, 2017) associates the platform with the white straight masculinities of geek culture that fuel its binary gender dynamics, sexism, and aggression with racist overtones, a point we address further in chapter 6. NSFW content is, not surprisingly, a staple feature of Reddit, which, according to its policy, is "a platform for communities to discuss, connect, and share content" that "might be funny, serious, offensive, or anywhere in between" (Reddit 2017). In 2017, the policy banned illegal content, involuntary pornography, posts that encourage and incite violence or involve harassment and bullying, spam, impersonation, and the leaking of personal and confidential information. The policy also requires, "Content that contains nudity, pornography, or profanity, which a reasonable viewer may not want to be seen accessing in a public or formal setting such as in a workplace should be tagged as NSFW. This tag can be applied to individual pieces of content or to entire communities" (Reddit 2017).

The photo-sharing app and website Pinterest (est. 2010), on the other hand, is advertised as a "catalogue of ideas" yet targets markedly female users with default interest categories such as fashion, style, food recipes, and inspirational quotes. Pinterest's terms of service simply state, "don't post porn" (Pinterest 2018b). No further definition of pornography is provided, yet displays of sexual representation are further unpacked in the site's community guidelines under the "Safety" category, which states,

> Our team works hard to keep divisive, disturbing or unsafe content off Pinterest. Some types of content we delete, other stuff we just hide from public areas.
>
> We remove porn. We may hide nudity or erotica.
>
> Most artistic, scientific or educational nudity is okay on Pinterest. We may hide this and other explicit content from public places so people don't run into it accidentally. Paintings, statues and other real world art, and content that shows breastfeeding or mastectomies are always okay.
>
> We always remove images of explicit sexual activity or fetishes, and nude or partially nude people in sexually suggestive poses. (Pinterest 2018a)

What might be too explicit for the community is left deliberately unclear—and, given the diversity of Pinterest's scope of users, this would be challenging to start with. Artistic images are allowed, but not in all instances. The dividing line between acceptable and unacceptable content ultimately involves commercial sex: visual materials relating to pornography and sex work are specifically weeded out.

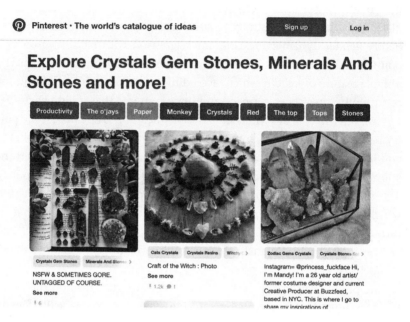

Figure 2.5
NSFW and SFW crystals on Pinterest.

A search for "NSFW" on Pinterest results in top hits on photographs and drawings of women in varying degrees of undress, cartoons with characters embracing one another, and a range of sexually suggestive textual quotes, as well as pictures of socks, jewelry, and balloons involving some sexual innuendo. The tag and the user expectations concerning it are also explicitly played with. One of the top hits leads to Milene Design's board, titled "knit and crochet" and described as "NSFW & SOMETIMES GORE. UNTAGGED OF COURSE" (see figure 2.5). Promises of porn and gore are connected here with images of tastefully displayed decorative crystals and mineral collections with implicit New Age connotations.

The leading image-sharing platform, Instagram, also refers to sexual content in its community guidelines, which state,

> **Post photos and videos that are appropriate for a diverse audience.**
> We know that there are times when people might want to share nude images that are artistic or creative in nature, but for a variety of reasons, we don't allow nudity on Instagram. This includes photos, videos, and some digitally-created content

that show sexual intercourse, genitals, and close-ups of fully-nude buttocks. It also includes some photos of female nipples, but photos of post-mastectomy scarring and women actively breastfeeding are allowed. Nudity in photos of paintings and sculptures is OK, too. (Instagram 2018)

Instagram is nevertheless particularly well-known for its range of selfies that constantly test—and, in many instances, clearly ignore—the boundaries of what the service deems appropriate. This has been the case with celebrities such as Kim Kardashian as it is with aspiring social media influencers of more local repute. The Finnish tabloid celebrity and blogger, Cheyenne Järvinen, known for her personal relationships, cosmetic surgeries, and reality television appearances, regularly poses topless images on Instagram (misscheyenne 2018). Reports of these images being removed and of Järvinen, incensed by this treatment, posting further sexually suggestive photos on the service, create clicks for the online news sites, her Instagram account, and Instagram as a service, resulting in a happy distribution of the fruits of the attention economy between corporate and private actors. A search for #NSFW on Instagram results in top hits of images of half revealed buttocks and breasts, nude selfies, and erotic art, along with a disclaimer that recent posts cannot be shown since they may violate the terms of use (see figure 2.6).

Such examples point out how the hashtag NSFW is not merely a neutral organizational tool but actively and performatively orients and generates meaning, invites attention, and creates expectation. At the same time, it also shows that #NSFW is an unfixed signifier with context-specific social functions. Other than an association with naked, sexualized bodies, often those of the female kind, there is little coherence across platforms about what actually is NSFW content. Reliant on tacit understandings of normative uses for coherence, hashtags may only be used to address a particular community of users (Bruns and Burgess 2012; Zappavigna 2011). Consequently, to use a hashtag effectively also requires social—and occasionally subcultural—literacy of the kind that Ryan Milner (2016) associates with the appropriate use of memes. This can involve the use of hashtags to promote posts independent of their content, as in the examples of "instalove" addressed above, just as it can mean the careful use, or avoidance, of #NSFW in order to conform to implicit, platform-specific codes of communication. The "untagged of course" statement on Milene Design's Pinterest board speaks explicitly of these tacit expectations.

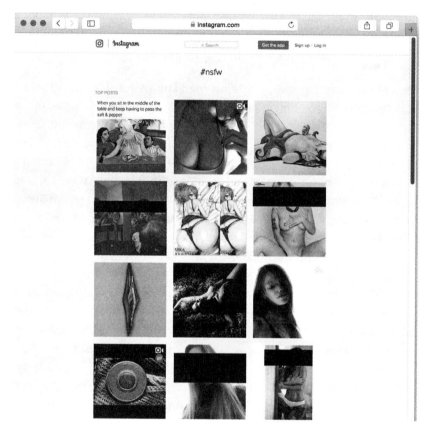

Figure 2.6
Top #NSFW posts on Instagram, March 2017.

A tag is creative in that it generates meaning, but in its reliance on shared understanding it may also be constitutive of association, connection, affiliation, community, and temporary publics. Rambukkana (2015a, 32) defines hashtags as "singular moments that coalesce into something new" in complex and even cacophonic media environments: as "threads of meaning that work to weave new abstractions into the world." These threads range drastically in their foci and performative force, lacking as they do any inherent or shared orientation and effect. Analyses of the particular functions of NSFW as term, tag, and hashtag therefore need to attend to how the sociotechnical politics of a particular platform render its categorization in particular ways, as well as how the addition of the tag comes to have meaning within particular user communities and interpersonal exchanges. User networks of NSFW content may come into being through the tag's deployment and policing. These networks, then, are marked by a shared sensibility about what is and what is not safe for work, producing and reproducing that cultural logic.

The tag then is part of a suite of digital and social technologies used to codify and police appropriate communication in networked communication systems through normative pressures. These systems have a long history in online communication and have taken many forms, ranging from the libertarian self-management associated with early Usenet and contemporary spaces like 4chan (Pfaffenberger 1996; Phillips 2015) to the FAQs, netiquette guides, and moderation of the online communities of multi-user domains (MUDs), object-oriented MUDs (MOOs), and commercial portals like AOL (Lambert 2008; Mnookin 1996; Postigo 2003, 2009). Increasingly, though, this norm setting involves the work of paid community managers and content moderators, as well as the labor of content filtering algorithms (Kerr 2017; Kerr and Kelleher 2015). The effort of establishing shared norms and rules of conduct based on established forms of sociability has in fact grown impossible on the most used social media services simply because of their vast size. At the time of writing this book, the market leader Facebook alone sported over 2.2 billion monthly users worldwide: clearly, no rules of conduct would be likely to organically emerge from interactions involving almost one third of the world's population in their own circuits of sociability divided along the axes of language, culture, politics, age, and religion alike.

At the same time, social media services all have community standards delimiting appropriate content and conduct that are regularly updated in response to feedback directly from users but also from wider social and political interventions. The increasing attempts to regulate the distribution of "fake news" and hate speech across a range of social media sites are key examples of these dynamics at play. These standards, though, emerge from and are drawn within corporate headquarters—they are not folksonomies, but taxonomies. Hashtags like NSFW may be shaped by social forces, but these dynamics are not necessarily emergent from the needs, beliefs, or desires of user groups. In the current context, the term "community" within community management, connoting as it does the longer history of online communities' organic self-organizing, performs a particular affective

framing of togetherness and care for the service and the interactions occurring within it, while masking the obvious fact that these standards do not
necessarily emerge from any shared communitarian efforts of users. It
is therefore clear that commercial agendas are key to understanding the
uneasy position occupied by nudity and sexuality and the logics of what
becomes tagged NSFW.

Disquieting, Naked Bodies

On February 9, 2016, the visual artist Illma Gore published on her Facebook
page a pastel pencil painting of Donald Trump in the nude, titled "Make
America Great Again," with the accompanying slogan, "Because no matter
what is in your pants, you can still be a big prick." Inspired by the highly
public, and broadly discussed, allusions to Trump's penis size during the
Republican presidential primary debates during which many saw the candidate as boasting about its capacity, the drawing featured genitalia of markedly modest size. Gore's image soon began circulating on other social media
platforms from Instagram to Tumblr, Twitter, and Snapchat. Only two days
on, it had been featured, with the necessary NSFW warnings intact, in
media outlets such as *Huffington Post* ("Artist Imagines What Donald Trump
Looks Like Naked and It Ain't Pretty (NSFW)") and *The Daily Dot* ("Realistic
Nude Painting of Donald Trump Will Make You Gouge Your Eyes Out").
Many similar stories were soon to follow.

    Very quickly after posting the initial image, Gore's Facebook account was
temporarily suspended for violating the service's standards and has been
blocked numerous times since. According to Facebook's community standards: "We remove photographs of people displaying genitals or focusing
in on fully exposed buttocks" (Facebook 2017). Gore's portrait of Trump in
the nude did not in fact violate these terms as she had covered Trump's genital area with a black block (Hoffman 2016). Nevertheless, it was deemed
a breach of these protocols. On March 3, she published an eBay listing for
the piece, only to have it taken down a few days later due to violation of
the service's policy on images of nudity, according to which "frontal nudity
is allowed in Art categories when the item is considered fine art, such as
Michelangelo's David, vintage pin-up art, Renaissance-style paintings, and
nude cherubs" (eBay 2017). Works not fitting these parameters should be
listed in the Adult Only Category. Within a week, Gore had been threatened

with lawsuits from Trump's legal team and also risked having her Facebook account permanently removed (Voon 2016).

While the image itself, with its acute timing, explicitly controversial, provocative style, and possibly visceral appeal, was a news item well suited for the dynamics of clickbait journalism, news of blocking, banning, and potential censorship—and those connected to Facebook in particular—invested the incident with a different kind of sticky attention value. In the course of all this, the image gained virality as people shared news items on the story, most of which featured an uncensored version of the portrait that consequently found its way to extensive distribution back on Facebook. In order to further fuel its dispersion, Gore put a high-resolution image file on her website for free downloading. By April 2016, the portrait was on display at the Maddox gallery in London, priced at £1 million (Greenfield 2016). All this exemplifies the intermeshing of attention value and monetary value through and within the fast speeds and economies of social media platforms, online news outlets, links, and clicks.

The image in question, situated in the realm of both arts and politics, is one in a long, steadily accumulating stream of incidents testing and challenging Facebook's community standards with images of nudity. At the same time, the incident is exceptional in that it focused on the nude body of a controversial male celebrity businessman, reality TV figure, and U.S. president-to-be. Like the NSFW tag, other controversies have predominantly focused on images of female bodies, as in the contexts of breastfeeding and breast cancer where bodily displays have been banned, even when connected to mothering and women's health. Similarly to MySpace (est. 2003) and LiveJournal (est. 1999) before it, Facebook has long weeded out images of breastfeeding (see Ibrahim 2012, 35–36). In 2012, a group of women gathered in front of Facebook headquarters in a collective breastfeeding protest opposing the company's policy of flagging and removing images of nursing. In a 2013 controversy, over 20,000 people signed a Change.org petition protesting the removal of images of mastectomy as obscene and hence as comparable to pornographic content. Facebook community standards have since undergone revisions. According to the March 2016 version,

> We also restrict some images of female breasts if they include the nipple, but we always allow photos of women actively engaged in breastfeeding or showing breasts with post-mastectomy scarring. We also allow photographs of paintings,

sculptures and other art that depicts nude figures. Restrictions on the display of both nudity and sexual activity also apply to digitally created content unless the content is posted for educational, humorous or satirical purposes.

Art remains a space where nudity fails to be automatically conflated with obscenity, yet social media community standards and terms of service routinely map out its confines and discontents in notably conservative, even retrograde terms. As mentioned, on eBay, this involves fencing off the obscene in contrast to "Renaissance-style aesthetics" and cherubs, even while the normative boundaries of art are transgressed by including vintage pin-ups within the category.

Image recognition software has been developed since the 1990s for the purpose of filtering out pornographic images through automated means (e.g., Iqbal et al. 2016; Ries and Lienhart 2014), yet Gore's blocked Facebook access most likely owes to other users reporting the image as offensive, and to company representatives screening the content then agreeing on the issue (cf. Summers 2009). As a mechanism for reporting offensive content, flagging is a "technical rendition of 'I object,'" based on user participation in the reification of social media sites' community norms (Crawford and Gillespie 2016, 414; Jarrett 2006). Kate Crawford and Tarleton Gillespie (2016, 411) show how flagging has become a ubiquitous mechanism of governance with a somewhat complex relation to community sentiment, consisting as it does of interactions between "users, platforms, humans, and algorithms, as well as broader political and regulatory forces." These are themselves inseparable from moral concerns and corporate strategies and routinely result in opaque decisions detached from broader negotiations and articulations over what is acceptable, offensive, or controversial (Crawford and Gillespie 2016).

Flagging may be a sign of objection, but it also involves more complex social dynamics and exchanges, many of which are inseparable from increases in attention value:

> Flags get pulled as a playful prank between friends, as part of a skirmish between professional competitors, as retribution for a social offense that happened elsewhere, or as part of a campaign of bullying or harassment—and it is often impossible to tell the difference. Flagging is also used to generate interest and publicity, as in the cases where YouTube put a racy music video behind an age barrier and promoters decried the "censorship" with mock outrage. The fact that flagging can be a tactic not only undercuts its value as a "genuine" expression of offense, it

fundamentally undercuts its legibility as a sign of the community's moral temperature. (Crawford and Gillespie 2016, 420)

The persistent hunt for offensive areolas and micropenises in the Facebook incidents discussed above is connected to broader boundary maintenance between SFW and NSFW content, and the platforms through which such content is distributed and accessed. While Twitter accommodates sexually explicit content, most other notable social media platforms go to considerable effort to remove it. This, combined with the increased concentration of ownership in dominant corporate actors (most centrally, Google/Alphabet and Facebook), has drastically reframed the operating possibilities of companies trading in pornographic content in stark comparison to the easy visibility afforded by 1990s Web cultures (see chapter 3).

Pornography, or even less sexually explicit displays of nudity, is weeded out from YouTube and Facebook through flagging and automated blocking alike. Should a Facebook user attempt to share a link to a pornographic site, the site responds with, "You can't post this because it has a blocked link. The content you're trying to share includes a link that our security systems detected to be unsafe. Please remove this link to continue." The umbrella of unsafety here encompasses anything from potential viruses to pornographic sites and drawings of nude cartoon characters. No further distinctions are available since such content is deemed not only NSFW but generally unsafe. In addition to limiting links to and shares of adult content, Facebook has, as of 2018, limited appropriate discussions on sexuality to those addressing sexual violence and exploitation:

> We recognise the importance of and want to allow for this discussion. We draw the line, however, when content facilitates, encourages or coordinates sexual encounters between adults. We also restrict sexually explicit language that may lead to solicitation because some audiences within our global community may be sensitive to this type of content and it may impede the ability for people to connect with their friends and the broader community. (Facebook 2018b)

Sexual communication other than that addressing violence and harassment is, in sum, deemed both unimportant and "sensitive" in the sense of risky. Labeled as "objectionable content," expressions of sexual likes or desires are framed out from exchanges allowed on the platform. Tumblr, which operated as a hub for the self-organization of diverse sexual cultures, similarly cut adult content that "includes photos, videos, or GIFs that show real-life human genitals or female-presenting nipples, and any content—including photos, videos, GIFs and illustrations—that depicts sex acts" from its palette of acceptability in 2018 (Tumblr 2018). The tangible tightening of community standards governing sexual content and communication online that has occurred in the course of writing this book speaks of the increased zoning out of sexuality from social media. Rather than being understood as key to people's self-definitions, central in terms of their wellbeing, and elementary in the building of social connections, sex and sexuality has become framed simply as problematic and offensive. The notable exception here is Twitter, which allows adult content and is a space where porn companies and adult performers can openly and explicitly promote their work, although since the 2018 introduction of the Fight Online Sex Trafficking Act and the Stop Enabling Sex Traffickers Act (FOSTA-SESTA) in the United States, these must stop short of soliciting sex work (see also chapter 5). Yet, as also discussed in the following chapter, Twitter has become a crucial platform for promoting new productions, building star image, and expanding one's fan base within the porn industry.

All in all, nudity occupies a tricky terrain in the borderlines between the SFW and the NSFW, especially since the criteria regulating obscenity are, due to the largest social media platforms' country of origin, overwhelmingly defined according to community standards specific to U.S. culture and suited for the preferences of their various commercial partners in a markedly conservative vein. Writing on the work of content moderation in social media—a topic discussed further in chapter 5—journalist Adrian Chen (2012) points out that "Facebook has fashioned itself the clean, well-lit alternative to the scary open Internet for both users and advertisers, thanks to the work of a small army of human content moderators." On Facebook, images of nudity and sexuality are removed much more carefully and easily than those involving violence, or even gore. According to the "abuse standards violations" manual leaked to Chen by a disgruntled, outsourced content moderator, "When it comes to sex and nudity, Facebook is strictly PG-13, according to the guidelines. Obvious sexual activity, even clothed, is deleted, as are 'naked "private parts" including female nipple bulges and naked butt cracks.' But 'male nipples are OK.' Foreplay is allowed, 'even for same sex (man-man/woman-woman)'" (Chen 2012). It then follows that not only breastfeeding but also "Blatant (obvious) depiction of camel toes and moose knuckles" and "Depicting sexual fetishes in any form" remain forbidden while "Gory pictures are allowed, as long somebody's guts aren't spilling out. 'Crushed heads, limbs etc are OK as long as no insides are showing,' reads one guideline. 'Deep flesh wounds are ok to show; excessive blood is ok to show'" (Chen 2012).

In other words, it is the NSFW, not so much the NSFL, that is weeded out from Facebook, with the implication that images of nipples represent more of a risk than those of crushed bodies. Despite the bizarreness of this association, it remains a central principle in commercially imposed content classification.

The Conservation Work of NSFW

As the discussion above makes evident, the norms connected to the tagging, flagging, and blocking of NSFW content are not confined to any particular digital image, text, or video files. They emerge from specific social contexts but also work to produce the texture of sociability they ostensibly reflect and the interaction options available to those contributing to it. While expressing the norms and putative community values of the site or service in question, tags, hashtags, FAQs, flags, and community standards all define legitimate experiences, as well as the contours of acceptable exchanges within those bounds. In this sense, they are performative, constituting the boundaries of that which they purportedly describe. While tagging practices may not produce a cohesive community, as clearly shown in our analysis of Twitter data, what gets collated under categories articulates a set of interpellating ideas about acceptable practices, even if only temporarily constituted. The values that tags and flags articulate serve as useful touchstones for understanding users and use cultures but also for seeing how wider social formations and politics—often those specific to the United States—are manifesting in corporate social media policies of global resonance.

The tag NSFW may be a mechanism through which to protect a site's codes of communication against legitimate, well-founded views that may be contrary to its internally produced status quo, regardless of whether that is generated organically through user interactions or imposed by platform taxonomies. Across the sites addressed in this chapter, NSFW tagging practices work to conserve and support the interconnections of risk, sexual titillation, and women's bodies and/or sexual activity. The uses of the tag make it possible for titillating or sexually arousing content to continue to circulate and, hence, to orient the data flows of attraction and repulsion that feed the online economy. At the same time, they code this content in ways that do not challenge orthodox understandings concerning its meaning and cultural value.

To use a tag such as NSFW is thus a layered act. It is to add a veneer of meaning by framing or associating the circulated content; it is to express but also to produce and reproduce particular social norms and forms of sociality; it is to capture attention and to add titillation to updates, posts, and tweets; and it is to engage with the management of communicative extensity associated with networked technologies. For all its associations with risky speech and "naughty" communication, the resonances of NSFW may therefore ultimately be quite conservative. NSFW is part of a suite of measures that facilitates the flow of data, ideas, and discourse within contemporary communicative capitalism. By sequestering supposedly polluting speech but not straightforwardly censoring it, the tag makes it possible for information and communication to circulate and multiply in ways that rearticulate existing social and economic agendas. Within this circulation, spaces of resistance continually emerge, take form, grow heated with activity, and then possibly fade away: these remain elementary to the communicative dynamics in which NSFW operates.

3 Pornographic Peekaboo

As a media genre and a field of cultural production, pornography can be considered NSFW on a number of levels. Perhaps most obviously, in terms of this book, the products of pornographers form the quintessential type of content to be tagged as NSFW. Given the degree to which the tag remains glued to sexual imagery, it is therefore unsurprising that content filtering activities and regulation routines connected to pornography are diverse, extensive, and ubiquitous. Access to porn is governed with firewalls, parental filtering software, and the use of browsers' safe search modes. Workplaces, schools, and public institutions block access to porn for their staff, students, and visitors, while companies from McDonald's to Starbucks, and beyond, block it for customers using their complimentary Wi-Fi (Chandler 2016; chapter 5).

In addition to the products of porn being consistently marked as NSFW, the labor of porn is associated with risks to sexual health, and the industry is perennially accused of exploitative labor practices. Understood in this vein, the work of pornography itself comes across as unsafe. At the same time, the shift and centralization of porn distribution onto key video aggregator sites, the majority of which are owned by the same company, MindGeek, suggests that there is much more to the labor of porn than the tasks of performers, producers, directors, camera operators, and other production staff and hence that the denominator of the porn industry may be in need of redefinition as to its occupational diversity and reach. The labor of porn is also centrally performed with and by algorithms and, in many ways, is inseparable from other forms of IT work.

This chapter zooms in on the ambivalent position and visibility of pornography in social media. Starting with considerations of content regulation and filtering, we move to address the uses of social media both in the promotional efforts of porn companies and in those of individual porn stars, issues connected to work safety within the contemporary porn gig economy, and the desktop labor of creating extreme animated pornography detached from the performances of human bodies. Throughout, we consider safety both metaphorically—as in the uses of the tag, NSFW, and the boundary work between acceptable and unacceptable that it entails—and more literally as an issue of occupational safety. Here, like elsewhere in this book, we ask why and how both sexually suggestive and sexually explicit media images become understood as not safe, and how the connections of safety and work might be thought of differently.

Rather than framing safety as a property of representational content, we argue for a more concrete take on risk and harm that acknowledges the complexity of contemporary porn labor as it is being reshaped by digital circulation and social media platforms. As Claire Potter (2016, 111) argues, this labor is generally rendered invisible: "[W]ork on porn sets is usually self-regulated, nonunionized, and without benefits or enforceable industry standards for wages and intellectual property." Such a combination of invisibility and opaqueness facilitates exploitative practices while the stigma connected to porn work "makes it difficult for people who are exploited to speak up" (Potter 2016, 113). It can therefore be argued that the default filtering and flagging out of NSFW content as risky, unsafe, unwanted, and at best problematic further feeds the stigmatization of both porn labor and the laborers of porn in unhelpful ways.

Adult entertainment companies have broad social media presence, yet, with the notable exception of content shared on Twitter, this involves sticking to the nonexplicit in order to accommodate the terms of service banning gratuitous displays of nudity and sex. Even in services where NSFW content is allowed, the quest for an optimal reach can involve a more SFW approach. @pornhub, the official Pornhub Twitter account titled Pornhub ARIA, tweets links to the company's content but, even more centrally, humorous lines disconnected from direct promotional practices, such as "Send nudes when you get home so I know you're safe!" (August 26, 2018) and "Netflix and Chill is just a D away from Netflix and Child" (August 24, 2018). Accounts such as @PornHubXXX and @PornHub_Vids are not operated by the company but rather by actors aiming to generate traffic through associations with it. Since a successful social media presence requires finding a balance between the content classifications of SFW and NSFW, this risks failure in representing porn brands' core features and assets. For its part, the official Pornhub Twitter account (also operating in Snapchat) simply states, "I'm Aria, no I don't do porn."

Furthermore, to consider how pornographic content may or may not be considered safe in the context of its online circulation, amateur production, and mainstreaming, as is the rationale of this chapter, means both addressing its changing labor dynamics and asking how the risks associated with the industry are being reshaped. An exploration of how these dynamics unfold among and in between the diverse human and nonhuman actors involved in the production, distribution, and consumption of porn shows a complex, and often contradictory, set of tendencies within the sector that usefully complicates the vision of what precisely is, or is not, NSFW about all this.

Keeping Us Safe from Porn

It tends to be common knowledge that the needs of the porn industry drove the development of Web solutions throughout the 1990s, well before the term NSFW was coined. Gaming and online shopping only popularized toward the end of the decade, and for quite a while pornography remained one of the few forms of content that users would pay for, necessitating improvements in the forms, technical quality, and speed of visual and audiovisual delivery. Safe credit card processing systems, streaming video technologies, and hosting services, as well as promotional techniques such as banner advertisements, pop-ups, and even mousetrapping, were first developed for, and used on, porn sites (Bennett 2001; Johnson 2010; Lane 2001; Paasonen 2018a). While pornographic content continues to quickly migrate to new technical platforms and media formats, it is however no longer accurate to claim that porn is the default winner application in new media—if, indeed, this was ever precisely the case. The role of pornography as a driving force in dot.com enterprise has clearly passed. In his coverage of the adult app store, Mikandi, *Wired* reporter Cade Metz notes how

> with the rising power of companies like Apple and Google and Facebook, the adult industry doesn't drive new technology. In many respects, it doesn't even have access to new technology. The big tech companies behind the big platforms control not only the gateway services (the iPhone app store, Google Search, the

Facebook social network) but the gateway devices (the iPhone, Android phones, Google Chromecast, the Amazon Fire TV, the Oculus Rift virtual reality headset). And for the most part, they've shut porn out. Besides, these giants now drive new technology faster than services like Mikandi or Pornhub ever could. (Metz 2015)

Porn sites are currently much more likely to emulate the technical solutions and revenue models of popular social media platforms than the other way around. Just as the traffic of views, links, and clicks connected to news items, memes, and video clips is driven through globally leading social media hubs such as YouTube, Facebook, Instagram, and Twitter, the traffic of online porn is increasingly centralized and organized through select video aggregator sites. This means that certain companies have considerable power to govern the accessibility of content and to modulate available user experiences and interactions while not needing to be transparent as to the parameters within which these occur. Since these companies are mostly unlisted, their specific flows of profit are also not public information. On aggregator sites, videos gain visibility through popularity calculated as ratings and views, by being displayed as sponsored content, as well as through more opaque algorithmic calculations that pull files from the sites' massive databases. All porn tube sites have, with small degrees of variation, emulated the design and operating principles of YouTube (est. 2005). Meanwhile, most porn sites modeled after other social outlets, such as Snatchly, PinSex, and Pornterest building on Pinterest, have folded after their initial news and attention value wore off. Their lack of success may be connected to porn consumption being increasingly focused on video clips and webcam streams rather than still images of the kind that dominated pornographic Web browsing throughout the 1990s.

Despite such emulation, pornography often sits uncomfortably in social media environments. As already pointed out, most key mainstream social media services weed out pornographic content with the aim of moderating the platforms' tones and styles of communication, as well as controlling their economic ties and associations. Since the services operate through targeted advertising based on analysis of user data, it is important for them to remain desirable to potential advertisers who, in most instances, are unwilling to be associated with sexually explicit materials because of the potential damage to their corporate image. Nike, Disney, Nestle, Starbucks, H&M, IKEA, or Marks and Spencer are unlikely to initiate advertising plans on platforms featuring content categorized as NSFW. Porn is warded off through flagging and filtering routines, as well as through terms of service that are policed by technical sanctions such as account suspension and deletion.

For its part, Google, YouTube's owner, has effectively banned pornography from its advertisements. In 2014 Google AdSense advised,

> The AdWords policies on adult sexual services (. . .) will be updated in late June 2014 to reflect a new policy on sexually explicit content. Under this policy, sexually explicit content will be prohibited, and guidelines will be clarified regarding promotion of other adult content. The change will affect all countries. We made this decision as an effort to continually improve users' experiences with AdWords. (Google AdSense 2014)

In 2018, the message on adult content included the following, again, effectively a continuation of a ban on pornography:

> Ads should respect user preferences and comply with legal regulations, so we don't allow certain kinds of adult content in ads and destinations. Some kinds of adult-oriented ads and destinations are allowed if they comply with the policies below and don't target minors, but they will only show in limited scenarios based on user search queries, user age, and local laws where the ad is being served. . . .
>
> Sexually explicit content . . . The following is not allowed: Text, image, audio, or video of graphic sexual acts intended to arouse. Examples: Hardcore pornography; sex acts such as genital, anal, and oral sex; masturbation; cartoon porn or hentai. (Google AdSense 2018)

Search engines have long filtered out pornography from their freely published listings of the most popular search terms, adding to the position of porn as a public secret of sorts (see Paasonen 2011, 32). The filtering out of sexually explicit content from results has, in practice, made it more difficult for users to find that which they are searching for. While this might be considered as a knowing design of a poorer service, such measures have, in fact, been articulated and motivated as improvements to user experience—as in the AdWords policy statement above. Google provides a SafeSearch option that filters out all, or at least most, hits to adult content. In earlier versions, safe searching was set as the default option and users needed to knowingly turn this filter off in order to access sexually explicit content. As that which SafeSearch filters out, sexual content is explicitly framed as unsafe and potentially risky. The implicit premise here is that aiding its accessibility conflicts with Google's corporate slogan of "don't be evil," even if that motto has not been in use since the spring of 2018. Should the user choose not to use SafeSearch, Google will "provide the most relevant results for your search and may include explicit content when you search for it." Searches on pornography can be tracked through Google Trends, which points to their perennial and even increasing popularity yet without breaking down these trends into actual numbers of searches unless one pays for the data. The uneasy visibility of pornographic content in searches and on social media platforms speaks of a gap between the normative, fictitious notion of a Web user—in accordance to which the services' "community standards" are generally crafted—and the diverse desires, inappropriate interests, and unruly titillations of the people engaging with the services in question.

While there is notable opacity to the notions of safety mobilized in social media governance, it is fair to say that images of nudity, and visual displays of pornography in particular, are at the heart of things to be deemed unsafe, and especially NSFW. As already mentioned above, Facebook's community standards categorize adult nudity and sexual activity together with hate speech, graphic violence, and cruel and insensitive content as "objectionable." The list of visual content categorized as "adult nudity and sexual activity" is lengthy, ranging from "uncovered female nipples except in the context of breastfeeding, birth giving and after-birth moments, health (. . .) or an act of protest" to "use of sex toys, even if above or under clothing," "[s]queezing naked female breast except in breastfeeding context," and "acts that are likely to lead to the death of a person or animal," dismemberment, and cannibalism. Exceptions include images that are "not sufficiently detailed" and where "only body shapes or contours are visible" (Facebook 2018a). Such decontextualized merging of images of female (but not male) nipples with animal torture and cannibalism conflates the obvious and drastic differences between the content, equating them all as similarly problematic, objectionable, and unsafe. While images of cannibalism are banned as assumed sexual fetishes, it seems unlikely that images of Hollywood films depicting the practice, such as *Hannibal* (2001) or *Alive* (1983), are to be similarly banned.

At the same time, available contextual expectations make evident the inherent difficulty in defining the contours of the objectionable. This difficulty is amplified by the mass of posts made daily by the two something billion active Facebook users that is impossible to manage through human means. Despite increased investments in the human labor of commercial content filtering—discussed in more detail in chapter 5—and the difficulties posed to computer learning by visual content, this quantitatively daunting task is also allocated to algorithms. Filtering software has long been used to detect images of child abuse, yet its range and scope are steadily broadening. In their expansive review of scholarship on computer vision–based pornography filtering, Robert W. Gehl, Lucas Moyer-Horner, and Sara K. Yeo (2017) point out that computers are trained to recognize, and hence to filter out, certain bodies and not others as pornographic. Explaining this focus through the broader straight male bias within the computer technology industry, the authors identify automated filtering as built on the assumption that

> pornography is limited to images of naked women; that sexuality is largely comprised of men looking at naked women; and that pornographic bodies comport to specific, predictable shapes, textures, and sizes. In other words, judging from their published works and conference articles, computer scientists appear to be training computers to see the narrow form of pornography (. . .) while dismissing a heterogeneous array of other forms of pornography (gay, queer, trans*, hardcore, fat, bondage, hairy, and so much more) as "noise." (Gehl et al. 2017, 530)

As in the case of Facebook (and Tumblr) content policy focusing on female and not male nipples, the female body remains the marker of sex and object of sexual desire, as well as symbol of obscenity, while—as discussed in more detail in chapter 4 in connection with naked self-shooting practices—male bodies are allowed a broader expressive spectrum ranging from the humorous to the erotic and the menacing. In fact, as Gehl et al. (2017, 536) point out, "CVPF researchers are not teaching computers how to see penises. Although a lot of attention is paid to skin, some to nipples and breasts, and a smaller amount is paid to female genitals, the word 'penis' does not appear in the 102 articles" that the authors analyzed.

Computers are taught to identify female body parts and not male ones, and this recognition is applied to a vast range of visual content of diverse origins and pictorial content in ways that render it a markedly abstract endeavor. These more abstract aspects of algorithmic image recognition and content filtering are rendered evident in Yahoo's 2016 open-source neural network, open_nsfw, which "scores images on a scale of 0 to 1 on its suitability for use in the workplace" (Goh 2016). The residual network applies machine learning to image classification and filtering:

> Automatically identifying that an image is not suitable/safe for work (NSFW), including offensive and adult images, is an important problem which researchers

have been trying to tackle for decades. Since images and user-generated content dominate the Internet today, filtering NSFW images becomes an essential component of Web and mobile applications. With the evolution of computer vision, improved training data, and deep learning algorithms, computers are now able to automatically classify NSFW image content with greater precision.

Defining NSFW material is subjective and the task of identifying these images is non-trivial. Moreover, what may be objectionable in one context can be suitable in another. For this reason, the model we describe below focuses only on one type of NSFW content: pornographic images. The identification of NSFW sketches, cartoons, text, images of graphic violence, or other types of unsuitable content is not addressed with this model. (Mahadeokar and Pesavento 2016)

Open_nsfw classifies images featuring genitalia—or things that might appear as such to the algorithms involved. Here, as elsewhere, pornography becomes the primary form of content deemed offensive, objectionable, unsuitable, and unsafe for any workplace. Testing open_nsfw with synthetic images generated through the parameterization of manifold natural images, computer scientist Gabriel Goh (2016) visualized some of its logic. By tweaking the NSFW neurons, Goh generated both SFW and NSFW visions out of images of beaches, museum and gallery display halls, coral reefs, concerts, towers, deserts, and volcanoes (see figure 3.1). The images to gain the classification 1—firmly NSFW—feature fascinating vistas of fleshy creases and reddish, tumescent bulbs folding into abstract patterns and textures reminiscent of cells seen through a microscope or visualizations of extraterrestrial landscapes and life-forms. In these synthetic visualizations, pornography opens up as a matter of patterns, shapes, and textures that are both generated and interpreted by algorithms. This fantastic landscape of the algorithmically unsafe sprouts genital resemblances that both illustrate the general principles of content classification and expand the notion of pornography in abstract, posthuman, and even surreal directions.

Online practices of tagging, flagging, and filtering similarly involve a radically decontextualized take on work and safety where NSFW visual content is concerned. In the logic of open_nsfw, as in Facebook's community standards, offensiveness and inappropriateness are seen as innate properties of pornographic images, and as such unconnected with the social uses or circulations that such images may involve or tap into. Yet as Goh's experiment exemplifies, the images categorized as NSFW in their sexual explicitness need not involve human bodies: they may just as well display variations of natural formations and architectural features, as long as they

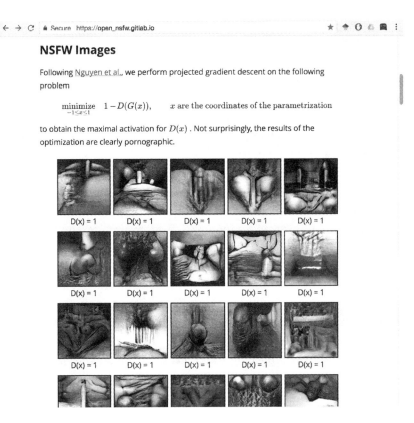

Figure 3.1
Gabriel Goh's image synthesis using Yahoo's open_nsfw.

fit the set parameters. More than an eccentric exception, this arguably absurd dimension of NSFW filtering points to the fundamental abstractness involved in automated content classification and the shapes it is primed to recognize. Detached from any contexts of content production, circulation, or consumption, the parameters of offensiveness become calculable as formal properties.

Branding Porn SFW

In its myriad forms, the filtering of pornographic content obviously has a negative impact on the porn industry's capacity to attract audiences and revenue streams from advertising and subscribers. The porn industry nevertheless is far from being a passive victim of these interventions. In fact, MindGeek equally trades in age verification with its AgeID product blocking access to adult content. At the time of this writing, the UK government was about to outsource its national online age verification to Mind-Geek, following the 2017 Digital Economy Act, opening up considerable, monopolistic novel revenue streams for the company. In addition to such flexibility in the products offered, the porn industry has adopted a strategic approach to negotiating its NSFW status, in effect playing an elaborate game of peekaboo in which it become both visible and invisible. This is particularly evident in social media, a landscape largely resistant to pornographic displays.

In February 2015, Pornhub announced that they were developing a wearable device titled Wankband that lets users charge their smart devices with the kinetic energy generated through the up and down motions of male masturbation: "Every day, millions of hours of adult content are consumed online, wasting energy in the process and hurting the environment. At Pornhub we decided to do something about it. Introducing the Wankband: The first wearable tech that allows you to love the planet by loving yourself" (Pornhub 2015). Producing 100 percent renewable "guilt-free electricity," Wankband is part of a longer chain of publicity campaigns profiling Pornhub's brand and services as fun, user-friendly, socially responsible, and risk free. The general mode of these campaigns might, in British English, be defined as "cheeky": witty bordering on the rude and the irreverent. They can be divided roughly into three categories: publicity stunts, social and environmental causes contributed to under the rubric "Pornhub Cares," and "Pornhub Insights," which, similarly to "Google Trends," consists of statistics and infographics detailing site traffic and user trends.

Pornhub's publicity stunts have included the 2013 SFW television advertisement featuring a senior couple sitting on a park bench accompanied by an R&B tune which, according to the company, was intended for broadcast during the Super Bowl but was rejected by CBS (Stuart 2013), although this seems highly unlikely given the advertisement's low production values. In 2014, Pornhub announced an open SFW advertising contest encapsulating its brand. The crowdsourcing call attracted some 3,000 submissions, and the short-listed proposals were widely covered in online news forums and clickbaits well beyond platforms considered pornographic or NSFW. The winning ad poster, designed by the Turkish copywriter Nuri Gulver and titled "All You Need Is Hand," was erected on the iconic location of Times Square to the backing vocals of Gotham Rock Choir's rendition of the Beatles classic *All You Need Is Love*, only to be taken down shortly after for unspecified reasons (Maskeroni 2014). In 2014, Pornhub also set up a theme song contest and gave out free premium memberships to celebrate Valentine's Day. The next year, mainstream news outlets from the *Huffington Post* to *The Express*, *Times of India*, *The Mirror*, and CNBC reported the company's plan to collect a $3.4 million budget through crowdfunding in order to shoot the first ever pornographic film in space.

Pornhub's social causes have ranged from the "Save the Boobs" campaigns collecting money for breast cancer research on the basis of the videos viewed in its "big tit" and "small tit" categories; to the 2014 campaign "Pornhub Gives America Wood," which involved planting trees for every 100 videos watched in its "big dick" category; and the 2015 "Save the Balls" testicular cancer awareness campaign. In 2015, the company gave out its first US$25,000 scholarship for academic studies on the basis of the candidates' videos detailing how they strive to make others happy—the rationale being that Pornhub itself works "hard to make millions of people feel happy every single day." The following year, a scholarship was given for women studying science, technology, engineering, or math, with the aim of advancing women's careers in the tech industry, and in 2017, for those "contributing to a better future for the world." In addition, Pornhub has joined in a campaign for saving sperm whales and, together with porn star and intimate partner violence survivor Christy Mack, has set out to fight domestic abuse.

Both Pornhub's PR stunts and social responsibility campaigns revolve around construction, management, and maintenance of a brand community, and news of them spread quickly through news hubs, blogs, Twitter, and Facebook by virtue of their easy combination of humor and porn. The social causes are additionally focused on constructing a socially responsible—and in this sense, respectable—corporate brand that contributes to making the world a better place, even if the sums involved in its charitable campaigns are on the modest side; in 2018, Worth of the Web estimated the value of Pornhub at US$4 billion (Worth of the Web 2018).

In February 2017, Pornhub launched their "Sexual Wellness Center," a sex education site with information on reproductive health, STIs, and relationships. The role of pornography as a form of sex education has long been a topic of debate among educators, journalists, academics, and concerned adults: in most instances, porn is seen as bad in its pedagogical output and its false, exaggerated, and generic sexual scenarios (Albury 2013; Spišák and Paasonen 2017). By inserting the professional angle of sex education into their palette of free services, Pornhub further aimed to bolster its image of public responsibility.

Yet probably the most successful form of the company's PR campaigns involves "Pornhub Insights," its widely circulated and diverse user statistics, infographics, and thematic reports, such as those published in its annual "Year in Review." The annual reviews summarize website traffic, search behaviors and trends, use patterns, and devices used and breaks down this data according to search terms and lengths of visits in different countries: in 2018, there were a reported 33.5 billion visits resulting in 30.3 billion searches and some 4,403 petabytes of data transferred. Such summaries of porn consumption are understandably attractive to international online news sites and blogs wishing to catch the fleeting attention of users while their already digested, easily understandable representation further fuels their spreadability. Given the general, and notorious, shortage of reliable data on the patterns of online porn consumption, Pornhub statistics are shared and referenced broadly as evidence on a global scale. It is hardly breaking news for social media sites to collect data on the devices and operating systems used, clicks, searches, comments, and connections made and to archive, mine, analyze, and sell this data for the purposes of targeted advertising. But Pornhub's manner of recirculating and feeding back this data to consumers as a form of self-promotion remains exceptional.

Cutting through Pornhub's PR efforts is the aim of overcoming the boundary between things deemed SFW and those not. The campaigns afford Pornhub broad, generally positive international publicity on markedly mainstream media platforms for virtually no expense. Facebook, for example, allows the sharing of news items on Pornhub even when blocking direct links to the site itself as unsafe. It would be highly unlikely for most news sites covering Pornhub's campaigns to accept the company's advertisements should these be proposed, yet they support the circulation of links to the company's stunts and initiatives. Pornhub's PR stunts are perfectly attuned to the click economy of social media: they feed clickbaits, and clickbaits feed (and feed on) social media traffic. This translates as added value to all parties involved.

News on Pornhub's various PR initiatives are suitable to be shared among friends and workplace colleagues. As a broad cultural phenomenon, porn consumption makes a SFW topic of conversation: statistics in particular facilitate a distanced range of discussion detached from personal likes, preferences, tastes, fantasies, or use patterns which, like sexual palates and habits in general, are seldom the stuff of casual social conversation. Discussing Pornhub data over an office coffee break assumes no intimate relationship to the site and its categories or services, and it necessitates no personal identification as a porn consumer. Given that no disclosure of dimensions of desire is required to consume, distribute, and discuss Pornhub's SFW branding exercises, these also allow for a detached public consumption of porn with minimized social risk. In doing so, they work to circumvent the filtering mechanisms that limit porn's audience and industry potential. SFW branding strategies like these make porn visible in a context where its profound entanglement with the label of NSFW may otherwise render it completely hidden.

Mainstreaming Porn

Pornhub's trend and traffic reviews also make the implicit—yet loud—claim that these practices are ubiquitous enough parts of the rhythms and flows of networked media use across national boundaries, during both working hours and leisure, and hence something ordinary and socially safe. This is a firm gesture of mainstreaming, of moving porn consumption from the so-called "dark" or marginal side of Internet use toward its central traffic while also reframing it as a fun recreational activity. Although porn has been part and parcel of the mundane Web use since the very early days of graphic browsers, it has retained an illegitimate conceptual status as perennially controversial and objectionable content. In an *Adweek* interview, Pornhub Vice President Corey Price explains that "We want to push the conversation into the general public as something that's acceptable to talk about, while letting people know that watching porn shouldn't be an underground activity that's to be seen as shameful. Everyone does it, why not just bring that out in the open? The reason it causes a stir is due to an already accepted set of social norms" (Monnlos 2014). The overall aim of the PR campaigns is to build up Pornhub as a stigma-free entertainment brand among others.

This is not an entirely unprecedented task, considering the respective success and mainstream recognizability of the *Playboy* and *Hustler* brands across decades (e.g., Gunelius 2009; Osgerby 2001). Once known primarily for their print magazines and audiovisual content, both have long since reinvented themselves as lifestyle brands expanding to casinos, t-shirts, coffee mugs, and jewelry (McKee 2016). In fact, *Playboy*, traditionally the brand out of the two keeping in line with the dictates of so-called SFW good taste (see Kipnis 1996), stopped publishing images of naked women on its pages in 2016 because of the resistance that they caused in the younger male readership. The company ultimately reneged on this decision but in a fashion that rebrands its nudity as desexualized and apolitical (Fisher 2017; Hefner 2017): according to the cover of the March/April edition of 2017, "naked is normal." At the same time, Pornhub, catering undeniably NSFW hardcore content, profiles itself as an entertainment brand that is increasingly desirable among women. Their "Year in Review" identified porn for women as the defining search trend of 2017. The inclusion and address of female audiences resonates with the longer normalization of sex and the framing of sex toys as safe, healthy, and fun (Comella 2008, 63). All this involves domestication whereby products, be these material commodities or media materials, that are deemed unsavory, inappropriate, and off the mainstream are rendered familiar, acceptable, routine, and ordinary, as well as increasingly safe to consume.

At the time of this writing, Pornhub's Alexa ranking was 27, sandwiched between Netflix and LinkedIn, which made it the most visited porn site globally. This notable popularity, combined with the site's brand-building exercises, has understandably made it increasingly lucrative as an advertising platform. Advertisements on porn video aggregator sites have conventionally consisted of pop-ups and banner ads for cam sites, pay sites, and adult dating services. However, in 2013, the food delivery app Eat24 launched an ad campaign on Pornhub after calculating that they could accomplish the same reach as with Google, Facebook, or Twitter for only one tenth of the cost (Truong 2013). The fashion brand Diesel followed suit in 2016. The gradual, albeit to date modest, migration of mainstream advertising on porn sites results from the attractive balance of cost and attention—not only the attention of the sites' users but also the attention that such campaigns gain in social media—as well as the added value of "porn chic edge" that the campaigns afford the companies in question.

These developments resonate with diagnoses made of the changing cultural role of pornography during the past decade or so through notions such as "sexualization" (Attwood 2009; Smith 2010), the "normalisation of porn" (Poynor 2006), "pornographicization" (Smith 2010), "pornification" (Gill 2008; Mowlabocus 2007; Mulholland 2013; Paasonen, Nikunen, and Saarenmaa 2007; Paul 2005), "porning" (Sarracino and Scott 2008), and "raunch culture" (Levy 2006). Despite their mutual differences, such conceptualizations aim to account for how pornography has grown mundane in its accessibility, how people of different ages and genders are routinely consuming it, and how the flirtation with both the sexually suggestive and the sexually explicit is ubiquitous in media culture. They identify the mainstreaming of pornography through its popularity (bearing in mind the annual volume of Pornhub traffic alone), as well as the general visibility of pornography in the guise of porn stars turned mainstream media celebrities; in its aesthetics circulated in films, television shows, and journalistic overviews; as well as in art projects grown fascinated with its imageries (Attwood 2009). As a long-standing media cultural trend, flirtation with pornography is telling of the perpetual—albeit also regularly uncomfortable—public presence of sexually explicit materials, the simultaneous fascination and aversion that they entail, as well as the constant labor involved in drawing pornography apart from mainstream media.

In other words, sexual imageries and routines long considered obscene—literally, ones to be put "out of sight"—have gained a new kind of visibility, or "onscenity," within media culture (Attwood 2009, xiv; Williams 2004). The mainstreaming and domestication involved in Pornhub's SFW media stunts dilute the scent of forbidden fruit that has contributed to the allure and overall cultural status of pornography as that which necessitates specific policing, censorship, flagging, and filtering (see Kendrick 1996; Kuhn 1994, 23). These campaigns are highly savvy in increasing the brand's positive recognizability within social media's attention economy of clicks, links, and shares that the site's NSFW video content cannot enter. In doing so, they extend the brand of porn itself into wider contexts.

Work in the Online Porn Industry

Through mainstreaming, porn consumption may be losing some of its association with danger and risk, even in places of work. At the same time, the production of porn and the labor of porn performers retain their negative association with harm and danger. This is also an area in which digital technologies have been mobilized, or where they function by default to reduce harm and reorder the dimensions of risk and safety associated with porn work—and, as we discuss later in chapter 5, in sex work more generally. Intersections with social media have complex effects on how porn performers and industry workers manage and experience their careers. Beyond the increasing necessity of branding porn as mainstream and SFW, the labor of the porn industry itself is reshaped by both digital production and online distribution.

Alongside the concentration of porn consumption on select online platforms, corporate ownership has centralized within the industry. With the exception of XVideos and xHamster, the Montreal-based MindGeek (formerly known as Manwin) owns most of the key video aggregator sites including PornHub, YouPorn, RedTube, and Tube8, giving it a virtual monopoly in contemporary online porn distribution (Auerbach 2014). The company has also bought up a number of porn studios—such as the high-profile Reality Kings, Digital Playground, Men.com, and Brazzers—that have been struggling with the decreased profitability of pay content following the dramatic drop in DVD sales and increases in the free sharing of pirated content via aggregator sites and torrents which have contributed to diminished revenues from pay for views and premium membership fees. Analyzing MindGeek's dominant role in porn, technology writer David Auerbach (2014) notes that it has put "industry members in the paradoxical position of working for the very company that profits from the piracy of their work," leading to what he identifies as a vampiric ecosystem: "MindGeek's producers make porn films mostly for the sake of being uploaded on to MindGeek's free tube sites, with lower returns for the producers but higher returns for MindGeek, which makes money off of the tube ads that does not go to anyone involved in the production side" (Auerbach 2014).

Within this new centralized economic system involving a dispersed corporate structure, the work of contemporary porn models and performers increasingly means freelancing and self-employment. Exclusive studio contracts were standard up until the early 2000s when the U.S. porn industry partly emulated the star system of old Hollywood, but this practice is in decline. As the gay porn star Colby Keller explains, "The way that MindGeek works with Men.com is that they have a team of producers and the producer gets a deal, a certain amount of money, and they are responsible for finding models and budgeting it. . . . But there isn't a lot of transparency to it and even negotiating pay can be very stressful" (in Paasonen 2017a, 73). The lack of transparency connected to pay, which even seasoned, high-profile veterans such as Keller struggle with, accompanies a sense of precarity connected to the labor of porn.

As the profit balance of pornography has shifted significantly from production to distribution in complex ways, it is increasingly difficult for porn performers to create lucrative careers in making films alone. Consumers are still willing to pay for specialized, novelty, and niche content and for live webcam services, yet its abundant availability has eaten away at the general profitability of porn. Thus, while there is little doubt as to the impressive volume of porn consumption, this does not necessarily translate as generous pay for workers in the sector. As Heather Berg (2016) points out, porn work may be a central point of identification but is not necessarily the main source of income among performers. Instead, money is made from webcamming, escorting, and strip club performances managed under one's star brand, which in turn is maintained through social media:

> Porn work is, paradoxically, both the most prestigious sex work identity and the least remunerative one. Workers pursue alternative income streams for different reasons. Some take non-performing gigs in order to sustain themselves between film gigs or before the hoped-for take-off of their porn careers, while others remain in porn primarily so that they can increase earnings in these other gigs. Both approaches represent workers' creative strategies for navigating the terms of their labour in an increasingly precarious industry. (Berg 2016, 161)

On the one hand, contemporary porn's political economy builds on a reserve army of labor that is "willing to perform in porn even when pay and conditions are poor" and where workers are placed "in shifting positions as entrepreneurs, independent contractors, employees, contracted and freelance managers, and producers" (Berg 2016, 161). On the other hand, this freelance gig economy allows for flexibility and diversity in terms of star image and the projects and forms of employment that porn models are willing and able to undertake.

Porn stars build and manage their careers through diverse online platforms as independent entrepreneurs: in the case of Keller, who has training in both anthropology and the visual arts, this ranges from blogging and tweeting to the online sharing of his multiple-year, crowd-funded film project, *Colby Does America*, edited on a volunteer basis. Keller has been a fashion model for the designer Vivienne Westwood (in 2016) and a model merman for the visual artist Cameron Stalheim's 2014 MFA project, "and then I saw Colby on the Street and my fantasy died." His star image balances and combines the fields of art and porn while many other models combine porn with other fields of sex work. Porn models, mainstream and alternative, gay and straight, are using their films as advertisements while making money through escort services. Meanwhile, taking up porn allows for better wages as an escort (Berg 2016, 167–168; see also Auerbach 2014; McClean 2013; Salmon 2015).

All this marks a departure from the older practice of porn stars performing live for, and setting up webcam sessions with, their fans without engaging in paid sex with them. At least superficially, this change also suggests an increased risk in the labor of porn actors. The work of escorting and porn differ in terms of their legal status as well as in terms of control over wages, working hours, and conditions of labor (cf. Berg 2014; see also chapter 5). At the same time, different kinds of commercial sex work involve occupational health and safety issues ranging from legal hazards (escorting being penalized in many countries, the United States included), health and well-being (including strain and the risk of violence), and social stigma (see Alexander 1998; Rekart 2006; Ross et al. 2012; Sanders and Campbell 2007). In Ronald Weitzer's (2009) typology of different kinds of female sex work, he asserts that the further a sex worker is from the unpredictable activity of the street, the less likely she is to be victimized either physically or financially. As a form of indoor work, porn labor rarely takes place between complete strangers and may therefore be seen as safer in comparison to escorting. Nevertheless, as Berg (2016, 168–171; chapter 5) points out, alternative streams of income such as escorting also allow for larger degrees of choice and freedom over pricing, scheduling, location, and bodily performance in comparison to porn sets, particularly when these are organized through webcam platforms. The potential for harm associated with porn, camming, and escorting are thus bound to context and do not necessarily reflect a unidirectional move from conditions with less to more risk.

One of the often assumed risks for porn workers is the threat to health of sexually transmitted infections (STIs) or HIV transmission, despite the protection systems in place. In California, historically the hub of professional porn production, adult performers are screened for HIV and STI every

14 days. Following the 2012 Safer Sex in the Adult Film Industry Act, porn studios are required to use condoms in scenes involving vaginal and anal penetration in Los Angeles County. In 2016, Proposition 60, driving the similar condom mandate statewide, failed to pass after being vehemently opposed by porn professionals. The mandate was seen not only as opposed to freedom of expression but also as hazardous in that the extended use of condoms in penetrative sex gives rise to friction, burns, and chafing, making the labor of porn both risky and painful.

It is noteworthy that the performers themselves first initiated HIV and STI prevention measures within the porn industry. In 1988, Sharon Mitchell, former porn star with a PhD in sexology, founded the Adult Industry Medical Healthcare Foundation (AIM) that provided STI screening and sexual health information. Soon after AIM was closed down in 2011, the Adult Performer Advocacy Committee (APAC), similarly run by porn performers and consisting of an all-performer membership, was launched to provide career mentoring and information resources on sexual health both on set and off:

> The mission of APAC is to provide representation for performers in the adult film industry and to protect performers' rights to a safer and more professional work environment. We do this through education of each other and the greater community, development of ethical best practices, and fostering of solidarity. We review existing health and safety protocols, and will initiate new ones as needed. We are committed to working cohesively with all aspects of the adult entertainment industry and the public, strengthening unity between all performers, and maintaining a work environment where workers are valued, respected, and educated. (APAC 2017)

Such self-organization aims at the advancement of work culture where performers are treated and respected as professionals according to standards outlined in the APAC Model's Bill of Rights. As discussed in chapter 5, other bodies advocating the rights of sex workers have a similarly strong presence online. On Twitter, APAC (@apacsocial) campaigns for the bill and other interconnected issues such as nondiscriminatory pay and workplace safety. Contra to the lack of transparency connected to the employment patterns of much porn production, Twitter has also become a key platform for disclosures of the industry's working practices which can help mitigate risks for workers by creating avenues for worker solidarity and information exchange.

Given the multiple roles that social media plays in contemporary porn work, people within the industry greeted the U.S. FOSTA-SESTA laws, introduced in April 2018, with dismay and protest. In short, the acts render social media services responsible for online trafficking. This makes these services remove and ban all content related to sex work, even when such materials are not sexually explicit. In her interview with the feminist porn producer, Erica Lust, on the implications of the new legislation, journalist Emma Garland (2018) argues that "sex bloggers and smaller, independent companies—like feminist, body-positive, and fetish sites—which rely on social media to attract traffic will struggle, while inherently misogynistic mainstream sites can afford to weather the storm." Furthermore:

> In addition to harming consensual sex workers while pushing sex trafficking further underground, the legislation's broad language means that sites now seem to be over-censoring their users to ensure they're not liable for anything problematic. This has already led to sex workers' Google Drive files being locked or deleted, Patreon changing its terms of service to exclude pornography, and Microsoft prohibiting profanity and nudity on Skype.
>
> Needless to say, this affects the livelihoods of already vulnerable sex workers first and foremost. (Garland 2018)

Such enforced platform governance obviously further limits the spaces available for independent and freelance porn performers and producers on social media, given that Patreon has been a key revenue channel for independent performers. The legislation conflates all sex work with trafficking and, hence, with enforced, abused, and exploited labor. It equally supports, and amplifies, the general tendency to frame pornography out from social media and the online interactions deemed acceptable by hegemonic data giants like Facebook and Google. As such, the acts render visible more long-standing tensions between online pornography and social media, as well as the diverse ways in which they continue to intermesh.

Reputation Management and the Online Porn Industry

Twitter in particular has come to serve multiple communication roles in the online porn industry. On one hand, the platform has become a central actor in how both porn studios and porn stars construct and maintain relations with their fan base, build brands, and develop potential revenues. On the other hand, news of unethical or dangerous labor practices can travel quickly through its networks, reaching journalists, performers, and fans, impacting reputations and careers overnight. Since starting his career at the age of 18 in 2004, James Deen was hailed as the world's first male feminist porn star—"the Tom Cruise of porn: a performer who parlayed boy-next-door good looks into unlikely fame and success" (Carroll 2015). Deen's social media presence was greatly amplified by the animated GIFs and other viral content crafted and shared by his female fan base—self-identified as "Deenagers"—on mainstream social media platforms. As Helen Hester, Bethan Jones, and Sarah Taylor-Harman (2015, 362) note, such GIF generation and exchange is explicitly motivated by straight female sexual desire, and it has involved scenes from Deen's films "featuring a female co-star (often locked in a direct eye-contact embrace with his off-screen partner Stoya) being pleasured by him."

In November 2015, Deen's former co-performer and partner, the alt porn star Stoya mentioned just above, wrote two tweets accusing him of rape: "That thing where you log in to the Internet for a second and see people idolizing the guy who raped you as a feminist. That thing sucks" and "James Deen held me down and fucked me while I said no, stop, used my safeword. I just can't nod and smile when people bring him up anymore." Other female performers soon joined in with tweets reporting similar behavior on set and off, and adult companies, including kink.com, known for its elaborate BDSM scenarios, cut ties with Deen as a performer and producer because of his alleged disregard for consent. Following this Twitter-driven incident, kink.com revised its "model bill of rights" and further clarified issues connected to consent (Potter 2016, 112). In the course of all this, Deen's career suffered, yet this slump seems to have been only momentary, possibly since his star image had incorporated roughness and domination from the outset.

In a similar Twitter event, the porn star Nikki Benz accused director Tony T of choking and stomping on her head on set in a series of tweets on December 20, 2016. According to Benz, the session resulted in a nonconsensual rape scene shot for the high-profile, MindGeek-owned studio Brazzers, for which she was a brand ambassador. Her pleas for cutting the scene had been ignored, and the experience had been traumatic. Several female performers stepped up to disclose similar abusive treatment from the same producer, as well as the lack of interest that this treatment had been met with within the porn industry when reported. Brazzers responded with the tweet, "Hey @nikkibenz we're behind you and will never tolerate negative behavior towards stars by any 3rd party producer." The company also released a statement of having ended all collaboration, present and future, with Tony T:

> Brazzers, along with the entire adult community, was upset to learn of the recent events surrounding a film shoot involving one of our own, Nikki Benz . . . The moment that the disturbing details of the event were brought to our attention, we treated it with the urgency that it demanded and investigated the situation to understand what exactly had taken place. It appears that some of the alleged conduct could have occurred, and we took immediate measure to sever our relationship with the producer in question. Not only have we terminated all existing professional engagements with the producer, but any possibility for any future endeavors with this producer have also been quashed.
>
> We have also refused to purchase the scene in question as it stands in direct contrast with our mandate to ensure that performers' consent, boundaries and limits are respected. It is our commitment that this offensive scene will never find itself listed as a Brazzers property. (Brazzers 2016)

While apparently a powerful statement in support of porn workers, this is, ultimately, a cop-out. Condemning Tony T's unethical behavior, the company nevertheless failed to take responsibility for what had unfolded on set and, consequently, for that which may have unfolded in their outsourced productions more generally. The case of Benz is particularly noteworthy as she is a major star: if such abuse can happen to her, it may happen to anyone. Colby Keller similarly recounts how "All the horrible stories you can imagine in a porn company, I've experienced" (Paasonen 2017a, 74). This would imply that within the current system of production, porn studios do not protect the well-being of even their most bankable stars.

In the aftermath of Benz's disclosure, Brazzer's Twitter account that generally consists of promotional material grew rife with tweets defending the centrality of consent, the rights of women, and the unacceptability of violence and bullying within the industry (see figure 3.2). Benz's fan base, known as "Benzmafia," asked people to unfollow Brazzers and to unsubscribe from their membership services. Meanwhile, news items on the incident circulated widely across social media platforms.

Social media thus made it possible to highlight a particular incident of sexual workplace violence and even to partly police and amend labor conditions. Complaints of unethical treatment connected to porn production

Figure 3.2
Twitter support for Nikki Benz.

spread quickly and reverberate in social media in ways that are impossible for studios to control or manage. It should nevertheless be noted that it takes clout to raise a Twitter storm of such visibility. As an established and highly popular star, Benz has enough status to challenge a major studio whereas models lower in the food chain have fewer possibilities to challenge and question oppressive work conditions in ways that are likely to leave a mark. Furthermore, Twitter storms tend to have short life spans, even when these are intense—and, as the example of Deen illustrates, the critical exposures they afford do not necessarily have lasting effects. Still, in facilitating public discussion between workers within the industry, their fans, and the wider public, social media can contribute to the recognition and destigmatizing of porn work, and of the actors themselves.

Amateur Labors

The rise of amateur pornography in the context of global distribution giants such as Pornhub has also reframed the notion of porn work and its connections to risk. In the case of amateur porn, the production of images and videos may not be perceived as work but more as a public extension of sexual lives. Resulting from the broad access to digital video technologies, the ubiquity of broadband connections, and the ease of uploading and publicly sharing user-generated content, amateur pornography has, along with webcam sites, been a key porn trend for the past decade, and more.

The attraction of amateur porn and webcams builds, in diverse ways, on their sense of directness, realness, and authenticity. The appeal of non-professionally produced pornography is regularly, even routinely, associated with its unpolished aesthetics of domestic intimacy and rawness, as well as with its assumedly ethical principles and conditions of production (e.g., Hardy 2009; Hofer 2014; van Doorn 2010). This is exemplified in MakeLoveNotPorn.tv, which defines its amateur-produced but commercial content against notions of porn performance. It describes itself as "of the people. By the people. And for the people who believe that the sex we have in our everyday life is the hottest sex there is" (Make Love Not Porn TV 2017). Understood as quotidian, interpersonal sexuality, authenticity is a key selling point suggestive of intimate connection (see also Maddison 2015). On webcams, the ready availability of performers, and the possibility of direct communication with them, implies a similar, yet mediated, sense of intimacy.

Produced in private spaces alone or with people of one's own choosing, amateur porn work involves a different sense of agency than that attributed to porn stars working under contract with production studios and at the demand of directors. This is not to say that either amateur performers or cammers would simply operate autonomously. Amateur and pro-am porn performers with degrees of microcelebrity status (Senft 2015) shape their videos in accordance with fan feedback as part of their personal branding strategies, while webcam performers similarly act out scenarios desired by paying customers, even when these involve problematic gendered and racialized dynamics (Jones 2015). The maintenance of audience relationships is key to how independent models make money from the pornographic clips and shows they distribute online. This sense of mediated intimacy is akin to the interactions that porn stars foster on Twitter in order to build and develop their public personas, yet the forms it takes can be much more direct and taxing, extending to private messaging and texting at odd hours. In this way, social media porn work broadens into diverse forms of networked communication where the boundaries of work time and leisure grow ephemeral.

The same applies to the physical spaces of work. The labor of both amateur porn and webcam shows is largely situated in domestic spaces and hence detached from the production routines of porn studios that make use of rented apartments—and, occasionally, hotel rooms—devoid of personal décor and other material traces of everyday life. In contrast, textures of domesticity contribute to the appeal of user-generated content (Paasonen 2011, 98, 104). Some amateur porn is detached from the monetary flow of the porn industry in that its fruits are uploaded online for free without its performers and other creators receiving monetary compensation. User-generated pornography travels across platforms both freely and for money, and, given its popularity, it is neither marginal nor coherent as a field of practice.

In his exploration of the similarities between the acts, poses, and routines of amateur and professional pornography, Niels van Doorn (2010) points out that amateur porn both approximates the generic conventions of studio porn and provides alternatives to them as that which is assumedly more authentic and less acted out. In other words, amateur pornography reiterates mainstream conventions, as these have emerged through repetition and serial variation through decades of film and video production, in order to appeal to its consumers. At the same time, amateur porn needs to come across as more real in the bodies, acts, and relations that it conveys. In her analysis of Sell Your Sex Tape, Kristina Pia Hofer (2014) notes that the amateur videos published on the site perform pornographic heterosexual domesticity devoid of friction or compulsory routines. These mundane scenarios are also elaborately staged "to gloss over the fact that producing a pornographic video is labour" (Hofer 2014, 335, 343–344). In other words, it takes some work to develop a desirable amateur porn commodity, and the relatable authenticity of amateur pornography necessitates crafted performances of intimacy and domesticity.

All in all, amateur productions play a central role in the economy of contemporary online porn. The origins of Pornhub, for example, lie in the distribution of amateur content, pointing to the leakiness of divisions drawn between amateur and professional, independent and corporate, noncommercial and commercial porn—between labors of love and work tasks performed for profit (Paasonen 2010). All kinds of porn, new and old, homemade and corporate, are shared and consumed on the same, centralized platforms. This means that the products, despite their possibly drastic aesthetic and political differences, enter the same logic of operation and monetization. On Pornhub, amateur models are invited to upload their homemade tapes and make money—purportedly, up to $5,000 monthly—from the advertising revenue that the site partly shares with them. The invitation is for "Fun, Fame, Fortune" and getting "paid for doing something (and someone) you love." Amateur of the Month and Amateur of the Year prizes—also given out in the categories of newcomer and top video—range between $250 and $10,000. As is the case with You-Tube, only a small percentage of user-generated content attracts enough views to qualify for a percentage of advertising revenue though. In many instances, aspirations of Internet fame, or that which Pornhub calls "a taste of porno superstardom and mad cash," fail to translate as actual monetary profits (cf. van Dijck 2009, 53).

Porn platforms often retain the rights to distribute contributions in any formats and media that they see fit, so that users uploading their content may maintain precious little control over its later circulation and commodification. The situation is similar to that of mainstream social media services, such as Facebook, which reserve the rights to user-generated content and relies on unpaid user labor to both provide content and generate user data that can be sold to advertising, marketing, or data analysis companies. In most instances, users are unlikely to fully read through the terms of service or to pay much attention to the contractual details that govern their participation in social media. Put in Marxist terms, amateur online porn involves formal economic exploitation in that users are not compensated in direct correspondence with the amount of value that their videos generate. This effect is amplified when one takes into consideration the potentially long commercial lives of content that is housed in and retrievable from almost infinitely expandable databases. An amateur porn performer may find a company generating profit from their labor many years after its initial production. This exploitation thus also involves the alienation of porn performers from the products of their labor through the signing away of rights to it, typically in perpetuity.

The same dynamic manifests in the labor of site users. The revenues of platforms on which amateur content is shared are based on targeted advertising and premium memberships. As is the case with all commercial media, the rationale is to sell data about audiences to advertisers with the aid of content attractive enough to make users stay and return again (e.g., van Dijck 2013; Smythe 2014). Porn users whose clicks, search terms, and personal data form the economic basis of these sites—and that of social media—may also pay additional membership fees. Using Marxist terms again, once the data of users becomes commodified and marketable to advertisers, they are exploited laborers (Jarrett 2016). The dynamics of online porn use—ongoing cycles of attraction and distraction (Paasonen 2016)—readily facilitate the flows of traffic that can be repackaged as consumer information. The gradual entrance of mainstream companies into Pornhub advertising discussed above indicates the growth potential identified within this exploitative market.

Digital Modeling

Accounts of rape and assault on set, like those recounted by Benz, and of economic exploitation of amateur users and producers, only seem to confirm the very worst assumptions concerning the working practices of the porn industry. As such, they reinforce the connections of porn work, violence, and harm, as voiced in antipornography activism in particular. Some commentators understand amateur pornography as voluntary self-prostitution that is telling of how harmful pornographic conventions have become ingrained in culture and in women's self-perceptions (see Bray 2011, 164). Here, amateur labor comes across as indicative of false consciousness—and even as a form of self-abuse—while commercial porn labor is identified with sexual exploitation. Antipornography campaigners have accused the industry of being lacking in ethical principles, of trading in violence/crime, and of degrading women (e.g., Farley 2004; Reist and Bray 2011). The assumed riskiness of porn work resonates with concerns about the genre's allegedly harmful effects on individuals, relationships, and the social fabric at large.

It would be problematic, though, to claim that all workers in the porn industry are exposed to the forces of exploitation and alienation for the already established reason that the "porn industry" is not a particularly clear point of reference. With its connotations of factorylike centralized conveyor belt mass manufacture, the term "industry" seems to imply some unity in economic models, forms of labor, ethics, and aesthetics of production. While there may be more corporate centralization to porn production and distribution than ever before, a multiplicity of practices coexist under the umbrella term of the porn industry, not least because of the diverse production practices that digital media tools facilitate. This also has implications for how we understand the distribution of risks and safety in porn work.

Consider the case of animated pornography where the work of porn is detached from human physical sexual performance as such, involving instead visual modeling and occasional sound acting. Increasingly sophisticated in its audiovisual delivery, animated pornography spans myriad subcategories and genres, from adult parody versions of Disney characters gone wild to machinima (videos generated in real time with game engines and additional software) and the current wave of 3-D, high-definition bodies approximating photorealistic aesthetics. In the realm of computer-generated still images, comics, and videos, impossible embodiments and brutal scenarios abound. A Google image search for 3-D porn comics generates top hits on incest fantasies where minors sport massive genitalia and taboos function as key incentives for action. As in literary pornography (Marcus 1964), bodily capacities and desires know no bounds: this is a realm of unbridled sexual opulence. The pleasures involved in the processes of modeling the regularly unlikely bodies and acts of animated porn are a key motivation for the often unpaid, voluntary, and hobbyist labor required. In Tiziana Terranova's (2004, 84) terms, we "witness an investment of desire into production of the kind cultural theorists have mainly theorized in relation to consumption."

Studio FOW, established in 2014, is a specialist in crowd-funded Source Filmmaker (SFM) hentai monster videos set in game worlds. Their "born digital" machinima depicts spectacular, violent 3-D scenes of nonconsensual sex between female game characters, monsters, and demons, as well as human men, drawing strongly on the traditions of Japanese animated pornography (Hernandez 2015; Paasonen 2018b). Studio FOW's films generally involve a resampling and reimagining of game characters and events, and this is also where a central part of their attraction lies (Falkenstein 2011). As sexually explicit extensions of in-game events, the films focus on female characters, from Lara Croft to the female cast of *Final Fantasy*, set in elaborate scenarios of sexual humiliation, submission, and rape. As such, they seem to amplify both the sexualization of female game characters (e.g., Burgess, Stermer, and Burgess 2007; Stermer and Burkley 2012) and the toxicity of game culture (Consalvo 2012). At the same time, the female fan base of 3-D monster porn is suggestive of a more complex entanglement of sexual fantasies, desires, and identities. Furthermore, despite the visual—both affective and representational—plane of sexual extremity and risk, Studio FOW explicitly highlights the affordances of animation as a safe means to explore violent sexual scenarios:

> This medium allows us to explore fetishes in a safe environment where 3D models are used instead of actual people. . . . We aim to make movies for responsible adults . . . this medium bypasses the seedier facets of the pornography industry. In live action movies the viewer never really knows if the actresses are being exploited, especially in rape fantasies.
>
> We animate digital models in a safe environment, and the voice talent records from the safety of their own homes, which means that our medium is the ideal platform for exploring these darker themes with a clear conscience. (in Hernandez 2015)

Contemporary animated porn is fundamentally the work of algorithms and a means of exploring unlikely, fantastic, and extreme scenarios impossible to physically act out without censure or bodily harm. Unencumbered by the physical limitations of what human bodies may act out, animated bodies can, after all, stretch and bulge without tearing, bursting, or bleeding. Framing their productions through the discourse of work safety, the creators of animated porn are part of the informal and formal IT labor force contributing to the redefinition of the long-assumed relationship between the adult entertainment sector and workplace danger.

Protected by fair use copyright policies as parodies generated for non-profit purposes, Studio FOW's crowd-funded films can be freely downloaded and they reach an audience of millions across tube sites. These productions are enabled by fan contributions, and their collaborators include "animators, voice actors, and artists, who have come together to work on video game porn movies as a hobby" (Hernandez 2015). Studio FOW builds on voluntary participation and contributions characteristic of online platforms and fan cultures. Like the rise of online amateur porn, their success suggests many things in terms of how the work of porn entails "channelling collective labour . . . into monetary flows and its structuration within capitalist business practices" (Terranova 2000, 39). Both paid and unpaid work feeds into products shared for free, which, much like amateur porn, eventually generate value for tube sites making profits out of advertisement revenues. In other words, Studio FOW makes evident both the coexistence of highly different operating principles in the creation and distribution of online porn as well as the degree to which these forms intermesh, build on, and feed one another.

Porn as IT Labor

At the very same time, the porn industry is actively trying to refashion itself as a branch of the creative industry (see also McKee 2016). At least before the #MeToo movement gained momentum in October 2017 by highlighting expansive sexual harassment in Hollywood and beyond, the creative industries have seldom been picked out as involving specific risks of harm at the workplace. As early as 2012, Fabian Thylmann, then a 33-year-old managing partner of Manwin (now MindGeek), characterized it as essentially a tech company. At this point in time, the company was already running Playboy's television and online operations. Thylmann saw these as a gateway to collaboration with large tech and entertainment companies, including Google and Netflix, which would veer away from more explicit pornographic content but would "not be afraid of Playboy, though" (Morris 2012). MindGeek currently introduces itself as a company engaging in search engine marketing, hosting, security, antifraud, cloud service, advertising, media content delivery, data analysis, and customer support:

> MindGeek continues to drive the state of technology forward, developing industry-leading solutions enabling faster, more efficient delivery of content every second to millions of customers worldwide. The Company is committed to enhancing its technological capabilities and thrives on a sustainable growth trajectory built on innovation and excellence.
>
> With over 1000 employees worldwide, MindGeek continues its expansion with the acquisition and licensing of some of the most iconic brands in entertainment media. (MindGeek 2019)

As porn distribution has shifted online, the hard core of porn labor increasingly centers on IT skills, such as software engineering and information design, in ways that call for a redefinition of what is understood as the work of the porn industry. Labor in video aggregator sites largely involves tasks such as running servers, database maintenance, data management, and the tweaking of algorithms, as well as work tasks connected to marketing and legal affairs. Consequently, MindGeek's open positions involve careers in software engineering and programming, PHP and Web development, project management, customer service, sales, support, video editing, website optimization, mobile design, legal counsel, financial, data, security, Web analysis, marketing, and PR. Such skills, tasks, and professions form the backbone of Pornhub, and they differ little from those within other high-tech companies trading in social media and contributing to the datafication of everyday life.

If one ignores the nature of the audiovisual content with which their workers engage, there seems to be little unsafe in the white- or no-collar careers available at MindGeek: in this sense, occupational safety claims echo those voiced within Studio FOW's computer-generated pornographic animation. One might nevertheless speculate about the absence or presence of concerns common in the high-tech industry more generally, such as male domination, the cornering off of women's tech professions into PR and user testing, the difficulties in sustaining work–life balance, problems of burnout, and the individualization of risk (e.g., Martin and Barnard 2013; Marwick 2013b; Neff 2012; Webster 1996).

All in all, MindGeek runs hundreds of sites that consume more bandwidth than Twitter, Amazon, and Facebook combined (Auerbach 2014). This is not surprising considering that, along with humor and gossip, sites trading in streaming video require substantial bandwidth. Given the size of MindGeek and its operations, its public presence remains notably inconspicuous, especially when compared to the energetic brand-building activities of Pornhub. It also flies under the radar of regulatory authorities, allowing it to continue its growth and its industry dominance. Auerbach (2014) sees the taboos surrounding pornography, in the United States in particular, as a key reason for why antitrust actions against MindGeek are unlikely despite their factual monopoly status and their regular flouting of copyright legislation. According to Auerbach, were porn tube sites considered part of the mainstream of high-tech companies—rather than an NSFW glitch haunting their operations—antimonopoly and copyright motions toward tube sites would be more active. The fact that pornography is *not* perceived as a branch of the creative industries operating according to its general ethical and legal standards then facilitates highly visible, mass-scale content piracy on aggregator sites. At the same time, and possibly paradoxically, the dominant role of Pornhub in particular speaks not only of the unprecedented centralization in porn distribution but also of the mainstreaming and increased visibility of porn use as leisure activity. As discussed above, the latter also involves a process of knowing brand building that, in aiming to normalize and mainstream porn, may confront the industry with regulatory challenges.

Diverse Labors

Considered as descriptive of processes through which value is produced, the labor of online porn is a tortuous assemblage. It encompasses networks of people, software, and network technologies, diverse ethical and aesthetic principles, business models, labor practices, and financial goals. Pornography is performed by veteran stars and aspiring new talent, hobbyists, and algorithms and is produced for the purposes of money, social, and cultural capital alike, and in conditions both exceedingly safe and clearly not. Porn is consumed—and in fact also produced—at the office, on the street, at home, in cars, and in places of study. It is financed through crowdfunding, targeted advertising, and premium membership fees while the work required spans from highly demanding bodily choreographies to specified IT expertise. Discussing the field as a singular entity therefore comes with obvious problems, as does any discussion of the contemporary porn industry that continues to draw on the operating principles of print and video pornography based on the distribution of material consumables. At the same time, most available scholarly overviews on the porn industry are retrospective—as well as markedly U.S. specific—in their approach (Tarrant 2016).

The limited availability of information concerning the labor practices and financial arrangements connected to aggregator sites further complicates the issue. The flows of money involved in advertising and sponsored content remain unaccounted for, as does the overall profitability of online pornography. While corporate giants such as MindGeek fashion themselves as lifestyle brands and IT companies contributing to the creative industries, there remains much that is opaque in their principles of operation. Value creation within online porn is tied in with data and traffic flows (of the kind visualized by Pornhub Insights) as much as it is with particular commodities such as videos. This in turn impacts on the ways in which labor is organized in the occupational sector, opening the field to wider socioeconomic trends of freelancing and outsourcing but also to new modes of networking, publicness, and empowerment. All in all, it is fair to say that both the workplace and the consumption contexts of contemporary porn fail to sit seamlessly in any neatly predefined categories of SFW and NSFW.

The ways in which these dimensions of online porn intersect, overlap, and contradict each other make evident that the distribution of risk and safety has changed for producers and consumers alike. Consequently, blanket assumptions of harm associated with porn production need to be rethought, not least since some forms of work seem to be becoming safer while others shift toward potentially riskier forms, such as escorting or direct sex work (see chapter 5). Assumptions about the reputational risks of porn consumption—and what even constitutes porn consumption—equally need to be reexamined as the cultural products of porn diversify and are to a degree mainstreamed. All of this challenges the default labeling of porn as NSFW and as consistently worthy of filtering, raising questions of the validity and politics of such equations. The dynamics influencing the field of online porn intersect with wider transformations in labor relations, taste conventions, and norms concerning social propriety. In the following chapter we further explore these dimensions of NSFW social media. Beginning with an exploration of the ecology of sexually explicit user-generated visual content, we continue to question normative assumptions of what is unsafe about social media, and what other aspects of risk connected to content production and circulation may necessitate critical inquiry.

4 The Ambiguity of Dick Pics

As is evident at this point, #NSFW is a tool of classification in the convoluted visual landscape of social media where people, algorithms, organizations, and companies are constantly making judgments and taking actions concerning the appropriateness of the content that is circulated and rendered visible. This chapter shifts the focus to user-generated NSFW practices, their connection with the affective dynamics of humor, grossness, shame, interest, and desire, as well as their links with sexualities and gendered underpinnings. More specifically, we zoom in on the seemingly ubiquitous, yet ambiguous, object of the dick pic and the different social circulations—and degrees of publicness—it enters.

Identified by The Urban Dictionary as "a wordless suggestion of intercourse," the dick pic involves the male display of bodily goods. In its ubiquity, it remains a prime example of user-generated NSFW content. Despite the invitations for sexual intimacy that dick pics may involve, their purpose often remains obscure to recipients and the reactions they evoke do not all revolve in the positive registers of affect: this is routinely reported to be the case with images of the unsolicited kind (Waling and Pym 2019). Like the NSFW tag more broadly, the dick pic both catches and orients attention. At the same time, it involves gradations of risk connected to privacy, reputation, and professional status for the producers, recipients, and distributors of this visual social media content.

Dick pics are NSFW in a very literal sense as they are risks to employment. As listed by the male lifestyle magazine *Crave*, both female and male health care professionals have lost jobs after taking candid pictures of patients' genitalia as jokes and a range of workers have faced consequences after accidentally sharing dick pics with colleagues when the subject matter should have been something much more work specific. Still other have faced censure for documenting practical jokes involving a penis and the preparation of fast food at a chain restaurant. Sexting scandals have been known to hurt political careers and, in some instances, dick pics have blocked access to employment from the start, as when men have included such pics in their résumé or sent them to human resources personnel via SMS after mistaking their mobile phone number for that of a love interest. Since such circulation of private shots fills the criteria for harassment, they have invited corporate and legal intervention (Henry 2016).

Both solicited and definitely not, dick pics have entered the landscape of social media on Tumblr, through dating and hookup apps, as well as the diverse back channels afforded by Facebook Messenger and other personal messaging tools—networked spaces which, in the course of finishing this book, have grown increasingly scarce. Social media back channels are subject to the same community standards as posts visible in news feeds. They are scanned and regulated accordingly yet remain more leaky and porous in the visual communication they afford. In terms of community standards and terms of use, inappropriateness is not dependent on the solicited or unsolicited status of the image file in question: offensiveness is considered a property of representation rather than an issue of communicative consent or context. Visually harassing virtual strangers and sharing a dick pic with an intimate partner may therefore similarly result in one's account being suspended.

Circulating in public and in assumed privacy alike, dick pics combine the self-shooting practices of selfie culture with some of the visual codes and capacities of pornography (see Tiidenberg 2016). As we discuss below, dick pics evoke questions concerning the regimes of desirability involved in bodily exposure and the social norms connected to gender, sexuality, and sociability as these are constituted according to the platform or service in question and its community standards and terms of use, as well as the specific communicative functions that the images may serve. In order to make sense of all this, we start this chapter with a contextualization of the role and position of sexually explicit content and gross-out humor within the online attention economy of Web cultures of the 1990s to current social media before moving into a discussion of dick pics as figures of humor, harassment, fascination, and desire.

NSFW and the Attention Economy of Social Media

Awash with content available at scales too massive for human cognition to fathom, social media revolves around the constant quest of capturing and diverting attention; tracking it through the clicks, likes, shares, and recorded visits; and monetizing it (Gerlitz and Helmond 2013; Light and Cassidy 2014). Jodi Dean (2010) argues that the search for affective intensities drives the movements of users across social media platforms in search of both distracting thrills and more lingering attachments. When browsing through Facebook news feeds, trending tweets, or the top images of Imgur, most content flows by with little effect. When something does grab attention, it leaves some kind of impression, no matter how momentary or minor, that evokes a desire to engage. The logic is not altogether dissimilar from that of dating apps where the task is to find attractive options after being presented with a contingent mass of available choices by actors such as databases, social networks, likes, preferences, and algorithms. From the perspective of the platforms in question, content that grabs is valuable in the stickiness that makes users pay attention. This is explicitly the key aim of clickbaits that feed, and live on (and off), Facebook and Twitter traffic generated through eye-catching headlines and visuals promising affective jolts, shivers of amusement, interest, and fascination (Paasonen 2016).

That this attention economy is elaborate, is finely attuned, and operates at expansive scales and speeds is not to say that its principles of circulation and distraction would be entirely novel, or that it was suddenly born around 2005 with the coining of the concepts of Web 2.0 and social media. Content published in order to bemuse, cheer up, amuse, irritate, and shock has been shared on discussion forums and home page links of all kinds throughout the history of the Web—and, well before, in e-mail, bulletin board systems (BBSs), and Usenet newsgroups. What is novel is the increased and organized monetization of viral content that emerges and results from such circulation of data. Moreover, the content spread in social media has grown increasingly and characteristically SFW. Much of the meme production that has characterized platforms such as 4chan (est. 2003)—the home of not only Anonymous but also Pedobear and myriad strands of controversial humor—fit ill in the landscape of clickbaits that, for understandable reasons, prefer to avoid having their content flagged as controversial, obscene, or offensive and their user accounts closed on the platforms that are their main engines of traffic. As pointed out in the previous chapter, commercial partners do not, for the most part, want to be associated with content deemed obscene or otherwise controversial.

Exceptions do apply, of course. Established in 2009, Dangerous Minds is a news and media website—or, according to another interpretation, a clickbait. Operating a website, Facebook page, and Twitter account, as well as a Pinterest, Reddit, StumbleUpon, and (until 2019) Google+ presence, Dangerous Minds publishes content on music, visual art, and the mundane oddities of popular consumer culture. Like numerous other sites, Dangerous Minds trades in spreadable media, yet, unlike the more high-profile clickbaits such as BuzzFeed and Bored Panda, it regularly publishes content marked as "NSFW," "slightly NSFW," or "NSFW-ish" that leads to articles on vintage pin-ups, cross-dressers, and pulp fiction; films, paintings, and sculptures dwelling on the fleshly details of human bodies; and introductions to "the erotic art of the enema." In its combination of the artsy, the subcultural, the bizarre, the vintage, and the cultish, and by flirting with the boundaries of the risqué, Dangerous Minds contributes to and occupies a specific ecological pocket in social media's attention economy.

Despite the various titillations offered by the quintessentially NSFW genre of pornography, its visuals do not dominate most social media platforms precisely for the reason that #NSFW is also a technique of content filtering. Pornographic imagery has, despite its broad volume and perennial popularity, fairly seldom grown viral. In addition to the community standards policing appropriate content, this is equally a question of humor and the lack thereof. Memes, in general, live off their participatory possibilities of remix and alteration, and their appeal is centrally dependent on their ability to amuse (cf. Shifman 2013). Humor can intermesh with cuteness, as in the case of baby animal videos (Page 2017); it can be offbeat in its cuteness, as in the case of the meme cats, Lil Bub and Grumpy Cat; or it can be vitriolic, as in the case of pro- and anti-Trump memes. It can be cruel, heavy with offensive overtones, nostalgic, warm, or absurd. Sexism and racism tend to be mundane enough to be staple elements of much online humor and meme culture, not least in the United States (see Highfield 2016, 17–18; Phillips 2015, 97–98). As Sarah Roberts (2016, 151) notes, a great deal of popular user-generated content "trades directly on its disturbing racist, homophobic, or misogynist tropes and images. While social media platforms perpetuate the myth that such content may simply arrive on a site and become a hit due to serendipity or other intangible factors, the reality is much more complex and is predicated on a long tradition in American popular culture of capitalizing on media content that degrades and dehumanizes."

Independent of its particular edge or resonance, humor plays a key role in how online content catches attention and inspires likes, shares, and modifications through which it further spreads and prospers. When watched with the purpose of sexual arousal, pornography fits uncomfortably in the frame of humor: it is, after all, not routine to laugh at that which turns us on. The sexual fantasies and desires of others may nevertheless be a source of great amusement, especially when these differ from normative palates of straight vanilla sex. The clichés and conventions of porn can also be a laughing matter, as in the Brazzers Photoshop meme where the logo of the porn studio is pasted onto unrelated images, reimagining them as stills from a porn video and thereby sexualizing the interactions of the people, animals, and objects appearing in them (see figure 4.1). Since its invention in 2011, the

Figure 4.1
Kim Jong-Un Brazzers meme from Meme Center, circa 2015, combines current political events and their key figures with the conventions of American commercial porn, reframing them.

Brazzers meme has been liberally applied to the products of film and television fiction but also news events such as royal weddings and presidential press conferences. The Brazzers meme recodes sexually nonexplicit, markedly mainstream, and SFW images with the key aim of amusement. When it comes to visual content of the sexually explicit kind, though, the imagery to gain virality has typically belonged to the category of shock and gross-out, watched for reasons of bemusement and surprise rather than arousal.

The Appeal of Grossness

In addition to people knowingly seeking out sexual, explicit, titillating, or gross materials in search of sharp affective rushes of arousal, disgust, or laughter throughout the history of the Web, they have also shared links to so-called shock and gross-out imagery of a sexual nature as practical jokes. Whitney Phillips (2015, 19) identifies classic viral porn images such as Goatse (1999) and Lemon Party (2002) as key to prototrolling practices where users open a link of shock porn when expecting to encounter something altogether more innocent and SFW. These relatively early gross-out imageries notably often focused on male bodies coded as gay. Lemon Party, for example, features three senior men engaging in oral sex while Goatse, familiarized by the Stile Project, shows a man stretching his anus, revealing a broad expanse of his rectum. Meatspin (2005), a short video set to the 1985 Dead or Alive song "You Spin Me Round," involves a clip from the transgender porn film, *TSBitches*. It features a shot of anal penetration while the partner on top spins their penis round and round in circles. As Meatspin plays, a counter marks the spins made and, after 45 spins, a text appears stating, "YOU ARE OFFICIALLY GAY :-)." As is the case with "2 Girls 1 Cup" (2007), a one-minute video of coprophilic play once known as the most disgusting video on the Internet (Paasonen 2017b), links to these visuals have been shared with unsuspecting friends and colleagues with the overall aim of driving them to states of shock, disgust, amusement, and embarrassment—in different degrees and combinations.

The frame of grossness, often rife with homophobic undertones, works to cut off these images from sexual titillation while also demarcating the boundaries of bodies, desires, and sexual acts deemed appropriate. Yet grossness in no way automatically forecloses or excludes a broader range of titillations, homoerotic undertones included. In her analysis of sexual connections between straight white American men, Jane Ward (2015) points out that transgressions of the boundaries of heterosexuality—such as the insertion of fingers in each other's anuses, sessions of oral sex, or incidents of tea-bagging—that occur under the guises of humor, under the influence of alcohol, or within homosocial rituals of hazing work to reinforce rather than undermine the sense of straight white male identity. "That straight men are grossed out by men's bodies, that they appear especially obsessed with what is grotesque about their own and other men's anuses, and that they use homosexual sex to humiliate and demean and dominate one other are all important pieces of information for analysis, but they are not evidence that these acts are nonsexual" (Ward 2015, 145).

Ward (2015, 169) explains this simultaneous sexual flexibility and rigidity through a streak of childishness, an embrace of boyish sexuality among adult men, that is "implicitly heterosexual but primarily male-bonded, sometimes sadistic, and oriented toward an aggressive enjoyment of grossness and the anus." Hands-on play with other men's bodies is, as the title of Ward's book encapsulates, coded as "not gay" in balancing acts between interest, repulsion, and titillation. Disgust plays a key role in these affective dynamics, for "rather than a signal that straight men are simply 'not into' touching other men's bodies, [it] is also a fetishized and performative mode of encountering men's bodies, its own mode of sexual relating" (Ward 2015, 176).

Writing on sexuality and disgust, Beverley Skeggs (2004, 169–170) notes that the maintenance of tasteful distance toward sexual excess involves visceral intolerance toward the kinds of tastes than one does not share, as well as tenacious fascination toward that which is being expelled from view. Disgust marks the boundaries of taste, sexual tastes included, and not all bodies have equal position in the dynamics of grossness, fascination, and desirability that it entails. Accented expressions of disgust are a means of generating moral distance toward things seen as violating the boundaries of acceptability, good taste, or appropriate demeanor, as in displays of sexual explicitness and extensive bodily detail (Daniel 2011). Following Ward, it is nevertheless crucial to note the intermeshing of grossness, amusement, fascination, and desirability in straight male bodily explorations, as well as how articulations of repulsion may be a means to affirm and maintain the malleable boundaries of straight sexual identities. The surprise sharing of Meatspin, Goatse, or Lemon Party can be understood as cut through by a similar affective dynamic which, while dominated by exclamations of disgust, involves a broader range of affective intensities where only a thin membrane separates the straight male homosocial from the homoerotic or the homosexual (see also chapter 5 for a discussion on nimping and humor).

Grossness breaks against the norms of taste and is therefore titillating. The tag NSFW is one means to mark out such grossness and to invite certain modes for encountering content thus marked. The tagging practices on the GIF-sharing site giphy.com, for example, point to such interpenetrations of NSFW with the notion of grossness. Animated GIFs—both ones tagged as NSFW and not—are routinely used as reactions to posts, and they are tagged and searched specifically for such purposes. Massanari (2015, 100) notes that "a reaction GIF's effectiveness lives and dies by its ability to encapsulate a specific response creatively and precisely while still expressing a kind of universal sentiment with which others can identify." Such sentiments may not be precisely universal, though, but rather steeped in specific formations of gender, class, and sexual norms that become articulated predominantly through products of North American popular culture.

This is easy enough to identify in the common GIF reactions offered under the tag #NSFW. In the top hits of January 2017, the comedian Wanda Sykes frowns in dismay; the actor Adam Scott from the TV series *Parks and Recreation* pulls back from his desktop with his mouth open in an explicit expression of dislike; and Sponge Bob of the animated TV series digs himself into a hole in sand, which then becomes covered with the text "nope." In these instances, NSFW is something clearly unwanted, disturbing, and disrupting and routinely accompanied with further tags such as #disgusted, #gross, #ew, and #shocked. In one #NSFW GIF after another, people are shown to grimace and frown in disgust, shake their heads, and hide their faces in reaction to unappetizing things just seen and heard.

The second broad category of GIFs tagged as NSFW on Giphy, notably smaller in number than the first, features degrees of female nudity—most conspicuously displays of breasts and buttocks—with additional tags such as #censored, #boobs, #booty, #her, and #girls that echo those found in our Twitter sample discussed in chapter 2. While the first category of GIFs features reactions in the unambiguously negative affective register, with the aim of amusement and distancing the sender of the reaction GIF from the content commented upon, the second aims more at sexual titillation as that which is being shared between the sender and recipients.

A more specific search for "nsfw" and "men" results in GIFs from the alt-country band Indiana Queen's homoerotic black-and-white music video (other tags include #gay, #lgbtq, #connections, #gay men, #gay sex, and #twinks); a scene from a *Mad Men* episode where the actor John Slattery is shown sitting naked on the floor; one is of a topless Hugh Jackman as Wolverine; one with a group of men tying up another man snugly with duct tape; and another with a man dressed up as a giant bunny sitting on a toilet seat, inviting others to join in. There seems notably little place in these tagging practices for sexualized displays of male bodies as objects of desire without them being marked as either gay or creepy. None of these top hits are tagged as #hot or #sexy. While the sexualized female bodies we noticed here and in our Twitter sample become coded as NSFW by virtue of being objects of desire, in gross-out content, male (homo)sexual bodies become intertwined with concepts of horror and disgust and, through that, earn their status as NSFW.

As conveyed through reaction GIFs, hyperbolic, humorous expressions of being grossed out or titillated in potentially risky ways are thus in line with, and contribute to, broader affective dynamics that drive online exchanges forward and carve connections and detachments between different embodied identities, sexual palates, and broader taste cultures. Reaction GIFs, in particular, both frame and orient the flows that online exchanges may take. By rendering impressions of other people's posts visually tangible, reactions GIFs, similarly to the Facebook reaction options of "like," "love," "haha," "wow," "sad," and "angry," simplify the dynamics of online exchanges by pinning them down in quickly identifiable and clear-cut categories of feeling (see Paasonen 2016). Ambiguities do not easily prosper in such exchanges. At the same time, such ambiguities are rife in people's relations to each other's bodies and in sexual lives of all kinds, a fact amply demonstrated by the ambivalences identified in the valorization of nude selfies—and particularly in the diverse uses of the dick pic.

Nude Selfies and the Gendered Dynamics of Sexual Shame

With the rise of digital photographic technologies, what has been considered photo worthy has been expanded to include the everyday (Murray 2008; van House 2009). At the same time, the criteria of what qualifies as photo worthy remain subject to interpretation, as is notably the case with nude selfies and their circulation in social media. The spread of smartphones and image-sharing platforms has rendered selfie practices ubiquitous enough to cover contexts private and official, leisurely and professional. The phenomenon has evoked diagnoses of narcissism, yet the most vocal concerns have been targeted against nude selfies and their sharing through sexting, especially among young people (see Lee and Crofts 2016; Ringrose and Harvey 2015; Salter 2016).

Images not originally taken for public circulation can be made to enter it, as in the incidents of hacked naked celebrity pictures and revenge porn enterprises where images of former partners or more accidental encounters are posted online for the purposes of vengeance and/or profit, possibly along with the personal information of those depicted. Some revenge porn sites operate on leaked and hacked images with the main principle of extracting money from the people involved who wish to have the materials removed. Such blackmail enterprises trade in sexual and gendered shaming rather than revenge as such (Henry and Powell 2015; Stroud 2014). At the same time, nude images—selfies and other—are used to pressure, bully, and humiliate others without being categorizable as porn in any clear sense.

While public debates on revenge porn and the negative resonances of sexting tend to focus predominantly on heterosexual women, recent studies conducted in the United States and Australia show no gender disparity in the likelihood of being subject to image-based abuse (Kaszubska 2017; Lenhart, Ybarra, and Price-Feeney 2016). Importantly, lesbian, gay, and bisexual people are much more likely to face such abuse than straight women or men. In comparison to 4 percent of American Internet users—one in twenty-five—having been victims of threats or posts of nearly nude or nude images without permission, the figure was 17 percent among LGBTQ+ people (Lenhart et al. 2016, 4–6). In the Australian study, these figures were as high as 10 and 37 percent. Equally strikingly, abuse disproportionately targeted people with disabilities, 56 percent of whom had encountered image-based abuse in the form of nude images being taken or distributed without their consent, or having received threats to put such images into circulation. Among indigenous Australians, the figure was nearly as high: 50 percent (Kaszubska 2017). The findings further indicate that the likelihood of being victimized increases if the person in question has shared naked selfies (37 percent in contrast to 10 percent among those who had not). Furthermore, one in three people ages 16 to 19 and one in four between the ages of 20 and 29 had some experience of image-based victimization (Kaszubska 2017). All things considered, the risks were high among women ages 15 to 29 and among people with lower incomes (Lenhart et al. 2016).

All this implies that image-based abuse is disproportionately used against queer people under 30, women, people with disabilities, and racial and ethnic minorities in ways that both draw from and reanimate dynamics of sexual shaming, marginalization, violence, and hate. A broad range of image-based abuse works to truncate the agency of the people subjected to it. In the context of queer youth, this may involve violent public outing, which, given the discrimination toward sexual and gender minorities in the labor force, both feeds on and feeds off existing social inequalities. Queer perspectives, like those connected to disability and race, nevertheless remain notably absent in journalistic accounts on revenge porn and sexting that remain rooted in the framework of normative heterosexuality and notably often foreground the victimization of white, able-bodied, straight women by men. Without undermining the persistent sexism and misogyny of online cultures or questioning any of the damage that revenge porn causes, an exclusive focus on the experiences of white heterosexual women obscures the diversity of current image-based abuse. As the intersections of gender with race, age, sexual orientation, ability, and social class become sidetracked, if not effaced, so does the fact that people identifying as male are, according to the recent studies addressed above, equally likely to experience such abuse as those identifying as women. This works to support a binary, and ultimately simplified, understanding of the gendered and sexual dynamics at play.

Like racist slurs publicly shared on Twitter and preserved for virtually endless revisiting, shared traces and evidence of naked selfies stubbornly linger on, even when unsuspected. Social media data is, after all, characteristically tenacious. This applies also to services such as Snapchat that are built on the ephemerality of data that remains available only for a limited time. This has made the application popular in sexting inasmuch as such exchanges are allowed by the terms of use that ban pornography, violence, harassment, and infringements of privacy. But although ephemeral data grows inaccessible to users, it remains not only archived as corporate property of Snapchat but, possibly—and against the services' terms of use—stored in different applications developed for the purpose of further consumption and distribution.

Revenge porn practiced against people with nude photos of their own making involves an effacement of agency. Cut off from the authors' control, the pictures become evidence of sluttiness that is both titillating and worthy of blame, and this circulation may well involve an added layer of body shaming. People may be told that they need to assume some, if not all, responsibility for having consented to such images and videos being taken, let alone for having taken these themselves. This was a common response to the 2014 Fappening (a combination of "a happening" and "to fap," a term for masturbation) in which naked images of female celebrities, most notably those of/by Jennifer Lawrence, were hacked from iCloud accounts and distributed across the Internet through 4chan, Imgur, and Reddit (Massanari 2017). Celebrities whose images were shared in this way were berated firstly for having been stupid enough to take the image and secondly for not having secured their data well enough. Beyond the pernicious effects of victim blaming, such responses trivialized the experience of online harassment (Citron 2009b; Hess 2014).

While commonly produced and shared across occupational and educational strata, nude selfies are in obvious conflict with the norms of professional behavior, to the degree that they may even bar one's access to a professional workforce at the outset. Background checks on people's social media accounts have become a somewhat routine part of the job interview process, especially in the United States (Lee and Crofts 2016, 88; see also chapters 5 and 6). Public debates on naked selfies and sexting rely on the assumption that people—and young people in particular—are incapable of properly assessing their risks and harms when these images fold into future careers, relationships, and life prospects. For the most part, the perceived gendered risks connected to naked selfies remain asymmetrical in the sense that women's sexual subjectivity is framed as more fragile and because it requires necessary reputation maintenance concerning sexual availability, activity, and expression (for an extended discussion on straight female sexual agency, see Albury 2002).

At the risk of reiterating a binary model, it can be argued that male sexuality has, in a range of forms, been framed as something of a natural force that requires curbing more than coaxing—or, in its less normative forms, may become subject to violent forms of retraining. In contrast, nineteenth-century *scientia sexualis* figured female sexuality in terms of lack, inaccessibility, and dysfunction: there being, so to speak, necessarily no there there. Connected with unequal relations of power that result in forms of gendered discrimination, sexual harassment, and diminished bodily integrity in both private and public realms, these figures—as fantastic and binary as they are—have exercised considerable performative force in carving out patterns of available (if not necessarily appropriate) behavior within heterosexual relations. The traces of this false gendered divide seem to linger on in views of sexual self-shooting as involving clearly distinct gendered positions and available forms of agency.

Consider, for example, the cultural figure of the wanker, gendered male since the notion of the onanist was coined in the eighteenth century. While masturbating women soon grew into a popular pornographic trope in its own right (Laqueur 2003, 308–309), a stubborn cultural divide emerged separating gendered forms of self-pleasure. If the wanker has been a cultural figure of amusement and contempt, seldom pestered by other complications than excessive sexual desire, the female masturbator is a differently titillating creature engaged in self-exploration. In second-wave feminist texts, such as Nancy Friday's 1973 *My Secret Garden*, which mapped women's sexual fantasies, the female masturbator bravely stroked her way through unknown fleshy folds in the name of a sexual emancipation achieved by reclaiming her own body and desire. This dualistic gendered divide of the gross and the fascinating is premised on women having problematic, traumatic, or even plain clueless relationships with their bodies, involving a default inaccessibility of sexual pleasure. The divide may also explain why vibrators and lubricants targeted at female consumers have been made available in pharmacies in many Northern European countries whereas sexual aids for men remain the stuff of smuttier retail venues.

On the basis of existing literature, it seems that nude selfies by women are seen as indicative of sexual titillation and availability while similar images of male bodies—and dick pics in particular—open up a broader and more ambiguous spectrum of interpretations, from sexual invitation to harassment, gendered violence, and humor. At the same time, people of all genders are subject to such images being repurposed in abusive ways. As we have already noted, in heterosexual contexts, images of male bodies seem to easily border on gross-out, or at least on offensiveness, and considerably less often on sexual titillation or desirability. While the naked female body seems to be firmly associated with sexuality and the codes of pornography, the naked male body has more social mobility, as do pictorial representations thereof.

Women, and young women in particular, are regularly shamed for sharing sexually suggestive and explicit images with intimate others and, on occasion, with the world at large. This shaming involves the drawing of boundaries between the appropriate and the inappropriate, the publicly viable and the unsavory, the SFW and its opposite, as well as the boundaries separating sluts from decent female subjects. Open displays of nudity and sexual availability are incompatible with the conventions governing proper middle-class femininity grounded on the principles of sexual "restraint, repression, reasonableness, modesty and denial" (Skeggs 2004, 99). In other words, such bodily displays violate the class-, race-, and gender-specific criteria of respectability (see Skeggs 1997). At the same time, there may be pressure to send naked selfies to partners as indices of affection, desire, or trust.

For straight men sending dick pics, the risks are different and seem to mainly involve potential ridicule of penis size. The act of sending an explicit shot alone, be it requested or not, tends to be less a source of embarrassment than a potential source of laughter (Ringrose and Harvey 2015; Salter 2016). The ubiquitous dick pic thus emerges in a context charged with inequalities and cultural expectations that shape its production and reception in ways that complicate its meanings and social functions. As we discuss in more detail below, in the landscape of contemporary social media dick pics operate simultaneously as instruments of harassment, as objects of aesthetic and erotic appreciation, and as tools for hooking up with other men—to identify only some of their frequent applications.

Dick Pic as a Figure of Harassment

Balancing the more general self-shooting practices of selfie culture with some of the visual codes of pornography, and distributed both one-to-one and in online galleries, the dick pic emerges as a ubiquitous yet ambiguous object. Dick pics are rendered a topic of fantasy and curiosity that is open to commentary and comparison on Reddit, in queer dating apps, and on some porn sites. They are nevertheless rarely framed or accepted as objects of heterosexual titillation and desire, with young women in particular describing dick pics as confusing in their message and as troubling in their social resonances (Salter 2016; Waling and Pym 2019). At the same time, dick pics in (assumedly) heterosexual exchanges seem welded into the figure of sexual threat. As Jessica Ringrose and Emilie Lawrence (2018, 697) point out, when "positioned as a normative part of sexually predatory masculinity," dick pics retain "the binary between aggressive male sexual desire and passive feminine recipients."

Dick pics, or erotic shots of men alone, are forbidden in the submission guidelines of many straight amateur porn sites that only welcome videos of women, couples, and groups—the implicit assumption being that such images of the nude male body simply are not sexually arousing to either straight male consumers or the site's potential female audience. Contra to this reaction of disinterest and aversion, top Giphy search hits for "dick pic reaction" reveal degrees of ambiguity. Like a search for "NSFW," these hits result in GIFs expressive of women being grossed out but also in ones expressing lack of interest or attention. In other top hits, Dick Solomon of the TV series *3rd Rock from the Sun* bows with the caption "BEHOLD THE GLORY THAT IS ME!," while in another, the actor Dennis Quaid, in his role in *Innerspace*, happily declares, "[g]otcha!" In the clear-cut, yet sarcastic, visual culture of reaction GIFs, dick pics are connected to instances of gross-out aversion but also to (possibly misplaced) declarations of male pride and female titillation.

At the same time, it is somewhat difficult to find media accounts of women engaging with dick pics in a positive vein, largely since these focus almost exclusively on encounters of the unsolicited kind rather than on pictures that emerge as desired objects from mutual exchange or visual play. Unsolicited dick pics are identified as enacting online sexual harassment alongside negative social media comments, revenge porn, and gender-based hate speech (Vitis and Gilmour 2016). Understood in this vein, a self-made image of the penis becomes a figure of male power connected to a fundamental lack of sexual safety experienced by women in spaces both private and public. They serve as an online variation of catcalling: in both instances, the men involved may frame their actions as a compliment taking the form of sexual interest although these fail to be recognized as such. In the context of the #MeToo movement battling sexual harassment, dick pics have further become identified as a visual form of gendered abuse.

Anita Sarkeesian, the media critic at the heart of the Gamergate incident, has described endless accounts of men using social media to send pictures of themselves ejaculating on her image (see Jane 2016, 2; see also chapter 6). Ejaculations on other people's images may have been a form of sexual tribute and appreciation in amateur porn communities since Usenet by creating mutual loops of pleasure and desire (Dery 2007, 28), yet they are broadly used in far less supportive ways to fix women as objects of male sexual fantasy and control. In this context, the meaning seems to be far from a positive tribute. Rather, the penis—as conveyed in dick pics—becomes conflated with the phallus as a symbol of male power, dominance, and aggression and a tool for harassment.

Naming and Shaming

Naming and shaming is a tactic women use to reject the dick pic and to attempt to hold men to account (Waling and Pym 2019). For example, in a widely reported incident, Samantha Mawdsley received an unwanted dick pic through Facebook Messenger from a stranger after leaving a restaurant review and reacted by bombarding the man with equally unsolicited dick pics in return. After the exchange was through, she publicly shared the message thread with the man's name and image intact, and with the following description:

> My initial thought was to ignore it, as we females are taught from such a young age. But. . . . Nah! I decided to mess with him and call him out on all his ridiculous behaviours and double standards. To my delight, he was suckered into the debate! My favourite bit is "I just want to puke! Please stop!"
>
> It was 2am and I'd been drinking (Euros were on! This girl likes football!) so excuse some typos and autocorrects. And genuine apologies for all the pics of penis—I censored them because NOBODY likes an unsolicited d*ck pic!

Mawdsley's Facebook account was briefly deactivated because of the avalanche of pictures she posted—although she did use emojis to cover up the dick pics in order to comply with the platform's terms of use—yet the ban was soon lifted as news of the exchange grew viral. Details of the incident circulated with mainly laudatory headlines celebrating her reaction, as in, "Woman Receives Unsolicited D*ck Pic from a Total Stranger—Gives Him a Taste of His Own Medicine" (Gladwell 2016); "Woman Brilliantly Makes Man Regret Sending Her Dick Pic" (Jonette 2016); "This Woman's Response to Unwanted Dick Pic Has Won the Internet" (Browne 2016); and "How One Woman Got Justice When Unsolicited Dick Pics Went Too Far"

(Rose 2016). Thus heralded as a champion for gender equality, Mawdsley's actions were firmly framed as fighting back against sexual harassment by making it visible:

> "Men who do his sort of thing assume they have this anonymity and can invade our space. NO MORE!"
>
> Describing her viral post as "the equivalent of jumping back, pointing and screaming", Samantha said: "YOU exposed yourself to me, James!
>
> "So everyone has heard my scream and is turning to look at what I screamed at. This is on YOU!!!"
>
> She concluded: "Sure—not every girl will scream (or post it on their Facebook page) but if the threat of this response is what stops boys from doing it, rather than human decency and an appreciation of the equality of women, then so be it!" (Gladwell 2016)

With the aid of a plethora of news stories and clickbaits covering the incident, Mawdsley's public Facebook album was soon shared some 7,000 times.

For her part, the artist Whitney Bell turned her collection of circa 200 unsolicited dick pics into an exhibit titled "I Didn't Ask for This: A Lifetime of Dick Pics." In a *Vice* article covering the exhibition, Bell emphasized that the project "isn't dick-hating or man-hating. I love a good dick. I just don't love harassment." The article further summed up the essence of the matter: "[N]ow that everyone has a camera phone, dick pics are ubiquitous, despite the fact that most women really, really don't want them" (Stevenson 2016). In these incidents, the experience of receiving unsolicited dick pics was defined as unequivocally invasive, disturbing, and humiliating—as diminishing women's sense of sexual agency rather than contributing to it in any meaningful or pleasurable way. When perceived as involving more than an edge of male violence, the act of publicly shaming and ridiculing the man in question then becomes seen as not only acceptable but something to be collectively celebrated.

Some of this dynamic is evident in the Bye Felipe Instagram project (est. 2014) described as "calling out dudes who turn hostile when rejected or ignored." Bye Felipe consists of screen grabs of exchanges turned nasty, often with the names and faces attached, along with memes commenting on inappropriate online behavior (see figure 4.2). The materials submitted unfold as a relentless stream of come-ons turned vitriolic, dismissive, and unmistakably hostile: they are united by a sense of straight male sexual entitlement that, once challenged, flips into aggression. In her analysis of

Figure 4.2
Bye Felipe.

Bye Felipe, Frances Shaw (2016) defines it as an example of feminist discursive activism drawing attention to the sexual politics of online dating that makes use of public shaming as a political strategy. The project is kin to the earlier Douchebags of Grindr (est. 2009), which documents similarly undesirable and offensive behavior on Grindr: key tags include "femmephobia," "racism," "arrogant," "douche," "agism," "blockophiles," and "body nazi" (see also Miller 2015, 638; Shaw 2016, 2, 4). While on Bye Felipe an unsolicited dick pic can be compared to "textraping" and sexual assault (Shaw 2016, 5), as discussed in more detail below, in the context of gay male dating apps the sending of dick pics does not alone qualify as douchiness.

Anna Gensler's Instagram and Tumblr 2014 project, Granniepants, bears similarity to Bye Felipe. Gensler started to make unflattering nude portraits of men who have made sexual advances, objectified, or harassed her on the dating apps Tinder and OkCupid, and accompanied them with the man's first name and age, as well as excerpts from their exchanges. In addition to sharing the pieces in social media, she also informed the men of their sudden fame. Once the project went viral following a BuzzFeed article, one of the men began to bombard Gensler with graphic death threats and she realized that her contact information had suddenly become public. The project blog hasn't been updated since 2014, and Gensler has more recently focused on political cartoons critical of President Trump.

In their discussion of Granniepants, Laura Vitis and Fairleigh Gilmour (2016) identify it as a form of critical witnessing that makes visible the mundane harassment that women are subjected to and fights back through strategies of satire, reverse objectification, and public shaming, the impact of which is amplified through broad social media circulation. Similarly to Illma Gore's naked portrait of Trump discussed in chapter 2, Gensler's nudes make use of micropenises: in this sense, both projects can be considered as engaged in body shaming. Mockery of modest ("peanut") penis size emerges both as a particular risk of humiliation faced by young men sending nude selfies (Salter 2016, 2735–2736) and as a countertactic deployed by women in the face of online harassment. Mawdsley deployed similar tactics in bombarding the man in question with dick pics and comments such as the following: "Are you sending your little penis pics to people you think are girls?"; "Well . . . it's not big, let's be honest"; "It's smaller than the pics I sent you"; "Although to be fair, they're from a site for pics of 'large' penises"; "So an unfair comparison, I guess"; "Do you want me to send you small dick pics so you feel better?" By fighting dick pics with pictures of large penises, Mawdsley broke the desired mode of interaction as one revolving in the registers of heterosexually titillating show-and-tell. This disruption depended on the framing of the unsolicited dick pic as an object of symbolic violence. It was also premised on smaller penis size as being a topic of laughter and ridicule—and, consequently, a source of shame and embarrassment.

Addressing the social power dynamics of shaming, Skeggs (2004) draws a distinction between ressentiment as an expression of powerlessness and resentment as an expression of the powerful. For Skeggs (2004, 182), ressentiment is "a triple achievement, for it produces an affect (rage, righteousness) which overwhelms the hurt; a culprit responsible for the hurt; and a site of revenge to displace the hurt (a place to inflict hurt as the sufferer has been hurt)." Mawdsley's and Gensler's reactions to unsolicited dick picks followed the affective contours of ressentiment in their articulations of anger caused by sexual harassment, in their attacks against the culprit, and in the overall dynamics of revenge through public shaming. As an expression of the powerful, the affect of resentment is, for Skeggs, deeply tied in with moralism practiced by "those who feel they are losing the power that they once had (or would have had as a result of their positioning)" (Skeggs 2004, 182). Understood in this vein, the dynamics of shaming associated with nude selfies involve self-representation that is seen to violate the norms of appropriate gendered behavior. Moralizing involves dwelling in other people's shame (Warner 2000, 4). Shaming, then, becomes a means of putting subjects back in their place by failing to acknowledge the sexual agency that the circulation of the images may involve. Ressentiment and resentment, as outlined by Skeggs, are readily discoverable in debates on naked selfies: the shaming of dick pic senders is motivated by feelings of hurt whereas the shaming of women shooting themselves in the nude involves a different sense of entitlement.

The gendered and sexual dynamics at play are, however, much more complex than such neat gender divisions would allow—considering, for example, that women engaged in online shaming are also exercising social power and that image-based abusive practices disproportionally target members of sexual and racial minorities, young people, and people with disabilities, independent of their gender. Furthermore, the shaming of sexual harassers, fueled by the affective intensities of ressentiment, can be devastating in its reverberations, especially when such incidents gain positive viral circulation. In her brief account of online shaming, Emily van der Nagel (2016) notes how it can punish "people permanently and disproportionately to their actions." Attempts to call off disturbing behavior may become a form of online image-based harassment as stories circulate, accumulate, and become stored for the foreseeable future in social media data banks through which the people involved are perpetually discoverable, with negative social and economic consequences (see also chapter 6). As Frances Shaw (2016, 2) notes, gleeful coverage of women turning the tables on harassers may then take "joy in the practice of shaming itself," resort to patronizing and sensationalist tones, and indeed "reinforce or perpetuate some of the gendered harms of harassment by encouraging victim blaming and sexual shame" (see also Albury and Crawford 2012).

The Dick Pic Lovers of Tumblr

Andrea Waling and Tinonee Pym's (2019) study suggests that receiving an unsolicited dick pic is a ubiquitous experience for straight women. But not all dick pics circulate in the register of harassment irrespective of the gender and sexuality of the recipient. As any cultural studies scholar would add, the reception that a dick pic receives depends on the context—and, in the framework of networked media, on the platform. An unsolicited dick pic is unlikely to evoke enthusiastic responses, yet not all distribution is unsolicited and not everyone views dick pics just because they happen to receive one. Before changes to Tumblr's content policy in 2018, many a blog—from "Best Cock Pics!" to "Let Me Take a Dic Pic" and "Cock Pictures from the World of Penis Pictures"—was dedicated to the art of the dick pic, along with a plethora of tumblrs focusing on nude selfies and curations of amateur porn.

Tumblr's terms of service allowed sexually explicit content as long as it had been tagged as NSFW so that users who preferred not to encounter the material could avoid doing so. These tumblrs mainly consisted of images, text, and animated GIFs, as uploading sexually explicit videos was specifically forbidden. Due to its lenient content regulation, Tumblr became the hub for NSFW self-shooting practices, alternative and subcultural content, and diverse user-curated pornographic collections. Millennial women were reported as a particularly active user group for Tumblr porn (e.g., Moore 2015; Reid 2015) while the service's "queer ecosystem" was identified with the broader creation of minoritarian sexual publics (Cho 2015; Fink and Miller 2014; on counterpublics, see Renninger 2015). As all NSFW accounts were removed in December 2018, none of this rich culture remains.

As Katrin Tiidenberg (2014) points out in her research on NSFW self-shooting practices, the accepting sexual publics formerly afforded by Tumblr remain separate from the shaming, negativity, and snarkiness that characterize much of social media exchange. On Tumblr, sexual self-shooting allowed rendering one's body an object of sexual desire independent of sexual orientation (see Tiidenberg 2016; Tiidenberg and Gómez Cruz 2015).

Alongside the dynamics of shaming that cut through much of the debates on the public visibility of nude selfies, sexual self-shooting involves emancipatory potential in supporting body positivity in ways that do not simply reiterate dominant gender norms. This involves both platform and consent as these condition the kinds of social exchanges and uses that the posted images may enter. In this context, dick pics were not excluded from the realm of pleasurable posing, sexual titillation, and desirable gazing (Tiidenberg 2014). Here, #NSFW functioned much less as a warning than a delineator of a culture of tolerance, an allowance of vulnerability and respect, and a promise of certain conversations. In doing so, it opened "a door to a space where you can show parts of yourself that you would not show other mothers, other sisters, other daughters, other nurses, other professors" (Tiidenberg, n.d.).

Madeleine Holden's tumblr, "Critiquing Your Dick Pics with Love," was covered in social media as a body-positive response to sexting (Hamilton 2015; Sara, n.d.; Waling and Pym 2019). Rather than framing dick pics through aversion and shame, Holden motivated her enterprise through her love of a good dick pic and her desire to help men improve the aesthetic and technical quality of their intimate self-shooting practices for the benefit of all parties involved. Her blog consisted of submissions by those who wished to have their dick pic—either one of their own authoring or one they have received—critiqued on a scale from F to A+. In their analysis of this tumblr as a site of subversive feminist humor, Ringrose and Lawrence (2018, 699) saw it as working to reduce "a reading of the penis as object of power, threat, danger, sexual intention, etc. to one of relative beauty, vulnerability, delicacy, and style with the penis' sexual imperative being systematically redistributed in commentary as well as in some of the images themselves." In doing so, the tumblr opened "space for a more playful relationship to dick pics as non-threatening, funny, and aesthetically complicated" (Ringrose and Lawrence 2018, 701).

Given that Holden's focus was on photographic style, feel, and execution, she refused to critique the dicks themselves and explicitly resisted any normative criteria of a "perfect dick." A shot by a pre-op transman was critiqued for zooming in too close and for being slightly blurry, just as cisgendered men received critique for their distracting choices of background, poor lighting, and unimaginative angles, and a woman would get a B for her picture with a strap-on dildo for lacking "oomph." The feedback was constructive and appreciative, focusing on the strengths while raising suggestions for improvement. Holden received many more submissions than she had time to critique, and she also offered the possibility to receive private feedback or to get a guaranteed review in return for remuneration of US$10 and US$25, respectively. In a modest way, Holden's loving critique of dick pics itself became a form of paid work pivoting on NSFW content.

Tumblrs consisting of original submissions and reblogged content assemble images shot in different times, spaces, and locations, with different intentions and motivations, into thematic wholes that again feed other blogs in the movement of endless circulation characteristic of the platform. Writing on the curatorial principles of Tumblr, Alex Cho (2015, 46) points out how its locus of authorship "is less focused on the creation or capture of an original image and located instead around the personalized stream as a whole, a dynamic of constant movement and active selection." This curation and circulation give rise to blogs both specific and heterogeneous, both structured around a specific theme—be it pictorial or other—and catering to user curiosity with surprising and whimsical combinations of seemingly disparate elements.

Shared in this visual economy, dick pics were framed as desired, as appreciated, and as open to entering a range of social exchanges. Like naked selfies more generally, dick pics came in a range of tumblr subcategories, from general forums such as "Dick Pics," "Cock Pics," "Send-Ur-Cock-Pics," and "Amateur Cock" to blogs dedicated to celebrities, small or large penis size, and dick pics defined by their spaces and contexts of production. Consisting of images submitted by visitors and harvested by the bloggers themselves, the tumblrs often catered to male viewers in their penile aestheticization, but these displays were not necessarily coded as either straight or gay or as addressing people of any specific gender identification.

Especially in the context of this book, one notable subcategory of self-shooting tumblrs involved selfies taken in places of work. "Bored @ Work" and "Hot Girls Get Bored at Work Too" consisted mainly of topless—and some pantless—selfies taken by women assumedly in spaces of work even if these spaces were not necessarily easy to identify, given that the images were typically closely cropped to the body. Pictures were often taken in bathrooms but also in office chairs, by filing cabinets, and near keyboards. The names of the blogs proposed the taking and sharing of sexual selfies as a solution to boredom experienced at the workplace: as a pleasurable distraction breaking mundane routines of labor by bringing the element of forbidden, and hence titillating, sexual play to where it ought to remain absent. "Cock Out at Work" and "Wangs at Work" repeated the same concept and principle with dick pics. The rationales of these tumblrs were straightforward: "Get your cock out at work—send a selfie" and "A place to share your wang at work. Photo's [sic] of cocks out in the workplace. At the desk. In the bathroom or just a bulge around the office. Yours or a colleague [sic], lets [sic] see some wangs out at work."

The dick pics submitted and reblogged from other sources at "Cock Out at Work" covered a range of workplaces and occupational positions, even though bathrooms, with their mirror options, remained particularly popular locations for unclad self-shooting. Some images were anonymous and others much less so; some men posed at the warehouse and others at a real estate agent office; some smiled and others disguised their face; some men were young and some older; some wore the uniform of a firefighter, others those of a Marine private, a police officer, or a flight attendant, while yet others sported a neat suit and tie. Dicks were taken out in shared offices, on the roofs of workplaces, by communal coffee makers, and in car repair shops. Dicks were erect, semi-erect, and flaccid, fully out or candidly peeking from under the waistband so as to go unnoticed by coworkers who may or may not have been part of the visual economies of desire (and the image frame). In one animated GIF, a man was shown masturbating, cropped from chest to thigh, by his office window and shooting his load on its glass; in another, a man casually stroked himself by the urinal; in a third, a man masturbated standing squarely in a room resembling the office of a storage facility, his facial expression ranging from concern to indifference and questioning as he looked around, at the camera, and at his penis.

Most images had no captions, but some provided a minimal frame of action, as in "Work Got Boring, So Here you Go"; "BW—celebrating the last few minutes before vacation"; "Cock out at work and on the fit secretary's desk"; "Flashing co-worker"; "Meet Chester—young, hung security guard, bored at 4am, while working 7–11"; and "Strapped into a swing-reach lift. 40 feet in the air." Like other tumblrs dedicated to naked selfies in spaces of work, these captions evoked boredom as a key motivation for whipping out the cock while also introducing social dynamics with coworkers as essential fuel for selfie desire.

Writing on Tumblr's nonlinear "queer reverb" of "repeat and repeat," Cho (2015, 46, 47) identifies it as a "palpable, subterranean rhythm"; "dark optimism of a hovering possibility for community, the release of self-expression . . . and the potential for kinship and intimacy outside of heteronormative family and relationship structures." The exchange and circulation of dick pics taken at work, motivated by boredom and the pleasure of showing off, may at first glance seem quite detached from such emergent sexual publics resistant to sexual normativity. It is nevertheless possible to see them as gradations of the non-identity-based sexual reverb that Cho maps out, and as equally involving, and being driven by, an affective charge of potentiality. Dick pic after dick pic, captured in one space of work after another, gave rise to affinity and sameness across scales of variation without anchoring their interconnections in any particular sexual identity, orientation, purpose, aim, or desire. It was the male body, and the penis in particular, that remained the key focus of attention and curatorial effort. These Tumblr displays of appreciation remained detached from the figure of harassment that dominates journalistic coverage of unsolicited dick pics in heterosexual exchanges, as discussed above. Instead, they offered the penis as object for any willing gaze that could be endlessly reblogged and hence recontextualized, independent of the interests and desires of those uploading the file (cf. Renninger 2015, 1525). The intended audience remained open while the publics that the blogs comprised were both ambivalent and heterogeneous.

Dick Pics in Dating among Men

In sexual cultures among same sex attracted men, attitudes toward and practices regarding the presence, sharing, and circulation of the digitized dick are also complicated—though in certain ways no less SFW or easy to swallow for some. Dick pics are pervasive within dating and hookup apps used by same sex attracted men and, as such, an integral and accepted part of this sexual infrastructure. This is in contrast to social contexts and sexual cultures where the introduction or ubiquitous presence of dick pics is viewed as much more problematic or at least ambivalent in their assumed grossness. If we begin with those "with dick, for dick," though, we can see how consumption of the dick pic is a central feature and enabler of digitally mediated sexual cultures. This has been the case since the emergence of the Web and other computer networks.

Early studies of online community such as that of David Shaw (1997, 139) show the presence of the dick in the use of pseudonyms, for instance, where one user calls themselves "Meateatr," and in common discourse: "Scorsese" informs the researcher "You've heard of 'IRC inches?' . . . somebody says eight and you know it's probably five." John Campbell (2004, 70) similarly points to the role of the dick in certain elements of gay online culture where a user jokingly asks another if they are "still cruising for cock" and yet another, when asked how he identifies his gender on IRC, simply responds with "my dick." The early practices of those seeking to hook up on the now defunct French Minitel system further allude to inscriptions of the dick. As Anna Livia notes, numbers (between 10 and 25—referring to centimeters) and/or the abbreviations BFT (*bien foutu*, which means "well-hung") and TTBM (*très très bien monté*, which means "very very well hung") are used in complex codes of expressive pseudonyms to denote penis size (Livia 2002, 210, 214). Indeed, in an Australian study, 80.5 percent of survey participants reported that they viewed the explicit pictures—dick pics included—on chat profiles when preparing for meeting potential sexual partners in person (Murphy et al. 2004). Similar language is evident in Sharif Mowlabocus's (2010a) study of the cybercottage Uni_Cock. The name of the cybercottage itself suggests the central role of the dick in same sex attracted men's digital culture, while individual posts include references to a "6" cut cock," "8½ inches of cock!," and "nice cock" (Mowlabocus 2010a, 139–140).

In the late 1990s, dating sites such as Gaydar (est. 1999) and Squirt (est. 1998) emerged, introducing a profile-centered database logic to hooking up in addition to the online chat facilities (Fletcher and Light 2007; Light 2007, 2016a; Light, Fletcher, and Adam 2008; Mowlabocus 2010a; O'Riordan 2005). This early hookup app culture introduced further forms of the shareable dick through the deployment of digitized photography, video chat, and the writing of dicks into software menus. Gaydar's profile template, for instance, invites users to provide a description of themselves, including an indication of penis size and circumcision status, preferred sexual role, and attitude toward safe sex (Cassidy 2013, 2016; Light 2007; Mowlabocus 2010a). Guides to using Gaydar further explicate and foreground the importance of the dick in hookup culture: "Mr Right Now wants to see your cock—not a pic of you cuddling Aunty Ethel on Christmas Day. Mr Right might be put off by a cock-only portfolio. Though no gayer has ever not fallen in love with another for having a whanger like a can of coke with a still-beating lamb's heart stuck on top" (JockBoy26 2010, 17).

In the early days of Gaydar, and before the advent of the widespread uptake of digital cameras and smartphones, members would offer to take and digitize pics for those who did not have access to the necessary technology, such as flatbed scanners. Gaydar also provided chat rooms where links to MSN accounts were shared freely in order for members to engage in camming. Camming often focused on the dick rather than on faces unless trust was negotiated between participants, resulting in the common question—"Face?" Such networked visual sharing of the dick continues in full force today. As Kane Race (2015) asserts, the practice of camming partly appeals to users because it allows for erotic interactions without any overflow into other parts of their lives or intimate relations. This ability to archive and access sexual partners, as afforded by networked communication, has significant social, personal, and communal impacts and potentials for generating novel forms of sexual publics—or "publics of privates" (Race 2015, 505).

Race (2015) conceptualizes sexual media, such as hookup apps, as forms of sexual infrastructure which allow for new modes of participation in gay sexual culture, as well as for the emergence of new forms of community. Even given the ready access to camming and high-quality video made possible via technological developments such as apps, smartphones, fiber optics, and 4G, the static dick pic continues to have value within hookup cultures among same sex attracted men. The Squirt app exemplifies this continuing presence and circulation of dick pics, alongside more novel visual innovations such as "sexicons" (see Light 2016a). Sexicons, a play on emoticons, are shareable GIFs portraying particular sexual proclivities that include the dick as a mode of communication in a variety of ways, as shown in figure 4.3. The GIFs reference the early days of online sexual play among gay men where such assemblages were featured in order to add liveliness to predominantly textual environments through the ability to share grainy animated shots of the self (see Campbell 2004).

On Squirt, face pics are often stored privately and made available only to those who are serious about hooking up: profiles often feature a dick pic instead. The reasons for this vary in that some users of the app are not

Figure 4.3
Sexicons on Squirt.

open about their sexual preferences in everyday life, some are married to or in partnerships with other men or women, and because the activities associated with the app are not necessarily socially or legally acceptable (Light 2016a).

That dicks are so pervasive in dating and hookup apps used by same sex attracted men, however, does not imply they are universally welcomed or greeted with uniform appreciation. The visual presence of the dick has, in fact, long been contested. The practice of displaying a dick rather than a face has occurred with Squirt since the site's inception, as it has on Gaydar. Despite this penile ubiquity, many members have resisted the tendency not to post facial profile pictures and continue to do so. Some members even refuse to respond to messages from people who do not have a picture of their face but only one of their dick (see Light 2007). On Gaydar, it is not uncommon to come across users who refuse to respond to "faceless" browsers and the phrase "No Pic? No Dick!" occurs regularly (Mowlabo-cus 2010b). This practice is equally evident in the sites' chat rooms, where interaction with those not having "face pics" is often refused. Those who offer a dick pic or a torso shot instead are often not openly gay (or out) and do not post a facial picture for fear of being identified (Light 2007). Con-sequently, these members are marginalized within what they may perceive as a safe environment and one which is favored over traditional meeting places such as bars (Bolding et al. 2004). The situation persists with apps such as Grindr (est. 2009) where members using face pics are reportedly seen as more genuine and honest and where users are wary of, or do not talk to, those without face pictures (Blackwell, Birnholtz, and Abbott 2015).

However, it is not just users who seek to regulate and relegate the dick in same sex attracted men's hookup contexts: platform owners and app stores are equally key actors (Light 2014, 2016a; Roth 2015). The mobile version of Squirt, for example, operates as an HTML5 site. Unlike apps such as Gaydar and Grindr, Squirt does not offer members the option of downloading it from the Apple App Store or Google Play. This configuration creates a set of very particular associations. Squirt is uncensored, barring only certain forms of illegal imagery such as the inclusion of minors and bestiality, and dick pics can therefore be viewed on the opening geo-locative grid that displays user profiles. The app can operate in this way because it does not have to conform to the regulations or community standards posed by Apple or Google (Light 2016a). Squirt (2016) reinforces this in their FAQ section relating to mobile use: "Currently, apps that contain adult material are not allowed in the App Store or Google Play. Squirt does not believe in censorship. We are pro-sex, and we celebrate sexuality. Having to offer Squirt with no nudity in the pictures, or having to police what members put on their profiles for simple profanity or the frank talk about the kinds of sex that we look for is not an experience we want to bring to you."

In contrast, Gaydar and Grindr are subject to app store rules. At the time of this writing, Apple's App Store Review Guidelines (Apple App Store 2018) state that app developers should not include "Overtly sexual or pornographic material, defined by Webster's Dictionary as 'explicit descriptions or displays of sexual organs or activities intended to stimulate erotic rather than aesthetic or emotional feelings.'" The Google Play (2018) Developer Policy Center states, "We don't allow apps that contain or promote sexually explicit content, such as pornography. In general, we don't allow content or services intended to be sexually gratifying." The strict implementation of this policy would, in fact, not allow for the existence of Gaydar or Grindr in the Google Play store, making it clear that a factual gap exists between the policy and actual practice.

Both apps exist within these stores and can be freely downloaded. While the apps emphasize connection making, and while it is known that some users engage with them on purely platonic terms, they definitely do suggest the possibility of sexual gratification for many. Clearly, an element of flexibility is being deployed within the regulation of these online stores. The Apple App Store Review Guidelines offer further insights into why and where dick pics might be allowed in their services: apps themselves may not contain overtly sexual or pornographic material, yet this can be present in the content generated by users. However, going beyond the regulation of dicks out of the app itself—which it effectively conceptualizes as a container—the Apple App Store (2018) also engages in relegation work by stating, "If your app includes user-generated content from a web-based service, it may display incidental mature 'NSFW' content, provided that the content is hidden by default and only displayed when the user turns it on via your website." In other words, Gaydar and Grindr are allowed to be present in app stores as long as dick pics are not seen in publicly accessible profile pages within the app. For example, the Gaydar (2014) FAQ in this area states,

> Sadly, due to Apple's content restrictions, any photos uploaded to Gaydar profiles will appear as XXX [be replaced with an image depicting XXX] if we have classified the photos higher than our lowest rating [number 1], as below:
>
> Rating 1: Fully clothed, non provocative topless, non provocative in underwear
>
> Rating 2: Visible genitals through underwear and clothes, provocative topless, visible pubes
>
> Rating 3: Nudity, non-erect genitals, jock straps, bum shots
>
> Rating 4: Single and duo sexual scenes, erect genitalia, ejaculation
>
> Rating 5: Hardcore, group scenes, fetish.

In apps, dick pics are allowed only behind the scenes—where they do abound. If a user accesses a Gaydar profile via the desktop version of the app where dick pics have been uploaded via the app store version and marked for public consumption, then these are visible. On Grindr, dick picks are shareable in private messages only because the service was "born app" and there is no associated desktop version to allow for a different set of governances to be enacted. As these summaries suggest, is not only in the communities of hookup apps that the politics of dick pics become complex. Even in the relatively fixed and formal contexts of platform policies, the actuality of dick pics is layered and nuanced.

The Attention Economy of Dick Pics

The visual ecology and economy of social media both revolve around the imperative of capturing and optimizing user attention. If visual content fails to somehow stand out and appeal to people browsing through sites and apps, it flows by, fails to circulate, and is soon enough forgotten. Despite the notable institutional and other contextual differences involved, this broad logic applies equally to journalistic photos appealing to the readership of online newspapers, viral Web content brands like Lolcats, Tinder profiles, and sexually explicit user-generated content such as dick pics. At the same time, the attention that dick pics garner across different social media platforms ranges not only in its intensities—from being ignored to evoking a torrent of responses—but also in its affective qualities. Unsolicited dick pics tend to come across as ruptures in networked communication that make expected forms of sociability come to a halt and be recalibrated, possibly in highly antagonistic ways. In contrast, requested and desired dick pics may smoothly facilitate intimate exchanges and accelerate the reverbs of sexual desire. Sent for the intention of trolling, a dick pic can amuse in its assumed grossness, cause offense, or be interpreted as an act of violence. Sent through a dating app, the one and the same dick pic can evoke sexual interest, curb it, or inspire other members to flag the user, depending on what the codes and conventions of that platform may be.

It would nevertheless be inaccurate to identify the dick pic as that which, in 1980s postmodern semiotic discourse, was known as an empty signifier that, lacking a clear referent, is forever open to new acts of signification without becoming stuck with any of them. To continue in semiotic terms, while the connotations of the dick pic—that is, the range of things and meanings it evokes in different interpretations and exchanges—vary drastically, its denotative meaning—that which it refers to or symbolizes—remains firmly recognizable and anchored in its gendered genital referents. Dick pics are ambiguous and malleable in their uses and meanings while simultaneously remaining literal, obvious, and fixed by that which they represent. This paradoxical ambiguous literalness is perhaps key to the frictions that the accumulation of dick pics in social media involves. It may also be the key to the stickiness of content tagged as NSFW more generally.

5 Negotiating Sex and Safety at Work

Early in the new millennium, a link to a website ending in "nimp.org" was circulated through e-mail. The link opened up a blinking image alternating between a rainbow flag and gay pornography on the user's desktop, accompanied by a three-second clip of a male voice, amped up high in volume, shouting, "Hey everybody I'm looking at gay porno!" In addition to the potential social awkwardness that watching this loud and striking media product may have caused in diverse spaces of work and leisure, nimp.org would routinely freeze and crash the user's computer by opening up new pop-up windows with the same content much faster than these could be closed. The computer's sound card could keep on playing the file even when all windows had been successfully closed. Allegedly connected to the intentionally provocatively named Internet trolling organization, GNAA ("Gay Nigger Association of America," est. 2002), the site's routine became known as a "nimp."

This nimp relied on the social embarrassment caused by loudly calling attention to pornography—and not just any pornography, that of the male homosexual kind—being consumed in spaces of work. In the early 2000s, these links were opened up on desktop computers and laptops, which, situated in offices (as well as homes, libraries, and schools), allowed for limited privacy and hence always entailed potential social exposure. In the office, becoming subject to nimping was literally not safe for work. It is perhaps needless to point out that this default inappropriateness was a key rationale and attraction for sharing such links in the first place.

As nimping demonstrates, work is often more than work in that it involves interpersonal relationships and interactions that extend beyond the strictly occupational. Yet institutions, managers, and even coworkers would often like to present matters differently—for instance, through enforcing normative standards of decency. Expectations of appropriate behavior with respect to spaces and roles of work have evolved over time, and they vary depending upon the specificities of organizational cultures. Perceiving oneself, or being perceived, to be going beyond the boundaries of appropriate demeanor evokes risks of reputational damage, especially to those workers whose sense of humor or sexual desires veer beyond those stipulated by often narrowly defined workplace parameters.

In this chapter, we explore these organizational contexts and consider what "not safe for work" means in occupational frameworks through the interconnected themes of sex at work, risqué humor and harassment in the workplace, and the processes of organizational governance at work. This involves a somewhat literal take on the notion of NSFW that is used to consider the experiences of sex and sexuality in occupational realms, as well as in connection with social media and networked connectivity. In keeping with the association drawn between risk and sex in common uses of the NSFW tag, our focus is on the functions served by sex and sexuality at work, on the diverse risks they involve, and on their intermeshing with both workplace humor and harassment, as well as on the mechanisms through which they are policed, negotiated, and managed. Here, our interests expand beyond online exchanges to the resonances of sex—be these deemed safe, unsafe, or ambiguous—in diverse contexts of work as these intersect with digital media.

As the example of the nimp exemplifies, this chapter looks backward at the role of sex and, in particular, at its use in the context of workplace humor preceding the ubiquity of social media in order to ground current developments in a broader context. We do this with full awareness of the significant transformations that have occurred in definitions and practices of work since the 1990s. These include a growth in flexible work arrangements, home working, and the capacity of the Internet and mobile technologies to facilitate these practices (McDonald and Thompson 2016). Furthermore, social media have increased the number and types of people engaging with online content in both personal and work capacity. Where once only white-collar professionals enlisted mobile phones and laptops to enable mobility in their work, today those in other occupations, such as cleaners, tradespeople, and taxi drivers, are engaging with these same technologies. This social dynamic of mobile technology follows similar trajectories to that previously connected to the now-defunct object of the pager: hailed as a time-efficient tool for doctors and a labor-enhancing device for mobile professionals such as plumbers in the 1970s, some two decades later the pager had become identified with the notably risky work of inner-city drug crime (Kotamraju and Bruszt 2003). Crucially, such changes in the uses of information and communication technology are today connected to an increasing variety of occupational cultures with different expectations around what is safe for work, or not.

At the same time, social media continue to erode the boundaries of personal and work life in myriad and complex ways. As previous research has shown, network sociality is characterized by a combination of work and play (Wittel 2001), the performance of digital connectedness functions as a contemporary indicator of employability (Gregg 2009), informal networking improves job seekers' chances of securing a position (van Hoye, van Hooft, and Lievens 2009), and social media facilitates employee connectivity on the job (DiMicco and Millen 2007). These technologies also enable greater degrees of surveillance in and outside of the workplace, leave persistent traces of worker interactions, and collapse the distinction between work and not-work. Consequently, workers are increasingly required to manage not only their occupational uses of social media but equally their personal activity in line with organizational expectations. This often necessitates elaborate processes of disconnection through privacy settings and personal discipline (Light 2014).

Processes of classifying social media content and activity in the workplace require attention because these are used in identifying workers, in undertaking surveillance, and in exercising control—for organizations both to check up on people and to build trust (*Economist* 2013). They can be used punitively and as forms of managerial coercion. Meanwhile, employees may develop personal and group classifications of social media use, establishing their own distinctive safety parameters and practices. Such ongoing classification by employees, employers, and platforms impacts the ways in which the boundaries of appropriate work behavior become articulated, connected, and blurred. It is this fluid legal, cultural, and technological organization of contemporary occupational life that forms the backdrop, sometimes literally and sometimes figuratively, for what is tagged and flagged as NSFW.

Sex, Harassment, and the Workplace

Underpinning the NSFW hashtag is the specter of workplace sexual harassment, defined as "any type of unwelcome sexual behavior (words or actions)" that creates a hostile work environment (Gerberich et al. 2011, 294), but that may also extend to physical violence. This is the dark underbelly of working life—and one strikingly illustrated in the #MeToo movement—impacting the gendered dynamics of labor. Sexual harassment, or indeed any kind of workplace harassment, makes the recipient's work life unsafe in terms of career advancement, occupational esteem, and/ or personal security. As we discuss more in the following chapter, it can also be a persistent feature of work for people whose labor is primarily online and hence unbound to traditional spaces of employment.

Sexual harassment is typically targeted at those with lesser agency. A study of occupational safety among educators identified greater rates of sexual harassment among employees "who were female versus male; not married versus married; and those who worked as substitute versus part-time and full-time" (Wei et al. 2013, 76). Disclosures of nonstraight sexual orientation and nonbinary gender identification can also subject people to increased risks of bullying at work (see Collins 2013). Perhaps unsurprisingly, gender, sexual orientation, relationship status, and professional precarity—in connection with age—result in higher risk of workplace harassment. In other words, the dynamics of bullying, discrimination, and harassment at work follow the familiar fault lines of identity categories through which social relations of power are constantly articulated and reproduced.

In most workplaces in the industrialized West today, a series of institutional and state policies are in place to protect workers against sexual harassment, intimidation, and violence of this kind. While diverging in details, equal opportunity legislation or specific sexual harassment provisions exist that make employers responsible, or at least vicariously liable, for ensuring that individual workers are not disadvantaged because of harassment, either through exploitation by a superior or through the development of a hostile workplace. Employers are also typically required to do more than simply have a policy in relation to sexual harassment but to proactively foster a positive workplace culture through training and taking reasonable steps to ensure equity in treatment for all employees. Nevertheless, sexual harassment and other forms of harassment remain a workplace risk. It then follows that sexual innuendos—not to mention sexual approaches—at work are highly contested and risky as they are always potentially bordering on harassment.

Overt displays of sex, sexuality, and sexual organs are generally considered unsafe in the workplace, even in those where discussions of bodies and sexuality are normalized or crucial foci. In 1983, at the Urodynamics Society meeting in Las Vegas, Professor G. S. Brindley first announced to the world his experiments on self-injection with Papaverine. The drug, Professor Brindley argued, could be injected into the penis to produce an erection. In order to demonstrate the success of his procedure, Brindley had injected himself with Papaverine and attended his talk dressed in loose fitting jogging pants that illustrated its effects. However, the professor decided that having his erection covered by the jogging pants was not sufficient, and so he lowered them to his knees during the demonstration. As one audience member recalled,

> [T]he mere public showing of his erection from the podium was not sufficient. He paused, and seemed to ponder his next move. The sense of drama in the room was palpable. He then said, with gravity, "I'd like to give some of the audience the opportunity to confirm the degree of tumescence." With his pants at his knees, he waddled down the stairs, approaching (to their horror) the urologists and their partners in the front row. As he approached them, erection waggling before him, four or five of the women in the front rows threw their arms up in the air, seemingly in unison, and screamed loudly. The scientific merits of the presentation had been overwhelmed, for them, by the novel and unusual mode of demonstrating the results. (Klotz 2005, 956–957)

One might think that a group of clinicians with interests in erectile dysfunction would not be disturbed by examining a penis, erect or other. Brindley apparently felt he was on safe ground and prefixed his demonstration by suggesting to his audience that no normal person would find giving a lecture to a large audience to be erotically stimulating or erection-inducing. However, as the account illuminates, he clearly crossed a boundary, not just because the partners of clinicians were in the audience, but also because he exposed his own genitals in the flesh. His demonstration was deemed decidedly not safe for work. Thankfully for Professor Brindley, it occurred before the ubiquity of digital cameras, smartphones, and social media platforms, so that no persistent visual record of his act remains or circulates.

There is, of course, more to sex and sexuality at the workplace than the unexpected and challenging bodily exposure described in the Brindley case or in the cases of inappropriate or inadvertent dick pics discussed in chapter 4.

Not all forms of sexual behavior at work fill the legal criteria of harassment or are psychologically experienced as harassment—one needs only to consider the seeming ubiquity of workplace flirtations, romances, and consensual sexual arrangements (e.g., Franke 1997; Schultz 2003). Neither is sexual behavior at the workplace a novel development (Berebitsky 2012). In some work contexts, such as commercial content moderation (CCM) and sex work, which we discuss later in this chapter, dealing with sexual expression may also be part of core business.

Furthermore, sexuality manifests in the workplace and takes many forms with multiple, and contradictory, meanings and consequences (Williams, Giuffre, and Dellinger 1999). Advertising, for example, can make use of sex more or less indirectly on corporately determined "safe terms" even while sex at work would not be approved (Hearn and Parkin 1987). Organizations can safely evoke and deploy sexual images—such as that of a scantily clad woman, symbolizing sex, draped over a car signaling that an automobile enhances its owner's heterosexual allure—without overtly calling attention to sexuality or licensing it among their employees. There are also more directly carnal reverberations to the interconnections of sex in work. Within the restaurant industry, the division of labor, hiring, the design of uniforms, the business emphasis on customer service, and the wage–tip relation can all influence the nature of interactions with customers and facilitate harassment at work. Even interactions that are identified as sexual harassment can be perceived as part of the job and something merely to be expected (Matulewicz 2016). Since harassment comes and is experienced in myriad forms, sexist, homophobic, racist, sexually suggestive, or risqué jokes may also occupy a gray zone between symbolic harassment and the social lubrication particular to specific work cultures (Hemmasi, Graf, and Russ 1994; Holmes and Marra 2002). Sex can equally play a crucial role in academic inquiry, from studying the clients of sex workers by becoming a client (Stewart 1972) to studying swinging practices by becoming a swinger (Palson and Palson 1972) and having sex with research subjects as a planned research strategy, an afterthought, or an opportunistic residual benefit (Goode 1999).

While it may be instinctive to assume that sex and sexuality necessarily lie outside of workplace norms, they may in fact be deeply embedded in work contexts. Sex may be an integral part of corporate sociality in the form of humor; it may be the focus of work itself; and it may be a site of corporate policing; also, the workplace can be a site for meeting sexual partners. Each of these dimensions of workplace sexuality is shaped and reshaped by digital media technologies in ways that illuminate key dynamics of how workplaces are made "safe" in the context collapses of social media.

Humor and the Workplace

Humor in the workplace provides one arena for negotiating, expressing, and challenging sexual tensions and dynamics, but it can also be a key tool in aggravating them. Risqué workplace humor thus involves varying degrees of safety and serves various purposes: it is used for building social bonds and excluding others and for social positioning, and it can be a form of labor in itself, as in the work of comedians. It is also inherently fraught in the heterogeneity of a work context as that which any person considers funny, and what he or she may deem offensive, is particular, shaped by personal tastes and social locations, as well as the power relations within which jokes are articulated. With a contingency to its meaning matching that associated with sexual expression, and as a key form of its articulation, humor is a quintessential lens for considering how the ambiguities of sex enter into, and are managed, in the contemporary workplace.

In management and organizational research, studies of humor have been less concerned with its specific qualities than with its instrumentality in enabling productivity, participation, resistance, and the maintenance of hierarchies in the workplace. Although the requirement to remain productive and to avoid offense can inhibit, restrict, and direct fun (Fincham 2016), humor remains a key ingredient of effective workplaces. According to functionalist perspectives, it has three impacts: if you make people laugh, they will work harder for less money; if you make people laugh, they will buy your product; and if you laugh, you will be more effective (Rodrigues and Collinson 1995). The ability to innovate, often associated with productivity, has also been linked with humor's capacity to release tension and is considered a central feature of "strong" corporate cultures (Deal and Kennedy 1982).

Humor can also be classed as productive in that it sells products to consumers and markets the firm in question for recruitment purposes. It can be integral to corporate brands, as in the example of Diesel's SFW XXX viral advertising campaign discussed in the introductory chapter to this book. The video's humor, resulting from a bricolage of vintage video porn footage, both encouraged people to share the link and successfully contributed to the company's ongoing brand-building efforts as an edgy urban fashion label. Similarly, albeit hardly identically, Pornhub—as discussed in chapter 3—actively builds its brand through witty SFW social media campaigns drawing on combinations of humor and sexual references with the central aim of framing the company, and the services it provides, as an entertainment brand rather than a sleazy smut operation.

While having fun, or having too much fun, at work may conflict with corporate objectives, it can also be an expected part of the job. In such instances, expressions of fun become a form of affective labor, as with the perpetually smiling faces in service organizations such as airlines (Hochschild 2003), Disneyland (van Maanen 1991), and McDonalds (Ritzer 1993). Fun and humor can be sanctioned where they are valuable to the delivery of products and services in organizations. This is particularly evident in the deployment of emotional labor associated with the staff operating social media accounts on behalf of organizations, particularly those engaged in customer-facing functions—what has been termed "social customer service" (Blunt and Hill-Wilson 2013). In these instances, social media presence becomes, in effect, the Mickey Mouse costume of an organization, the corporately determined fun persona one might engage with at Disneyland.

Humor also serves other workplace functions. Relief theory is one of the three so-called classic or grand theories of humor, along with those of incongruity and superiority (see Shifman and Blondheim 2010). This theory describes jokes at the workplace as a means of decreasing social tension, generating relief in potentially straining situations, and lightening the atmosphere, thereby enabling wider participation. Managerial humor, for example, can make an organization more participative and responsive: it can generate energy, dispel nervousness in subordinates, and make managers more approachable. This, in turn, can enhance team spirit and involvement: humor can therefore be a means to "humanise the hierarchy" (Barsoux 1993, 54). Humor may equally "lubricate" meetings, relieve tedium, playfully subvert relations of control and authority, and help in negotiating paradoxes and ambiguities in the workplace (Hatch and Ehrlich 1993; Watson 1994).

Humorous exchanges can create release and relief from the mundane rhythms of work while also supporting and facilitating forms of social bonding. Moments of relaxation involving humor, such as instances of nimping, and others, such as Christmas and office parties where alcohol-infused coworkers may engage in flirtation and sex or take photocopies of their derrieres, can be seen as potentially carnivalesque moments in the wider culture of organizational surveillance and regulation. The regularity of such hiatuses and the willingness to go back to the status quo after a period of humor and misrule allow for the organizational iron cage to function (Holliday and Thompson 2001; Rippin 2011). Indeed, as we shall discuss below, the extent to which any fun can be had with social media, irrespective of the occasion or aim, may rest with the extent to which its usage is moderated by organizational technical blocking and broader policies of access.

According to a recurrent theory of workplace humor, employees' oppositional or resistant joking is ultimately manageable, controllable, and therapeutic. Humor should therefore be allowed, under certain conditions, as a nonthreatening way for subordinates to "let off steam," and be encouraged by managers where they seek to defuse tension and conflict. The release of frustration and grievance in and through humor can, however, also be a means of rendering subordinates easier to monitor and control, hence leading to a much more disempowering effect (Powell 1988). Managers can also use humor as a more direct means of exercising discipline and control (Dwyer 1991; Pollert 1981; Westwood 1984). As Ben Fincham (2016, 151) suggests, "When we have fun outside of institutional settings the anticipation of what possibilities there are for situations or actions are far greater than when we are in institutional settings."

Workplace humor can certainly also serve a primarily conservative social effect. By inviting us to laugh at the misfortunes, absurdities, or stupidities of others, humor built on superiority creates divisions between "us" and "them." Jokes at work may therefore involve laughter at the expense of other people, building a sense of superiority toward those who are the butt of the joke, creating divisions, and becoming a means of reinstating formal hierarchies of the workplace. To the degree that joking tends to be the prerogative of those in authority (Coser 1959), the paternalistic humor of superiors can establish in subordinates a family feeling of belonging from which others are excluded (Zijderveld 1968). In addition to bolstering occupational and managerial hierarchies, workplace humor may carve out a range of other social divides along the axes of gender, ethnicity, sexuality, religion, and nationality, possibly in violent ways. Nimping, for example, can be seen as reinforcing the bonds of straight male homosociality through gross-out humor. At the same time, its assumed impact is premised on the grossness of gay men, gay sex, and the embarrassing inappropriateness of consuming gay pornography, especially in spaces of work.

Additionally, the problems of context collapse, combined with overly stringent organizational policies regarding social media usage outside of work, can further limit the potential of humor to challenge hierarchies. Humor may, instead, potentiate further power dynamics when managers and coworkers are connected beyond the workplace. As one participant in Ben Light's (2014, 107–108) study of social media disconnection practices recalls,

> When I was off sick after my partner died I used it [Facebook] as a link to people and a bit of fun. I'm sat here every night on my own, so it was just a bit of a way to socialise, but not leave the house. [I was] careful not to put anything that even slightly make me happy because I was off [work] with depression and bereavement, so I daren't even put anything happy or positive on, but then I don't like putting all miserable stuff on. Yeah. My friend had taken me shopping and, in Asda, she takes stupid photographs of me in Asda. She found a packet of cock-flavoured soup; it has a picture of a cockerel on the front, which she made a post with it. So I'm like that, with this cock-flavoured soup. So she posted it on Facebook and I'm like "But I'm supposed to be off sick with depression!" So I were waiting for the backlash off that, but no one ever said anything. (Julie, health care assistant, 35–44)

The fear of surveillance by managers and colleagues alike evidenced in Julie's response works to nullify, or at least diminish, the potential for humor in social media to describe spaces of self-articulation, such as grieving, outside of corporate and capitalist agendas.

The perspectives introduced above emphasize the control effects of humor to the neglect of its oppositional potential. In attempting to render workplace humor predictable and controllable, organized fun undermines its spontaneity, which is a central characteristic of joking and its potential for generating change rather than reinforcing the status quo (Rodrigues and Collinson 1995). Nevertheless, humor may still facilitate resistance to heavy workloads, hierarchies, and challenges to women's authority in male-dominated work environment and contribute to participation and resistance alike (Griffiths 1998; Watts 2007).

In practice, the diverse roles and forms of humor at work are often diffi-cult to pry apart from one another. In the example of the nimp, its key effect relies on incongruities: between appropriate computer use in the spaces of work and the consumption of porn for sexual titillation and masturbatory release; between the content suggested in the shared link, its actual content, and user experience; between the publicness of the nimp and the assumed default privacy, or even secrecy, of porn consumption; and between the presumed normative heterosexuality of the workplace and the loud rain-bow flag and gay porn effects of the nimp in question. At the same time, the nimp also builds on superiority—on laughing at the person subjected to the nimp and, only slightly more indirectly, at gayness. In a successful nimp, the user is caught unaware and left helpless in the deluge of pop-up windows, unable to rectify the situation or to save face. Nimping owed its power to the premise that being thus "caught" watching gay pornography by one's peers would be a source of mortification and social amusement (Jones 2010, 128). Such trolling actions, conducted in the framework of straight male homosociability, tied gay porn and displays of gay male sex-uality more generally to the affective registers of grossness, shock, disgust, and embarrassment. Normative hierarchies are thus rearticulated in the use of such a joke and in the requirement of recipients to respond with "appro-priate" shame, mortification, or amusement.

Considered in isolation from broader occupational social dynamics, a smutty joke, a nimp, or a series thereof can come across as sheer fun. Yet humor is centrally about communication aiming to evoke certain responses in its intended audience, and, like all communication, it gives rise to social proximities and distances. Workplace humor—of whatever tone and how-ever distributed—can sustain mutual relationships, forms of collaboration, and sense of belonging but equally create social exclusions and divides, relations of control, and discrimination (Holmes and Marra 2002). Sex-ist humor, for example, can perform both of these functions, enhancing male in-group cohesion (Thomae and Pina 2015) as well as operating as a tool of gendered oppression (Moloney and Love 2017). The hypersaturated communication contexts of social media offer a broad range of such tools indifferent to any divisions between working hours and time off, spaces of work and those of leisure, thereby extending the social dynamics of the workplace to the broader textures of people's lives. Humor at work is, then, not an issue to be taken lightly.

Hooking Up at Work

Not all invocations of sexuality at work are intended to serve a humorous function, nor are they steeped in gendered relations of power and practices of sexual harassment by default. The organization, and enactment, of sex and sexuality at work may be linked to workplace inequality, stratification, and discrimination—as well as to job satisfaction, self-esteem, and happiness (Pierce, Byrne, and Aguinis 1996; Williams et al. 1999). Many people experience sexual innuendos, disclosures, desires, fantasies, suggestions, and acts at work as meaningful expressions of sexuality, but as shown in the case of Professor Brindley and his demonstration of the effectiveness of Papaverine, the lines between what is enjoyable, tolerable, and unacceptable are constantly being worked out. These boundaries are context specific, vary for different categories of workers, and alter in accordance with transformations in social norms, such as those connected to gender and sexual equality (Williams et al. 1999). Sexual and sexist jokes, innuendos, and motions considered routine and unquestioned in spaces of work in past decades may be currently unacceptable, yet not all forms of sex are considered not safe for work.

During the past decades, guidelines for engaging in workplace romances have focused upon aspects such as navigation of office norms, risks to career advancement, and the forbidding of relationships with senior colleagues or mentors (see Mainiero 1989, 259–264). At the same time, managers may have even aimed to deploy knowledge of sexual relationships in an instrumental fashion to secure organizational stability. In one study, an executive in a telecommunications firm in the United States reported, "We believe . . . that there are a number of trends that suggest that developing policies for married couples working together is a good thing. . . . Our analysis of demographic trends shows more couples will be geographically restricted, and this may serve as a means to achieve starting stability for the firm" (Mainiero 1989, 7). According to another study, the incidence of sexual harassment is low in comparison to the number of relationships initiated in the workplace, and by prohibiting sexual activity at work, organizations make it more exciting and desirable (Hearn and Parkin 1987). More recent studies have suggested that because many workplace romances lead to marriage or long-term partnerships, a ban on workplace romance is antisocial (Boyd 2010).

The frisson of illicit sex at work is illuminated by the case of a couple whose relationship was discovered via on-site surveillance cameras:

> "[The couple] adopted a habit of staying late in the office after hours. After everyone had left, Dan and Selina made good use of the company's exercise room in the basement of their building as a place of rendezvous. They had regular trysts together on Monday and Wednesday evenings. I know, because once I saw them going downstairs together when I was working late." But Dan and Selina neglected to realize one very important fact: Their office building was equipped with a new, high-tech security system—complete with video cameras. "The cameras tracked all the floors, including the basement," said my friend. "Their night time activities were recorded on more than one occasion by security personnel. Can you imagine? Their affair actually was recorded! And they never knew it." . . . The common joke was, "Will the tapes be out on VHS or Beta?" said my source, laughing. (Mainiero 1989, 173–174)

This incident of sex in the staff gym predates social media, the turn to apps, and the ubiquity of mobile devices. In workplaces now saturated with these devices, questions arise regarding the notions of privacy and the ability to seek out and enact clandestine sexual relationships. One might think that mobile media instantly afford more discreet engagements with sexual content because these devices can be accessed surreptitiously, under the desk, in a toilet, at the photocopier, or on a lunch break. This is in stark contrast with nimping, which was only effective given the semi-public nature of the screen of a desktop computer. Furthermore, the intimacy and individualization of mobile devices allow for more covert communication and thus may also facilitate sex at work.

This, of course, is not always the case. The use of dating and hookup apps is a clear example of how a small, discreet device can become decidedly unsafe for work. As we discussed in chapter 4, dating and hookup apps began to appear in the late 1990s when they were bound to desktop machines. Such dating websites, or portals as they were then known, were often viewed as for use by desperate people—those who would not easily get a date any other way, weirdos, and, of course, gay men who were typified as having a voracious appetite for sex, 24/7. As social media expanded and uses of the digital for sociality gained traction across populations, dating via the

Web and apps became both commonplace and socially accepted. One only has to consider the success of Tinder and how safe, in reputational terms, such an app has made meeting partners online. This represents an interesting counterexample to the shifting lack of reputational safety associated with the pager as it gradually moved from professional business to the context of inner-city drug crime in the United States. That said, the enlistment of Global Positioning System (GPS) technology and hacking occurring in this space point to a destabilization of dating and hookup apps accessed on supposedly personal and private mobile devices as something safe for work.

GPS allows for locative grid sorting (Light 2016a), effectively placing a user's profile among others in a grid for another user to browse based on proximity. Studies have argued that apps for men who have sex with men, such as Grindr, allow for a feeling of belonging in otherwise heterosexually dominated spaces *because* they use these geo-locative features (Blackwell et al. 2015). One cannot, however, ignore the possibility that questions of safety may arise, possibly in acute ways, from their use (see Light, Mitchell, and Wikström 2018). Browsing Grindr in a toilet at work, for example, will allow anyone else to see and communicate with that user's profile. This may "out" an otherwise private sexual preference, which, in turn, may become unsafe professionally, personally, or both. It may be that the person in question is not using a face pic on Grindr (but a dick pic instead), offering another form of "outing." Such inadvertent opening up of oneself at work clearly demonstrates the threats posed by dating apps.

Many dating apps are now premised on GPS technology in a variety of ways, and so it is not only men who have sex with men who may find themselves in public view at work. Even if one would not be concerned about revelations concerning one's particular sexual orientations, preferences, or likes, and fear for safety as a result, there are other risks. Dating apps are also used for extramarital affairs. While this may facilitate in-work connections, it may also increase the chance of being found out, given that the GPS may act as a contemporary surrogate for the security camera in the staff gym.

Furthermore, even if one is careful with the uses of a device or app and seeks to cover up extramarital activity, the case of the Ashley Madison hack further reveals how matters may be taken completely out of a user's hands. Ashley Madison provides a dating and hookup desktop website and app for people to create a "discreet connection" and is widely associated with extramarital affairs. The site operates similarly to many other dating apps—users can create a profile, search for connections, and communicate with connected users in a variety of ways. The site also provides the explicitly gendered Traveling Man functionality that encourages users to "pursue a little something on the side" while safely engaged in business travel (see figure 5.1). This feature is also available for women (see Bort 2013).

In mid-July 2015, hacker group The Impact Team warned Avid Life Media, the company behind Ashley Madison, that unless the service ceased, a large amount of data about its operation and customers would be released. This data was said to include employee documents and e-mails, as well as the real names, credit card information, addresses, and sexual fantasies of users. The rationale for the hack was reportedly to halt the company's exploitation of future users. In the words of the hackers, "We did it to stop the next 60 million [users being exploited]. Avid Life Media is like a drug dealer abusing addicts" (Cox 2015). Avid Life Media did not comply, and, on August 4 and 18, two data dumps were posted on the dark Web that rapidly became

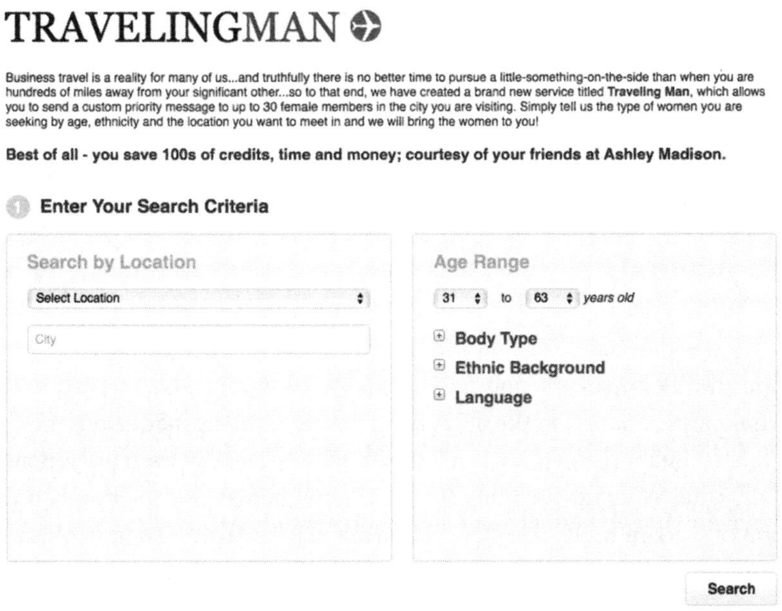

Figure 5.1
Traveling Man functionality on Ashley Madison.

available across the open Web (Newitz 2015b; Zetter 2015). In the region of 37 million account records were made public, along with company documentation. Within these released records were the identifiable details of users with work accounts associated with U.S. Homeland Security, as well as those of several churches.

Alongside the threats posed to professional reputations by this hack, it brought to the fore the role of nonhuman actors such as bots and hookup site user profiles on the site (Light 2016b; Newitz 2015a, 2015b, 2015c, 2015d). Both the fake profiles and the bots were almost all identified as women and configured to entice straight male users. While the hack aimed to expose "cheaters," it revealed an abundance of straight men chatting with social bots to make money for Avid Life. The leak also profited other businesses working with app data such as Trustify, a network of private investigators in the United States, who used the hacked data from Ashley Madison in two ways. First, an Ashley Madison user could pay to find out if their data has been released by the hack. Second, anyone could check up on someone they suspected to have used the site (despite the fact that Ashley Madison did not have a validation process in place, so no authenticated links could be made between users and their e-mails). As part of its advertising, Trustify (2017) states,

> If you suspect that you are being cheated-on by your spouse, or that your partner is on Ashley Madison, then you are not alone. The Ashley Madison data breach includes over 32 million users, and millions of Americans are cheated-on by their significant others on a daily basis. Many of these victims of infidelity cite that the worst part is not knowing if they are being cheated-on. They just want to know the truth. Trustify's Network of Licensed Private Investigators can help you get the truth today.

On the one hand, having (unsafe) sex at work through hackable platforms can be personally and professionally costly for those engaged in the extra-marital affairs. On the other hand, money is being made from the one trying to establish such illicit relationships. Sex at work becomes a potentially value-generating activity for various companies and thus, arguably, a form of work in itself. Therefore, while sex may be facilitated in workplaces with social media, it is connected to these questions of vulnerability to outside agents, as well as to the internal discord of surveillance, harassment, and inequality. Consequently, the management of the threat posed by social media continues to be an institutional focus, ensuring that abstract policies relating to harassment and equality are not the only technologies deployed in attempts to make our engagement with social media safer.

Policing Sex and Humor (with) Social Media at Work

It is perhaps needless to point out that the types of jobs people have affect what is deemed safe for work and what kind of mechanisms are used to police that boundary. In some white-collar work contexts, to be merely seen as having risqué fun at work may risk compromising one's professional status (Fincham 2016). In more blue-collar contexts, pin-up images decorating the walls may be accepted, expected, and deemed safe for work (Epstein 1992). While women would usually be those thus objectified, calendars depicting (usually) hypermasculine men have also risen in popularity over the past decades—often under the guise of a charitable association, marking them as safe for work, and possibly suitable for office decoration in female-dominated professional contexts that, by implication, become coded as heterosexual. For example, the internationally recognized *Dieux du Stade* (Gods of the Stadium) calendar, first published in 2001 as a charity commission, features nude and semi-nude photographs of members of Stade Français, a French rugby team.

In a more regional context, the Greater Manchester Fire Service released a similar charity calendar in 1999 only for it to be withdrawn after two years of fund-raising because of management's concerns about the lack of political correctness. In 2005, the calendar was reintroduced with, according to the project coordinator, Steve, more of a focus upon work than bodies (although bare-chested pictures were still included). In a news article, he stated, "The bosses decided we were not the image they wanted to project for the brigade at the millennium—white, male and heterosexual—but now they have changed their mind. We raised £10,000 for the Fire Service National Benevolent Fund with the last one. . . . Our last calendar was very popular, especially with women. This one is more a desk top calendar than for hanging on the wall" (*Manchester Evening News* 2005). Such sexual representation is clearly considered not only safe for the work of these firefighters but also for those who keep the calendar on their office desks.

What is deemed safe or at least appropriate for work also concerns the structures of the work performed. These structures may relate to the actual work itself: for instance, it may not be appropriate to be seen on your phone or to access social media in service professions, even if coffee and lunch breaks, as well as trips to printers, bathrooms, drinks machines, and photocopiers, allow for covert access during the working day. Assessment of risk and safety connected to social media sexual content can also relate to the physical environment of the workplace, particularly the consideration of who may be able to see NSFW content popping up on a screen (Light 2014). Self-management, personal discipline, and strategic subterfuge (such as using toilet breaks to engage with social media) can be key tools for managing the risks of social media at work.

For its part, organizational management regularly controls access to social media, thereby governing appropriate behavior through formal mechanisms. Employers can bar social media use for the sake of work efficiency and screen people's online behavior for the purposes of organizational reputation management. First, this can entail policies that disallow social media access through organizationally owned technology and employee-owned devices, such as mobile phones. The use of personal devices can also be constrained in other ways: having a cell phone on one's desk, or even inside the office, can be cause enough for a warning. In other instances, data protection or confidentiality considerations may prevent employees from discussing their work on social media. Large U.S. companies such as General Motors, Target, and Costco have social media policies that ban employees from publicly discussing work-related matters or disparaging coworkers, bosses, and the company, despite federal regulators ruling such policies illegal (Greenhouse 2013). Second, organizational control may involve the more intrusive tactic of technically blocking social media access, possibly in combination with a policy on use/nonuse. This can result in practical contradictions, as in employers referring to their novel social media campaigns without allowing employee access to them at work, or in institutions carefully locking down network access without accounting for the traffic that may simultaneously take place via personal smartphones (see Light 2014).

This paradox is common. At the same time as employers attempt to set the terms of engagement with social media once staff are employed, they are increasingly happy to use these same media to assess the suitability of staff during the recruitment process—to ensure that the candidates are indeed safe for work. Job applicants' social media profiles are routinely screened prior to employment (Preston 2011), although notably this practice is banned in Finland. A 2016 survey undertaken on behalf of a U.S. human resources software provider, CareerBuilder, suggests that over the preceding decade, the use of social media to screen candidates increased by 500 percent. More specifically, the top two pieces of information that "turned off employers" were provocative or inappropriate photographs, videos, or information (46 percent) and information about candidate drinking or using drugs (43 percent). A 2017 UK survey further revealed that half of employers are prepared to research job seekers using personal social media profiles (Robert Walters 2017).

Obviously, potential damage can lie in users' revelations of illegal activity such as drug taking, but it may even lie in self-disclosure of physical or mental health status, multiple gender identifications, or sexual tastes. To protect themselves, people may engage in disconnection practices such as setting up strict privacy parameters, managing multiple accounts, or simply logging off (Karppi 2011, 2014; Light 2014). However, these strategies can also become unsafe if the absence of a visible social media presence raises suspicions for a potential employer. For young workers and especially for those whose work calls upon communication skills, a managed online presence is therefore increasingly standard, a point we develop further in chapter 6.

Within the formal workplace, employers may use social media technology to monitor and control staff. In addition to media content breaching equality and harassment policies being deemed unsafe, more socially benign uses that contravene a company's brand or challenge institutional authority may also be cause for censure. The digital environment allows for extensive surveillance of employee activity, from the archiving of e-mail on company servers to GPS tracking of corporate phones, using keylogger technologies to map individual keystrokes for assessing content or general levels of activity, and using trackers to monitor and maintain individual workers' health (Moore 2017; Moore and Robinson 2015; Till 2014). In January 2016, the European Court of Human Rights ruled that employers did have the right to read private messages sent by a worker through Yahoo Messenger while the worker was in the workplace (Rawlinson 2016). In other words, communication channels deemed private fail to be such in spaces of work, and the possibly NSFW exchanges taking place within them can become objects of organizational scrutiny.

Organizational surveillance also extends beyond the formal definition of work time. The "presence bleed" (Gregg 2011) associated with mobile technologies' capacity to move work into our private lives stretches the working day well beyond the formal workplace. There are many documented cases of significant costs for uncensored online activity by individuals outside of work and on personal devices. In 2013, InterActive Corp fired PR executive Justine Sacco for a "joke" tweet she sent expressing a hope that she would not get AIDS while in Africa, adding that it would be fine because she was white. The tweet went viral while Sacco was in transit and incommunicado, unaware of having become an online hate figure. This furor, combined with what her inappropriate social media behavior indicated of her character, led to her dismissal (*Guardian* 2013; Ronson 2015). Sacco later claimed that the incident, and her ensuing online notoriety, not only cost her a job and career she loved but also hurt her dating options (Waterloo 2015). People have also been fired for much lesser offenses committed on personal social media accounts. U.S. teacher Ashley Payne, for instance, left her post after one of her pupil's parents spotted Facebook photos of her holding alcoholic beverages while on holiday, and she was offered the option to resign or face suspension by the school principal (*Daily Mail* 2011). Legal systems across the globe are still coming to grips with defining where employee privacy ends as cases mount of social media posts critical of workers' employers resulting in termination or censure (Mayer Brown 2011).

With the persistence and searchability of social media content, activity undertaken outside of the formal time of employment readily becomes unsafe for work. Overt or inadvertent revelations of sexual preferences, mental health issues, drug dependencies, or legal histories may all become grounds for dismissal or have a chilling effect on careers. In this way, corporate policies and norms about harassment, equality, and workplace culture can extend themselves into all facets of life, demanding ongoing self-policing which becomes yet another tool for managing the risks of social media in connection with the contemporary workplace.

The Dirty Work of NSFW

In managing the threats of social media's sexualized content, organizations are aided in policing by platforms themselves. This, in turn, creates both paid and unpaid jobs where managing and policing the safety of social media exchanges is the central task. NSFW and NSFL content is filtered out in social media through both flagging and tagging, but given both the volume of files uploaded daily on the most popular platforms and the insufficiency of automated image filtering software to pick up content prohibited by any platform's terms of use, this is centrally a field of human labor. More specifically, content moderation is human labor of the outsourced and offshore kind, particularly to countries such as the Philippines and Morocco where costs remain low and pay is as little as US$1 per hour (Breslow 2018; Chen 2012; Roberts 2016). It is also labor on a massive scale: already in 2014, over 100,000 people—that is, about the same number of people employed by social media companies for other tasks at the time—were estimated to moderate social media services, apps, and cloud services (Chen 2014).

In addition to screening content flagged by users, content moderators screen posts for pornography, gore, violence, racism, sexual solicitations, animal torture, and sexual content concerning minors. The work of watching such content all day long, day after day and week after week, is understandably taxing. Content moderation companies offer counseling services in order to help employees manage their labor, but as journalist Adrian Chen (2012, 2014, 2015, 2017; see also Buni and Chemaly 2016) notes, the emotional toll remains difficult for many to manage. Content management is part and parcel of social media services' brand and reputation management, as well as a mechanism necessary for securing the lawfulness of their operations. When conducted properly, such work remains invisible in the sense that users do not encounter forbidden or unsafe forms of content or gain knowledge of the volumes in which such content is steadily being uploaded, screened, and removed. As Sarah Roberts (2016, 148) points out, "The sign of a good CCM (commercial content moderation) worker is invisibility—a worker who leaves no trace."

In addition to the work being done by companies specialized in delivering CCM services, decisions over content deletion and banning are constantly being made by social media companies, dating sites, and discussion forums. As discussed in chapter 2, since the pre-Web days of Usenet and BBSs, moderation has been a task taken on by users themselves. From the 1990s, moderation in discussion forums and online communities has remained typically a voluntary task performed by active members with some status among other users, and with a good understanding of the platform's codes and conventions (Pfaffenberger 1996). Peer moderation is less easily understood as censorship than similar interventions made by paid staff. Volunteers moderate discussions on Reddit as they do on apps like Jodel. Such free labor is understandably appealing for the sites in question. It speaks of users' attachment to the service through their willingness to donate considerable time and effort to the maintenance of community standards while also removing the necessity for companies to pay employees for performing such tasks. This nevertheless involves degrees of vulnerability: Reddit, for example, was partly shut down in 2015 when many volunteer moderators closed their subreddits to protest the company firing a popular employee (Chen 2015).

Especially on the most popular forums and during heated moments of debate, the sheer volume of posts can be such that these human efforts fall short. Start-ups are applying machine learning that is promised to weed out hate speech and sexual or violent content according to a forum's specific needs, standards, and codes of communication. Utopia Analytics, for example, claims that their application can automatically moderate 90 percent of all posts while leaving only the most ambiguous cases for human screening. Automated moderation is gaining ground in textual data but is much more cumbersome with audiovisual content in particular. While YouTube remains a prime example of how labor-intensive content moderation in social media can be, Facebook, which has received plentiful bad publicity due to its users' live-streaming videos of murder, suicide, and rape, recently recruited 3,000 content moderators in addition to the 4,500 already employed to remove objectionable material (Solon 2017). The task in question is, however, not necessarily a straightforward one, for

> there are real monetary and other kinds of value that can be assigned to content that is sensationalistic, often on the grounds of being prurient, disturbing, or distasteful. In other words, it is this content that can often be a hit, driving eyeballs and clicks to a site or platform. For this reason, CCM workers find themselves in a paradoxical role, in which they must balance the site's desire to attract users and participants to its platform—the company's profit motive—with demands for brand protection, the limits of user tolerance for disturbing material, and the site rules and guidelines. (Roberts 2016, 149)

The attention economy of social media—thriving as it does on clicks, likes, and shares—involves some affective complexity in that content that makes users angry, sad, or disgusted can well be the content that is amply commented on and shared. Content of this kind can potentially capture broad attention and accrue the kind of affective stickiness that is highly valued (Paasonen 2015, 2016). Weeding out all controversial content would therefore be simply bad for business.

It should also be noted that identifying what visual content would be generally identified as racist, sexist, or hateful is not necessarily that easily accomplished, especially when such images are embedded in the framework of humor. Also, while we note in chapter 2 that sexual content is more readily removed than violence and hate, the types of sexual content that are deemed controversial by moderators are often shaped by particular politics, especially those related to nonnormative sexualities. These interpretations may well compete with the intentions of the content creator and the contexts of consumption. LGBTQI+ activists, for instance, report being blocked for using terms like "queer" and "dyke" in Facebook messages, with impacts on their political activism (Dottie Lux and Lil Miss Hot Mess 2017). This is an issue of both cultural specificities of the people using and those screening the services, and one of corporate conservatism characteristic of the U.S.-based companies running them.

This is also a question of context given that sexist, homophobic, ageist, ableist, and racist humor, in different degrees and combinations, is more than rife on online platforms. The mastery of such humor can be elementary to some platforms' default codes of communication, and part and parcel of what gets defined as online humor in the first place. The forms of exchange on platforms such as 4chan and Reddit are regularly opposed to any notions of political correctness while explicitly testing the boundaries of so-called good taste (Massanari 2017; Phillips 2015). The same applies to many an online humor site, discussion forum, Facebook group, and Twitter account. As Roberts (2016, 157) argues, it follows that in these contexts, "racist, homophobic, and misogynist imagery and content becomes reified as a norm, and the structures that abet it are cloaked and invisible, suggesting that the existence of content is just some kind of natural order of things and not, for example, potentially hugely profitable."

The opacity of CCM labor helps to sustain such an impression. As Chen (2017) points out, "the labor of content moderators is pretty much invisible, since it manifests not in flashy new features or viral videos but in a lack of filth and abuse." The work of CCM is invisible also for the reason that the companies paying for the labor are unwilling to identify their services with the broad accumulation and circulation of such "e-bile" (Jane 2014b). Furthermore, "Silicon Valley's optimistic brand does not fit well with frank discussions of beheading videos and child-molestation images. Social-media companies are also not eager to highlight the extent to which they set limits on our expression in the digital age—think of the recurring censorship controversies involving deleted Facebook pages and Twitter accounts" (Chen 2017).

Content moderation is a form of gatekeeping, yet the exact parameters of activities such as the "selection, addition, withholding, display, channeling, shaping, manipulation, repetition, timing, localization, integration, disregard, and deletion of information" (Barzilai-Nahon 2008, 1496) are not necessarily transparent to the users. In fact, moderation, which primarily involves the removal of content, needs to be understood as only one form, and mechanism, of gatekeeping of sexual content within a broader array of practices and tasks performed by both human and nonhuman actors. Information architecture, for example, already conditions what is readily available to users for commenting, sharing, and liking, and in what form that is distributed. Algorithms similarly govern the visibility of social media content based on estimates made of users' interests on the basis of their previous behavior (Jarrett 2014). The human laborers of the CCM industry are thus one more cog in the vast array of control mechanisms that manage the intersections of work and appropriate, safe communication, not least because their work is defined by that role. By functioning as another filtering layer, they work alongside the NSFW tag, corporate harassment, fraternization and social media use policies, information architecture and blocking technologies, and self-policing by users, to reduce the institutional and personal burdens of managing sex in the workplace.

Sex as Work

Finally, when considering sex and sexuality as directly implicated in the provision of a product or service in combination with networked media, commercial sex work performed on, or facilitated through, online platforms is an obvious area of focus. In fact, a book addressing sex, work, safety, and social media would be starkly incomplete without an examination of how sex work fits, or fails to fit, into all of this, as well as how safety and risk may be distributed within this realm of labor that has often been deemed unsafe by default. In discussing sex work primarily conducted on a freelance and gig basis, attention shifts from organizational and managerial control to platform governance, namely, the ways in which regulation practices connected to NSFW content limit and orient sex workers' uses of, and access to, social media. It equally involves the question of how networked communications have impacted the occupational safety of sex workers and the forms that their labor takes. This implies a drastically different notion of workplace harassment than the one addressed in the context of white-collar labor above, given that these sites of work are multiple, mobile, and mediated. Having discussed the impact of social media on the porn industry in chapter 3, we move here to further address the broader field of sex work, from escorting to webcamming.

The potential reverberations of the U.S. FOSTA and SESTA acts, also addressed in chapter 3, are particularly severe for those engaged in both direct and indirect sex work—that is, both for those soliciting sexual services online, and those performing them online. Sex workers have harnessed social media both to increase their agency and to generate safer working conditions. Consequently, by making platforms liable if sex work is facilitated on them, the FOSTA-SESTA acts reduce the capacity for sex workers to filter clients, to manage their careers independently, and to solicit trade. Direct sex workers use online platforms and apps to inexpensively and directly advertise their services (McClean 2015; Navani-Vazirani et al. 2015; Ray 2007; Sanders et al. 2018). Not only does this provide financial security by avoiding the skimming of profits practiced by pimps, brothel owners, or managers but it also allows for greater control over the working environment and the schedule of the working day. Escorts use digital media to screen clients and to compare notes on them, as well as to connect with "buddies" as safety guarantees, applying long-established off-line practices to networked communications (Sanders et al. 2018, 96–105). Sex workers assess the "vibe" of potential clients through SMS, phone calls, e-mails, and private messaging or by googling personal names, e-mail addresses, phone numbers, and usernames. Screening may also involve checking industry boards and forums—"bad date lists"—for community-developed red flags relating to particular clients (Ray 2007).

Online sex workers report fewer instances of violence and assault than other sex workers (Sanders et al. 2018, 90), implying that the aims of FOSTA-SESTA fail to meet occupational realities. Streetwalking remains the most unsafe form of sex work. Digital technologies have nevertheless opened up new economic avenues for these more marginalized sex workers. In his study of young South American migrant men in Dublin, Paul Ryan (2016) recounts that soliciting through Grindr and Instagram allows for reduced social and financial costs of entry into sex work, while also expanding the potential spaces where physical contact with clients may occur.

While intended to reduce the harms of sex work, FOSTA-SESTA in fact introduces danger for the workers on an international scale. As the legislation equally bans nonexplicit content addressing sex work, it may influence online coalition-building toward sex workers' rights (Kabeer, Sudarshan, and Milward 2013; Ray 2007; Sanders et al. 2018, 45–47). Rights bodies, such as the International Union of Sex Workers, use digital technologies to publicize the needs of sector workers, lobby for better protection of sex work by demanding coverage by industrial relations protections, and to advocate decriminalization. Their websites also serve as useful information kiosks for workers to learn of their rights. Online platforms remain equally central for distributing health information, particularly related to HIV and STI, to direct sex workers (Chaiyajit and Walsh 2012). Industry forums, particularly those that facilitate anonymity, can also provide spaces for peer interactions and thus cater to the emergence of collective action at the level of policy or policing. Mireille Miller-Young (2010, 227) notes that young women entering the sex industry, particularly black women, are "hurt by a culture of silence about wages, exacerbated by a stigmatized and complex field of work." The greater the information circulating on online industry forums like Stripperweb and AmberCutieForum, the more empowered and autonomous sex workers can be in making decisions about their labor. By increasing communication between clients and workers, especially about non-sex-related topics, these forums can also help humanize workers and reduce both their objectification and the legitimation of violence associated with it (Ashford 2008).

Equally importantly, online platforms allow for sex workers to tell their own stories, to speak of the matters that affect them, and to advocate for change in their contexts of work—all possibilities at risk with the current FOSTA-SESTA legislation (Feldman 2014; Rekart 2006). The closing down of sites such as Craigslists Personal Ads and Redbook to the advertising of sex work, as well as discussions focusing on it, directly limits communication among sex workers that could contribute to workforce solidarity and make a difference in how sex work is experienced. In effect, social media has allowed sex workers to express the agency denied them in too many policy, media, and research contexts. In cutting sex workers off from these platforms, the new legislation transforms their terms and forms of communication.

These implications are no less acute for those engaged in commercial webcamming, which, because of its mediated nature, occupies something of a gray zone between pornography and live performance. Since camming does not necessarily involve sex with other people on camera, it increases the possibilities of control and the reduction of harm for the individual sex worker. Camming has opened up possibilities for financially viable and independent sex work for black women who remain relatively marginalized within the porn industry (Reece 2015), and compared with other kinds of sex workers, cammers generally have a good deal of influence over the types of acts they undertake. As we point out in chapter 3, clients or platforms may demand particular acts or actions (Jones 2015; Senft 2008), yet, as Theresa M. Senft (2008) notes, cammers are regularly in charge of the camera's off button and focal range and hence control the parameters of their own mediated performance. While threats of physical violence from customers are typically minimized in webcamming because of the limited possibility of physical harm (Jones 2016, 247), the work also entails specific risks, such as "capping" (being recorded and distributed without consent). Capping may cause economic harm since selling videos is a key revenue source, even though it can also work as a promotional tool driving traffic to cammers' sites. Capping may also risk wider social reputational damage due to social exposure and the stigma associated with sex work.

Angela Jones (2016) contends that, contrary to many assumptions about the psychic distress of sex work, the work of webcamming can also be understood as pleasurable for the workers and not merely for the clients. Rather than disassociating dimensions of their body and self from the commercial sexual activity, she argues that the technological interface works as a psychological barrier that makes it possible for cammers to more fully engage with their sexual activity. Workers in her study report that arousal and orgasm are typically not simulated, creating a context of mutual pleasure between themselves and their clients. Some also described increased sexual satisfaction in their noncommercial sex lives after beginning a camming career. Empirical studies do not therefore support assumptions according to which sex work categorically involves disassociations generative of psychic harm, nor do they support an understanding of all sex work as trafficking, that is, as trade in illegal goods.

While there is little doubt of FOSTA-SESTA having a negative impact for online networking, support, and career building within sex work, it does not exhaust the possible uses and applications of social media. A recent study of UK sex workers found Twitter to be the most popular social media service in career building and advertising but even more centrally in connecting with other sex workers—a function equally associated with private Facebook and WhatsApp groups. The role of private groups was more important among transgender sex workers who did not find similar degrees of support from industry forums (Sanders et al. 2018, 39–44).

At the same time, social media also involves acute risks to privacy, as in one's occupation being revealed to others against one's will. Social media presence exacerbates the risk of "doxing"—release of personal contact details of those working in the sex industry with associated fears of physical violence—and various kinds of online harassment. Consequently, some sex workers choose to opt out from social media entirely whereas others manage the risks through solutions such as the creation of multiple accounts (Sanders et al. 2018, 112–114). This risk, though, is not specific to sex work. The strategies here echo those of the many workers described above who consciously manage their online presence, avoid posting sexual content to open groups, or otherwise limit their social media engagement to circumvent workplace surveillance as a strategic response to policies and policing that impact their workplace safety.

Balancing the NSFW

Addressing networked communications and safety in the context of sex work is a means of uncoupling risk from sex, as implied in the notion of NSFW, in order to pose an additional range of questions about what may or may not be safe about certain occupations and labor practices. A focus on the toll of commercial content filtering similarly helps in expanding considerations of risk and safety in social media from pictorial qualities to labor practices, namely, the concrete work of social media moderation. Considerations of sex, humor, and social media at work similarly extend analytical attention to organizational dynamics, governance, and harassment. This both grounds the uses of the tag NSFW in diverse occupational contexts and helps in articulating the complexity of where, how, and for whom sexual media content becomes deemed risky. It also illustrates the key point of this book, namely, that sex and sexuality are not inherently risky, or something to be equated with the notion of risk. As our discussion above indicates, sexual expression at work—whether it takes the form of circulating NSFW media content, risqué joking, or attempts at sexual intimacy—may be desired or unwanted, risky or safe, appropriate or inappropriate, but something that seldom remains simply absent in occupational contexts. This makes it central to shift attention onto issues of consent, reciprocity, and pleasure in considerations of both sex and sexually explicit media content at work.

Media content, humor, and sexual interactions deemed safe or unsafe for work differ in drastic ways across occupations, from soft-core porn calendars hung on the workplace wall to the strict filtering of access to adult online content to the impacts of government policy, each involving social hierarchies and institutional control. What constitutes appropriate humor or sexuality in relation to social media is thus bound to particular organizational cultures and the ways in which content is categorized and allowed to circulate within them. The blunt mechanisms of institutional firewalls and abstract interpretations by content moderators do not seem adequate to the subtleties of such a task.

In critiquing some of these practices, we hardly aim to diminish the value of the mechanisms in place for protecting workers or to undermine the problem of workplace sexual harassment. Dangers in work are manifold. In 2011, there were more than 330 million work-related accidents per year worldwide, with a total of 2.4 million people dying because of unsafe work conditions (International Labour Office 2012). While it may be tempting to juxtapose such risks with the safe, shiny, and frictionless machines of social media, its production and consumption are not free of risk—a point amply illustrated by the work of CCM. Considering risk and safety primarily in terms of physical harm and damage also obscures the ubiquity of bullying and harassment experienced in work life. According to the 2016 work condition barometer by the Finnish Ministry of Economic Affairs and Employment, for example, accounts of physical violence were particularly common among nurses, social workers, teachers, guards, and policemen, while more than half of all survey respondents had encountered bullying or emotional violence at work (Mähönen 2017). With this backdrop, managing unsafe social media use in the workplace is indeed an admirable goal.

What we do wish to highlight, though, is how the NSFW labeling functions as a prophylactic device in occupational contexts, but one which is contestable. Much of the media content associated with the hashtag invites censure and punishment in the contemporary workplace by contravening Internet use policies and equality policies or for being evidence of unprofessional and unsanctioned behavior carried out on company time. Mobilizing the tag can thus have useful effects in preventing the kinds of harms corporate policies seek to avoid, in supporting equality measures, and in generating safer, happier, more secure workplaces for all.

However, the mere existence of the tag NSFW (no matter where it gets deployed), as well as the emergence of industries and technologies that work to filter such content, also implies that users continue to circulate media materials that are beyond the limits set by organizational masters—after all, if all such content were unavailable or inconceivable in work contexts, the tag would not make sense. In the wider environment of extensive workplace surveillance, it is possible to read the sharing of content labeled NSFW, or indeed the viewing of it, as acts of resistance. This does not mean that content thus labeled is somehow inherently progressive, given that it is routinely racist, sexist, ableist, or otherwise demeaning of subaltern groups. Rather, engagements with unsafe social media content, or even engagements with social media during work, articulate a speaking back to power. At the very least, using NSFW is a recognition of the potential for surveillance in everyday workplaces, as well as a sly nod to the possibility of transgressing its ever-encroaching protocols.

6 The Political Economy of Unsafe Work

In November 2015, Meriton Apartments employee Michael Nolan called feminist columnist Clementine Ford "a slut" on her private Facebook page. It is perhaps ironic that this was as a comment on a post sharing sexually explicit abuse that Ford had previously received. A few days later, Ford, self-described "Feminist Killjoy to the Stars" known for her aggressive engagement with commenters across her various platforms, shared screenshots of the exchange. In this message, she also tagged Nolan's employer (indicated on his profile) and asked if they were aware of their employee's actions on Facebook, which also included racist statements. Meriton responded first by suspending Nolan from work and then, after a short investigation, firing him (Ford 2015; Levy 2015).

For Ford, receiving online abuse is unfortunately common, and, in this scheme, Nolan's transgression was minor, leading some to question her right to involve his employer in an ostensibly private exchange. In her *Daily Life* column in the *Sydney Morning Herald*, Ford explained her decision to act in this case:

> I did it because I'm sick and tired of men abusing women online and continually getting away with it. I can bear the brunt of this behavior, but I'm angry about the number of women who tell me they can't. Too many women are harassed into silence by men who flounce about the place doing and saying whatever they like. When we complain, we're told to "get over it' or 'harden up", two retorts that completely miss the irony of the fact that the most thin skinned, sensitive and retaliatory people online are white men aged between 15 and 35. (Ford 2015)

After Nolan's sacking, the backlash against Ford was immediate and vitriolic, some of which is documented in the companion blog to Ford's book, *Fight Like a Girl* (2016).

This unfortunately not uncommon incident demonstrates a variety of ways in which a workplace can be made a space of danger, fear, or risk when it intersects with social media. On one hand, we have Nolan, whose misogynist and racist self-expression on and through a personal Facebook profile became linked to his service-industry employer, subsequently becoming a liability for that company's public image. Workplace surveillance discussed in the previous chapter is implicated here. On the other hand, we have the online workplace of Ford herself, which is regularly experienced as unsafe through consistent threats of rape and other forms of physical violence. This also includes the inflicting of symbolic violence in the form of name-calling and shaming, a practice in which Ford also engages. Ford's experience in addition reflects the misogynist silencing of women also seen in high-profile harassment incidents such as Gamergate and The Fappening (Chess and Shaw 2015; Jane 2014a; Marwick 2013a; Shepherd et al. 2015; see also Massanari 2017; Moloney and Love 2017).

Harassment is a widespread dimension of the contemporary digital workplace. Despite this ubiquity, the common definitions of NSFW we have thus far explored focus primarily on expressions of nudity, sex, and sexuality and tend to ignore other forms of social media content that symbolically, or quite literally, make occupations unsafe. This is therefore the focus of this chapter. Making use of NSFW again as a framing device, we move away from discussions of sex to those of sexism with the aim of highlighting some of the key risks and power dynamics in careers built in and through social media.

Mapping the affective and political economy of harassment in a historical framework, we set out to place the aggressive policing of certain kinds of digital labor performed by women and minority groups within the economic logics of contemporary capitalism. We focus particularly on online misogyny as one example of how work can be rendered unsafe through its intersection with the political economy in which social media functions. Here, the symbolic violence that is generally overlooked in definitions of NSFW emerges as both cause and effect of the overstretched flexibility and forms of economic agency common in today's workplaces, and as connected to increasing precarity and anxiety. Social media, which is growing ever more central as a field of labor and profit generation, regularly plays a key role in how white- and no-collar labor turns literally not safe for work but in ways not necessarily connected to sexual content.

The Intersectional Spectrum of Harassment

As Alice Marwick, Lindsay Blackwell, and Katherine Lo (2016) note in their Data & Society "Best Practices for Conducting Risky Research and Protecting Yourself from Online Harassment" guide, marginalized groups such as people of color, women, and LGBT people are particularly subject to repeated online harassment as it makes use of

> networked technologies to threaten, maliciously embarrass, or attack another individual. It includes behaviors that range from merely irritating to life-threatening. Some typical techniques include "doxing," or revealing personal information publicly; "brigading," or when a group of people work together to harass an individual; "revenge porn," or disseminating private photos (real or falsified) without the individual's consent; and "swatting," or reporting a false threat to local police, prompting an emergency response team to the individual's home. (Marwick et al. 2016)

Such best practices documents are valuable to scholars working on sexuality, gender, multiculturalism, immigration, and racism who become bullied and more systematically harassed, not least when speaking out in the media. It is equally the case with journalists investigating Brexit, Russian and U.S. politics, as well as with female bloggers tackling the gender dynamics of the game industry and gaming culture. While beyond the scope of this book in their complexity, scale, and reach, such "webs of hate" (Kuntsman 2010) form a crucial context for our following discussion of the affective dynamics connected to online misogyny in particular.

While online harassment, both spontaneous and highly organized, has increasingly become a matter of public concern, actions for fighting it seem consistently to drag behind (Vitis and Gilmour 2016, 2). Possibilities for reporting bullying and harassment have been developed on Twitter and Facebook, largely in response to earlier measures, such as users blocking one another, being deemed insufficient. Social media sites have balanced the principles of freedom of expression, as guaranteed by the First Amendment in the United States, with demands to protect their users as well as to comply with hate speech legislation in other regions.

In May 2016, Facebook, Twitter, Google (as the owner of YouTube), and Microsoft cosigned a voluntary "Code of Conduct for Countering Illegal Hate Speech Online" as part of the European Union's Internet Forum between the EU, national governments, Europol, and tech companies (see

Aswad 2016). Motivated by the increase in racist, xenophobic, and anti-immigration activities following the political and military upheavals in Syria and Iraq, the code tackles the issue by defining hate speech as "all conduct publicly inciting to violence or hatred directed against a group of persons or a member of such a group defined by reference to race, colour, religion, descent or national or ethnic origin" (European Union 2016).

The fact that the code does not recognize hate speech targeted against people on the basis of gender or sexual orientation is not surprising, given its focus on fighting racism and xenophobia, as well as the more general exclusion of gender from definitions of hate speech. This nevertheless remains noteworthy, considering the intense volume in which gendered harassment in particular has been reported and debated in social media, newspapers, TV features, and scholarship (Mantilla 2015; see also Jane 2016). Just as racist content routinely falls outside the scope of the marker NSFW, sexist, misogynistic, homophobic, and transphobic content falls outside the definitions of hate speech.

Such separation of identity categories in connection with definitions of online hate and harassment is highly problematic since, by necessity, such categories intertwine with and are bodily inhabited as intersectional identity formations (see Lähdesmäki and Saresma 2014; Mäkinen 2016; Sundén and Paasonen 2018). As we noted in chapter 4, image-based harassment is disproportionally targeted at queer people, people with disabilities, and those marked as racial others. Racist slurs, for example, stick differently to and linger in dissimilar ways on bodies differently gendered, classed, sexed, and sexualized (Ahmed 2001; Kuntsman 2010; Tyler 2006). Misogynistic hate, again, resonates differently with bodies distinctly marked in terms of ethnicity, religion, or race. And, as Adrienne Shaw (2014, 273) points out, violent sexism and misogyny online is "compounded with racism, homophobia, ableism, and all other forms of hate." These forms of hate build on and amplify one another. Decoupling their interconnections therefore cuts short the affective circuits involved while, to a degree, also prioritizing certain forms of online hate as more pressing public concerns than others.

Hate erupts, sticks, circulates, and layers with different speeds and in different cycles: as organized, collective multiplatform enterprises where user accounts are generated in diverse social media services specifically for the purpose; as seemingly spontaneous incidents of provocation and trolling;

and as the means of generating personal microcelebrity, visibility, and following on online platforms. Vitriolic attacks against women and sexual, racial, and ethnic minorities operate with notably similar dynamics across national borders, yet such circuits of hate can also be highly convoluted when it comes to categories of identity. The issue becomes further complicated when hate is used as a brand marker in the NSFW online economy.

Consider, for example, the case of Milo Yiannopoulos, self-identified on his YouTube, Facebook, and Pinterest accounts as "the most fabulous supervillain on the Internet," who worked as senior editor at the alt-right news site Breitbart from 2014 to 2017. Also titled a professional alt-right troll and leader of an online mob, Yiannopoulos has published articles on the success of fat shaming and the ability of birth control to make women unattractive, likened feminism to a disease, and connected transgender identification to sociopathy (BBC 2017; Grady 2017). Known for his misogynist and anti-Muslim attacks in particular, Yiannopoulos was an early leading figure in the Gamergate controversy and was permanently banned from Twitter in 2016 due to his articulation of sexist and racist abuse toward the *Ghostbusters* star Leslie Jones. That the openly gay Yiannopoulos may have some Jewish ancestry and perform on live television in pearls and bangles has not kept him from speaking against gay rights, or those of any other minority group. Nor has his status as a British citizen residing in the United States kept him from playing an active role in Breitbart's anti-immigration campaigns. Yiannopoulos is manifestly propatriarchy, cis-gendered, and able-bodied, yet his particular intersectional identity formation also highlights the importance of broadening analyses of online hate and relations of dominance and power to account for such intersections (Shaw 2014).

Late in 2016, Yiannopoulos signed a US$250,000 advance book deal with the publisher Simon & Schuster. The contract was canceled only two months later after video clips emerged of him addressing his early teen sexual experiences with a Catholic priest in an upbeat manner and defining pedophilia as "coming-of-age relationships" facilitating self-discovery in young boys (Politi 2017). Due to the ensuing uproar, Yiannopoulos resigned from his post at Breitbart while denying his support for pedophilia. The incident makes evident that while it is possible, and even highly profitable, to build a career on vitriolic attacks on virtually any minority group without public condemnation, similarly sharp lines of provocation connected to adolescent sexuality—let alone that of gay orientation—and child abuse are not protected in the name of free speech even by the hubs that routinely engender and amplify similar antagonisms. The culturally abject, monstrous figure of the pedophile had particularly strong resonance when evoked by Yiannopoulos whose nonnormative sexual identification had already marked him apart from other leading alt-right spokespeople.

Nevertheless, for social media influencers such as Yiannopoulos, whose brand has been built on "monetisable notoriety" (Lynskey 2017) and click-bait provocation, the triggering, circulation, and amplification of hate online has become not merely an anonymous hobbyist preoccupation but a well-paid occupation with enhanced public visibility. In other words, his highly successful career trajectory preceding the pedophile controversy stands as an example of how trolling—partly in connection with the spread of disinformation—has become an effective arena of political work (Bershidsky 2018). The fruits of such labor effectively render other forms of online and digital work much less safe for those subjected to the harassment. Spilling from online platforms to off-line spaces of work and leisure, harassment effaces such conceptual divides, bringing material social and economic consequences for its participants. This can be clearly seen in the effects of online misogyny.

Online Misogyny

Despite early promises that the Internet could facilitate the articulation of discourse unfettered by the codifications of bodies, genders, races, and abilities, that it would open up of spaces for feminist and feminized speech, and that digital technologies could facilitate complex rearticulations of gender and sexual identities (Hawthorne and Klein 1999; Plant 1995; Rheingold 1994; Stone 2000; Turkle 1995; Wakeford 2000), the medium did not fulfill its liberatory potential. Rather, the Internet and particularly the Web rapidly reproduced and retrenched gender, sexed, and raced power relations (e.g., Nakamura 2002; Paasonen 2005). Early studies of online communities and communication either explicitly discussed the harassment experienced by women or set their case study against this assumed backdrop. They demonstrated that, despite the claims of the famous 1993 *New Yorker* cartoon, on the Internet, it was unlikely nobody knew you were a dog (see Nakamura 2002, 35).

Writing in 1995, Dale Spender placed digital media within the long history of the gendering of technologies, including the technologies of writing such as grammar and print. According to Spender, computers and their networks are "the world of men. . . . Men have more computers, spend more time with them, and are the dominating presence in cyberspace" (Spender 1995, 165–166). But it was not only access to computers and confidence in their use that excluded women. Spender went on to describe the toxic atmosphere facing women in both university computer science labs and in public online forums: "From schoolgirls to seasoned professional women, the virtual reality is the same. There is no female who has worked on a networked system who has not been subjected to harassment, flaming, or other intimidatory tactics" (Spender 1995, 202).

Similar experiences were already documented in the context of Usenet. Women's accounts of the sense of agency emerging from the mastery of computers and the social codes of Usenet, as well as from the interpersonal relations developed in newsgroups, were set against aggressive flaming, sexist speech, and persistent "wanna fuck" messages, the rejection of which often led to more aggressive tactics such as hacking and stalking (Camp 1996; Clerc 1996; Gilboa 1996; Sutton 1996). Despite confident Internet use in the workplace and enjoyable interactions on professional lists, women noted their reluctance to use anonymous chat rooms, MUDs, and MOOs out of fear of "online 'wackos', 'kooks', 'axe-murderers', 'rapists', 'child molesters', 'thieves', 'blackmailers' and so on" (Montgomery 1999, 108). The assumption of such spaces as potentially risky reflects contemporaneous mainstream media moral panics, but this aversion can also be likened to being "wary of strangers on city streets" (Montgomery 1999, 108; Spender 1995). The risk minimization strategies routinely adopted by women in public were echoed in their experiences of the digital environment. Policing yourself in how far, how often, and when you communicate online, making sure not to (ad)dress provocatively as you do so, was a default for female users, even in the halcyon days of the so-called "cyberspace."

It is in this context that we must place the experience of violent speech that has penetrated the lives of the increasing number of people whose work, like that of Clementine Ford, involves online creative expression or whose professional or occupational persona has a significant online dimension. Such harassment is clearly not a new phenomenon but has, perhaps, been enhanced and amplified by the expanding reach and the porous nature of contemporary networked communication systems. Harassment has certainly grown much more visible as celebrities, microcelebrities, and social influencers (see Abidin 2015), many of whom owe some of that fame to their work on and for digital platforms, have become its targets.

However, one does not need to be a widely known public figure to be on the receiving end of online harassment, or even a woman working in traditionally male-dominated fields like the technology sector; ordinary users who merely post in forums may also come under attack. These users may be self-identified activists or merely anonymous posters whose commentary is contrary to the prevailing discourse. In almost a throwaway remark in her discussion of people who call out misogyny, homophobia, or racism in online forums, Lisa Nakamura (2015, 108) notes that not only is this work unpaid community management of the kind discussed in chapter 5, it "often results in the poster being harassed, trolled, and threatened."

As users populate websites and platforms with their content and social interactions, their activity is increasingly defined as a form of labor (Jarrett 2016; Terranova 2000). Such interactions keep costs down for site providers by replacing the work of paid content producers with that of unpaid users. Small, unconsidered interactions of clicking links also contribute value as they generate data to be sold. If almost all online activity on commercial sites can be considered work in the sense that it involves the generation of value, then almost all experiences of online harassment can be interpreted as unsafe work. According to a 2014 Pew Research Center survey, 73 percent of U.S. Internet users had witnessed harassment and 40 percent had been recipients of it. Of the percentage who had witnessed online abuse, 25 percent had witnessed a sustained period of harassment; 24 percent had seen physical threats; 19 percent had witnessed sexual harassment; and 18 percent had seen stalking behaviors (Duggan 2014). Notably, young women were more likely to have directly experienced more aggressive forms of harassment. As vitriolic misogyny, homophobia, and racism become the "standard discursive move" (Jane 2014a, 558) in online exchanges, even a small amount of online work can lead to a sustained campaign of symbolic violence—such as that in the 2014 Gamergate controversy, which embroiled a vast range of famous and not-so-famous game designers, journalists, scholars, and gamers in an internationally distributed antifeminist crusade.

Emma Jane (2014b, 2015) characterizes the type of abuse received by women and other subaltern groups as "e-bile" in order to indicate its specific sexual and embodied quality. Despite its occurring across modes, platforms, and political spectrums, she typifies this form of speech by its "reliance on profanity, *ad hominen* invective, and hyperbolic imagery of graphic—often sexualized—violence" (Jane 2014b, 533). Such e-bile flows both in concert with, and separately from, online hostility and hate connected to identity categories such as race, ethnicity, religion, and nationality (e.g., Nakamura 2009), yet even these can take the form of the hyperviolent, sexualized terms associated with harassment online and off (Filipovic 2007). The "unwilling avatars" (Franks 2011) created using these identity markers function as index and cause of negativity and come under online attack. The embodied qualities of online harassment reach an apex, though, in doxing, where a user's personal contact details, often including their home address, are publicized. These acts place the physical body at the center of the threat, increasing the anxiety experienced by those who are harassed. When the material body comes under assault in this way, the intersection of work and social media becomes particularly unsafe.

Geek Spaces

Explanations for online misogynist harassment have connected it to the licensing of toxic aspects of geek masculinity on platforms like Reddit and 4chan and the bleeding of that culture throughout the Web (Braithwaite 2016; Massanari 2015). Sketching the nature of this form of masculinity is integral to understanding the economic dimensions of online harassment. Following Adrienne Shaw, it is important to note that online harassment is not merely a matter of trolling specific to social media platforms and their affordances of anonymity: "Like all racism and sexism, it comes out of a position of privilege that has been created via the same historical events that made 'tech culture' a particular form of masculine culture" (Shaw 2014, 274).

The nerd stereotype mobilized in popular culture aligns an interest in technology and computing with being white, heterosexual, and cis-male (Adam 2005; Adam and Green 2005; Kendall 2000, 2011). That this is also borne out in labor statistics of digital media industries is both effect and cause of this phenomenon. Geek masculinity is a particular version of the nerd stereotype. While "nerd" remains a pejorative, "geek" has more positive connotations aligned with the successful entrepreneurial ideal of the contemporary digital media sector. Geek masculinity is a hybrid composite, borrowing elements of normative hegemonic masculinity, such as the valorizing of technical mastery and rationality, while rejecting others (Bridges and Pascoe 2014; Connell and Messerschmidt 2005; Crawford, Gosling, and Light 2011; Ging 2017; Kendall 2000; Wajcman 1991). Unlike hegemonic masculinity, geek agency is not associated with physical strength and, indeed, often defines itself against that paradigm by privileging intellect, wit, and arcane knowledge (Massanari 2017; Nagle 2015). A good lulz—amusement derived at another's expense—by a troll, for instance, requires dexterity with language, technology, and subcultural codes along with a creative sensibility (Phillips 2015). Geek heteromasculinity, particularly in how it plays out in online cultures, is linked with cultural and intellectual capital expressed as a particular kind of aggressive communicative competence, which then becomes the domain of white men to be defended as such.

Geek masculinity is defined against a stereotyped, essentialized, and devalued feminized "other." In particular, this binary divide juxtaposes masculine, intellectual rationality against female, embodied emotionality. Women who do not meet the standards of this mythic femininity or who take on qualities associated with masculinity by, for instance, mastering online invective as Ford has done, effectively challenge the alignment of male bodies with privileged activity. They subsequently become objects of hate, "the wrong kind of women, who need to be put back in their place" (Braithwaite 2016, 1). Paradoxically, or at least ironically, women who do perform traditional femininity are also rejected because they fail to conform to, or are deemed incapable of understanding, the humor, practices, and beliefs of online geek culture. As online spaces become more mainstream and diverse, the threat of a difference that challenges the regime of geek privilege becomes particularly keenly felt (Evans and Janish 2015). The rejection of both gender-conforming and gender-nonconforming women ensures that only male geek bodies can retain the privileges associated with them.

Simultaneously, women are fetishized in this discourse, remaining impossible objects of desire who are discussed, criticized, and valorized in terms of their heterosexual appeal (Kendall 2000; Moloney and Love 2017; Nussbaum 2010). Moreover, women's bodies are defined in heterosexist terms as the natural prize for successful masculine performance (Chu 2014; Kendall 2002). The cry of "tits or GTFO" (show your tits or get the fuck out) that greets users outing themselves as female on some subreddits and game platforms is one example of geek masculinity's sense of entitlement over women's bodies (Phillips 2015).

It is also why so many attacks on Ford were based in her physicality and the attacker's judgment on, and preemptive rejection of, her heterosexual allure. In the "Dicktionary" chapter of her book, Ford (2016) catalogues key names she has been called: fat, hairy, lesbian, ugly, slut/whore, frigid, in desperate need of a root [Australian slang for sex]. On her Twitter feed, references have been made to her "probably stretched out vagina," having a "head like 10 miles of bad road," and being "a fat little troll" and a "whore." Some have suggested that she, or her attitude, would benefit from corrective rape or having someone "take a dump into that mouth," and that she should be thankful that her lack of desirability means men would never "be sick enough" to rape her. She has also been repeatedly told that she would not be "fun at parties" because she fails to appreciate masculine jokes, practices, and politics and so is too uptight and contrary to have any heterosexual social appeal.

Geek masculinity is heavily focused on claiming, asserting, and defending a sense of superiority. Angela Nagle (2015) describes how geeks in antifeminist online groups define themselves against what they call "normies" or those who express dominant, mass cultural tastes as opposed to the subcultural versions they advocate. Massanari (2015, 86) recognizes this phenomenon in some cultures of Reddit whose members view themselves as exceptional or special. According to Massanari, the subreddit /r/ gentlemanboners, which features fully clothed pictures of female celebrities intended for sexual titillation, encapsulates the complexity of geek masculinity's understanding of its superiority even when performing normative acts of masculine dominance. On this subreddit, "women are objects to be admired and exist for male satisfaction, but the men doing the ogling are nice, classy gentlemen wearing, metaphorically speaking, monocles and top hats" (Massanari 2015, 133). Such claims to superiority are particularly potent on sites that actively define themselves in relation to men's rights, the recuperation of male power and privilege which has allegedly been usurped by feminism, and those addressing the recovery of "true" masculinity (Ging 2017).

Meritocracy and Oppression

An individualized, libertarian ethos also figures strongly in gaming and open-source development communities where online misogyny is rife (Pfaffenberger 1996; Reagle 2013; Streeter 2011). Hacker culture's anti-authoritarianism and the valorization of radical free speech that animated Usenet (Pfaffenberger 1996) reflect and reproduce geek masculinity's belief in its own meritocratic distribution of power. This couples with the fetishizing of technology to produce an insistence that participation in digital spaces is a matter of individual choice and that status is entirely governed by linguistic or technical prowess. Regulation is therefore unnecessary and undesirable as good code or good conversation should speak for itself. In this liberal meritocracy, to acknowledge gender difference at all is considered sexist (Nafus 2012). The systemic effects of gender, sexual, and race politics thus go unconsidered. This assumption contributes to the disavowal of privilege and the need for its policing.

As Joseph Reagle (2013) argues, this apparent openness means that the rules governing sociality become implicit and remain biased toward white, masculine norms. In particular, he points to the aggressive, adversarial, competitive discursive style that dominates geek spaces. That Ford, for instance, remains and continues to engage actively on such antagonistic forums and through often aggressive modes indicates that masculinized speech is not the exclusive preserve of those who identify as men. But in order to function in those spaces, users are required to adopt at least some of these aggressive, middle-class, masculinized discursive practices. Those unwilling to speak back on these terms can become silenced, drowned out by louder voices, structurally excluded by technical affordances such as upvoting that privilege content aligned with majority views (Massanari 2015), or exhausted by the continual fight for discursive space.

People leaving these conversations, and sometimes the fields of work altogether, can be seen as performing personal choices rather than being forced out by structural issues. Consequently, environments like Reddit or 4chan, which are already dominated by performances of geek masculinity and in-group norms that value or at least support misogyny, racism, and liberal—or libertarian—principles, embed a definition of neutrality that "valorizes the rights of the majority while trampling over the rights of others" (Massanari 2015, 11). In such a meritocracy, anyone is fair game for lulz or threats and no one warrants protection. To express concern for others is to be too sensitive (like a woman) and to speak to the systemic inequalities is to engage in censorship. To react against the misogyny or racism is to "not get the joke" and restate your status as an outsider. In this way, openness becomes exclusive.

Despite its adoption of dominant positions against women and people of color and its unsympathetic relationship to the oppressions of people in these categories, geek masculinity nevertheless defines itself as oppressed (Kendall 2011; Phillips 2015). Geekiness has recently achieved a good deal of cultural visibility, but geek culture remains marginal and is celebrated for being so (Massanari 2015, 2017; Tufecki 2014). Consequently, it is simultaneously culturally subordinate, or "beta," and highly privileged (Ging 2017; Nagle 2013, 2015). As white, heterosexual, middle-class, and male, it can mobilize the social and economic advantages and entitlements of all of these social positions while simultaneously being dominated by, or believing that it is dominated by, normative heteromasculinity's greater social privilege and the assumed privileges accrued by women. This tension between subordination and domination, as experienced through personal life histories, can intensify the protection of power and status markers and produce aggressive defensive reactions when geek privilege is pointed out (Massanari 2015; Tufecki 2014).

It would be absurd, however, to trace all online harassment that makes the Internet unsafe to the politics of geek masculinity, as this would ignore entrenched sexism, racism, ableism, trans-, and homophobia across all sectors of society. It would also suggest that all who have harassed women online identify with or perform this particular type of masculinity. This claim would clearly be untrue simply given the wide scope of online harassment. It would certainly not capture the spectrum of harassment directed at Ford as these attacks have lacked some of the coordination and technical flair associated with geek mobs. Ascribing online harassment solely to geek masculinity also flattens out differences among users, ignores the intersectionality of identities, and fails to capture the movement between different identifications and practices in people's online activities. Certainly, it would be difficult to source the figure of Milo Yiannopoulos entirely within the politics of geek culture.

Nevertheless, geek masculinity remains an important source and index of the symbolic violence that makes digital work unsafe. It is also a valorized subjectivity in contemporary capitalism and aligned in its internal set of values with the dominant political economy. As a number of feminist and queer theorists have shown, economics and gender politics are deeply implicated with each other, with, for instance, the gendered division of labor that demarcates and devalues "women's work" being integral to capitalist development and its perpetuation (Dalla Costa and James 1973; Federici 2004; Mies, Bennholdt-Thomsen, and Von Werlhof 1988). From this perspective, expressions of white, masculine power online are not merely individualized expressions of misogyny but also have a particular economic function. In the next section, we move to ask how online harassment and the privileges of white heteromasculinity, both geek and hegemonic, are entwined within the political economy of contemporary capitalism, within the IT sector in particular. Through this lens, we can see precisely how online invective is unsafe for work.

The Economics of Harassment

Online harassment has personal emotional and psychological effects but also significant economic costs as victims move house, increase security arrangements, seek counseling, or incur legal expenses. Danielle Keats Citron (2009a, 2009b, 2014) and Emma Jane (2018) list these dangers and their economic implications, arguing also that the intensity of harassment can simply make women and other minorities stop contributing to online spaces. A past Pew Research Center study noted a drop in participation in online chat or discussion group from 28 percent of users to 17 percent, which they attribute entirely to women's declining involvement (Fallows 2005). One of the key harms of this harassment, though, concerns employment capacity.

Being forced off-line comes with extremely high financial and personal costs for people like Ford whose key employment involves writing for the Web. Victims must either continue to write and endure the sustained harassment or seek other forms of employment. When technology blogger Kathy Sierra stopped blogging in order to protect herself from the onslaught of e-bile, her online readership was not only deprived "of an apparently talented and enthusiastic blogger on software design" (Citron 2009a), but Sierra herself lost the opportunity to further enhance her reputation in the field and, subsequently, to develop her career. Prior to 2007, she had been "one of the most visible women in tech" (Sandoval 2013) but gave up that status, book deals, and speaking engagements in order to escape the threats. Sierra did not return to the Web until 2013, leaving a significant gap in her online presence. Gaps like this deflect professional trajectories, which, in turn, can damage career earnings for professionals or pro-ams alike.

A particular loss for those driven from the Web lies in advertising revenue. The income generated by most bloggers and vloggers is typically small because revenues are dependent upon audience size and click-through rates. For those who have reached the status of a social media influencer, though, advertising revenues may be significant, and to forgo them because of threats and harassment becomes costly. Established bloggers, vloggers, and instagrammers also generate revenue or receive in-kind goods by undertaking promotional activities across their online platforms or by establishing brand partnerships, leveraging their fame to generate profit (Abidin 2016a, 2016b; Abidin and Ots 2016; Abidin and Thompson 2012; Duffy 2017). However, as Brooke Duffy (2017) recounts, the economic leverage of influencers relies on the crude market metrics of the numbers of viewers and commenters associated with their accounts. Such all-important follower numbers can be easily damaged by the presence of trolls, hate posts, or hacks. Online harassment thus may render economic success or a sustained presence in this growing sector untenable.

It is not only those who actively commercialize their online activity who may suffer financially from online harassment. People working in fields as diverse as law, dentistry, teaching, and financial consultancy have all been impacted economically and professionally by their experiences at the hands of online mobs (Citron 2014). People have lost career opportunities or their jobs because of damaging and often untrue statements made about them. Some harassers have deliberately targeted employers and potential employers with e-mails detailing false accusations, hacks, or distributed denial-of-service (DDoS) attacks that saturate a company's website with so many requests that it effectively stops functioning. The persistence of information on the Web also means that such hateful information can readily be found by Google searches long after the original incidents. As Citron (2009a, 80) notes, "The damaging statements and threats may raise doubts about the victim's competence, or suggest the victim attracts unwanted controversy, causing the employer to hire someone else."

This effect is felt particularly keenly by those whose work involves online creative production, but it does not end there. Developing a vibrant social

media profile has long been important for career development in many
industries where work is based on networks and self-promotion (Duffy
2017; Gill 2011; Neff 2012; Neff, Wissinger, and Zukin 2005), but today
an effective online presence is important across a wide range of occupations. Globally, labor is increasingly managed through short-term, precarious contracts. Work is outsourced to self-employed freelancers, subsidiary
companies, or offshore service providers, hollowing out organizations and
leading to insecure, unstable work conditions. A career today is increasingly a portfolio of short-term gigs assembled from a variety of contexts
(Dyer-Witheford 2015; Huws 2014; Neilson and Rossiter 2008). Use of
information and communication technology is central to this kind of insecure work in a variety of ways (Huws 2014), but particularly for building a
successful, promotional online identity that can secure paid work. A strong
profile helps attract the next client, the next sale of your craft product, or
the next assignment from TaskRabbit. It can also secure work in traditional
employment contexts. Damage to that profile through lies, harassment, or
association with controversy can have lasting effects.

As white- and blue-collar industries have both become information
intensive, computerized, and flexible, the skills focus of various industries
has swung to matters of cognition, communication, and affect. This is the
shift toward a form of capitalism where global economic growth is assumed
to come from labor associated with these immaterial, feminized dimensions
of work (e.g., Adkins 2001; Hardt and Negri 2005; Morini 2007; Moulier-
Boutang 2012). This, in turn, has led to a focus on matters of human
capital—the "skills, knowledge, and experience of individual employees
within the firm" (Krebs 2000, 88). This means that online reputation systems that measure and make visible such forms of capital, albeit in particularly flawed ways, have become an aspect of how potential employees
are evaluated (Gandini 2016; see also chapter 5). Alison Hearn (2010, 422)
notes that reputation management is vital in the contemporary workplace:

> Human resources professionals also have come to recognize that an individual
> employee's skills matter far less than the depth and intensity of their social rela-
> tionships online, or, in more familiar terms, their social capital, which can be
> aggregated and expressed as their digital reputation. The number of times a name
> comes up in a Google search, an Ebay rating as a buyer or seller, the number of
> friends on Facebook, or followers on Twitter can all be seen as representations
> of digital reputation—the general public feeling or sentiment about a product,
> person or service.

This includes constructing and maintaining online profiles often in the time away from work or prior to securing paid work. The work of establishing a digital media identity can be considered as a form of "hope labor," the unpaid or undercompensated work undertaken for exposure in the hope of enhancing future employment prospects or securing employment with the particular service for which the unpaid work was performed (Kuehn and Corrigan 2013). For users who are driven off-line or who adopt pseudonyms that are disaggregated from their occupational identities in order to protect themselves, or who deflect critique by changing the markers of gender or racial identity, it can be difficult to establish positive sentiment that might spill over into employment opportunities.

The importance of maintaining "safe" online identities extends to occupations where surveillance of social media profiles by employers have an impact (see also chapter 5). In some areas of the growing platform economy, social media profiles feed directly into hiring and the potential to earn a sustainable wage. Peer or customer ratings of workers contracted by platforms like Uber, Upwork, and Mechanical Turk can determine whether that worker is allocated more work or can regulate the quality of the work he or she is allocated. Uber drivers, for instance, are policed by passengers' ratings, with drivers dipping below particular thresholds at risk of having their accounts deactivated, as well as a range of other invasive surveillance systems. Drivers can also have their fees for a particular journey cut if passengers provide negative feedback, such as claiming the driver took a longer route than necessary (Rosenblat and Stark 2016). The use of crowdsourced rankings and ratings such as these has helped solve the problems of trust in the emerging environments of online marketplaces, but it has also placed a premium on workers' digitally mediated reputations (Scholz 2016, 24). In the platform economy, you are only as employable as your online profile declares, and your income may rise and fall with that declaration.

Self-branding through social media is thus integral to the precarious, contract-based labor relations that are coming to dominate creative, knowledge, and service work, at least in the developed world; here, a worker's online identity is clearly an important asset. When these personal brands are damaged by harassment or false claims, or when a worker's online presence is diminished as a response to this harassment, his or her employability and financial security are also under threat. This is particularly onerous when harassment forces someone off-line completely, for the Internet "offers no viable alternatives to connect with others" (Citron 2009a, 68). If someone is precluded from building or sustaining an online identity, it can become difficult for that person to function effectively socially and (thus) to thrive financially. When it leads to the exclusion of its victims, online harassment constitutes a powerful economic weapon.

Yet suffering online harassment does not always have only negative economic effects. Part of what distinguishes the brand that is Clementine Ford is that she suffers from intense harassment and online threats and refuses to back away from the fight, taking her assailants on at their own game. This aspect of her brand has a positive economic impact, feeding the popularity of her 2016 book (which sold out in Australian presales) and her continued employment as a newspaper columnist. Rather than detracting from her employability, online harassment has, in fact, supported Ford's career. This is not to claim that Ford has cynically cultivated this hatred, exploited a victim status, or falsely leveraged the harassment for the purposes of economic gain. It is to suggest, though, that the fact of harassment is simply now bound into her online practices, her personal brand, and her career trajectory.

The case of Ford is very particular but also helpful in pointing to the spectrum of economic gains and losses for people experiencing online harassment. This clearly remains a continuum, though, where most of the activity is clustered in the end marked "loss." Given the high economic and social costs associated with online harassment, legal and policy contexts are important avenues for providing remedies or, importantly, protection for workers. However, the same global dynamics of precarity, self-management, and devolved risk that place a premium on strong online profiles also limit the protections available for workers.

(Un)Protected Settings

The nature of workplace antiharassment protections addressed in chapter 5 is much more complex when we more closely examine the types of labor that intersect with social media and that dominate in the contemporary economy. The legislation and/or policies associated with the workplace are limited in their effectiveness when dealing with social media, not only because anonymity renders policing difficult but also because of the labor context in which this harassment occurs. The conditions of contingent, freelance self-employment, short-term contract work, and "hope labor" have implications for how or whether a worker is protected from harassment and the legal remedies to which they have recourse. This complexity is particularly evident in the harassment case of Adria Richards, who in 2013 tweeted from the open-source conference PyCon a picture of two men she had overheard making jokes about "big dongles" and "forking someone's repo," protesting against the non-women-friendly conference environment, and blogged about the incident on *Hacker News*. One of the men was subsequently fired by his employer, PlayHaven, and a backlash began against Richards involving symbolic violence based on gender and race, as well as abuse taking the form of threats of sexual and physical violence. A DDoS attack was also launched upon her employer, SendGrid, which eventually fired Richards (Marwick 2013a; Zandt 2013).

There is a distinction to be made about the kinds of labor relations and protection environments at play in this story. In the first instance, we have Richards and the unknown PlayHaven developers as full-time employees of their respective technology companies. Here, state and institutional protections come into play to manage risks and police safety. For instance, Andy Yang, CEO of PlayHaven, explained his decision to fire one of the men criticized by Richards by referring to formal institutional policy. He says, "PlayHaven had an employee who was identified as making inappropriate comments at PyCon, and as a company that is dedicated to gender equality and values honorable behavior, we conducted a thorough investigation. The result of this investigation led to the unfortunate outcome of having to let this employee go" (in Milstein 2013).

Here we see legally enforceable regulations being invoked, but which only function to protect in the context of a formal employment contract. By virtue of the relevant state legislations, workplaces are protected settings where rules about harassment can be articulated, even if poorly executed, and clear lines of liability can be established (Franks 2012). Obviously, this did not assist Richards in managing the immediate matter of the conference sexism or the later online harassment, but it nevertheless demonstrates how formal contractual relations place risk management in the hands of corporations. Under U.S. law, liability for sexual harassment also lies with employers rather than the individuals undertaking the harassment (Franks 2012). To protect itself, PlayHaven was required to fire its employee for breaches of its stated policy (although the entire logic behind the dismissal remains unclear). At the same time, the tech sector, among many others, is increasingly casualized and propelled by gig, freelance, and outsourced labor in distributed workplaces. Here, the protections offered to paid workers become fewer and the lines of responsibility for managing workplace harassment become less clearly defined.

The second labor context—that of the conference—corresponds with the legal fuzziness associated with such contract work and other labor performed outside of physically defined workplaces. PyCon organizers had in place a code of conduct which was used to good effect in initially addressing Richards's concerns (Milstein 2013), but it was not legally enforceable nor actionable in the manner of state-mandated equal opportunity legislation, for instance. Here, community norms rather than legal obligations were the organizing principle. The insistence in the community that Richards should have dealt with the sexist speech on an interpersonal level rather than making the matter public also results from this logic (Blum 2013; Zandt 2013). The assumption is that she should have protected herself and personally absorbed the risks of managing the problem. Like the flagging of inappropriate content in social media platforms (Crawford and Gillespie 2016), dealing with sexual harassment in this labor context becomes a matter, firstly, of preemptively regulating the self in relation to community norms and, secondly, of taking on personal responsibility for policing those norms in others. Individualizing the management of risk and safety in this way immunizes the platform, or in this case the tech community, against responsibility or external regulatory oversight.

Finally, we reach the labor context where limited or no protections are available: Richards's unregulated, uncontracted, arguably voluntary labor on social media platforms and the similarly unregulated labor of her abusers. This is the context of the "hope labor" of building personal social media profiles. It is in this setting and in relation to a range of uncontracted work that much of the harassment documented in this chapter takes place. But it is also a space that remains unprotected in most legal contexts (Franks 2012). A key issue in implementing sexual harassment legislation in these instances is that it and its effects occur across multiple settings (in Richards's case, the abuse took place on various online platforms not formally linked to her workplace) and/or produces harm in a setting to which the harasser is unconnected (the abuse that cost Richards her job at SendGrid was conducted by people not connected to that workplace and thus not under control of her employer). As people increasingly become self-employed freelancers and gig workers in the online content production sector and elsewhere, there is ultimately no employer other than the abuse victim to be held responsible for ensuring a safe, nonhostile workplace environment.

In most jurisdictions, criminal or tort laws are the primary legal avenues for people suffering online harassment in or outside of their paid work context. Rather than equal opportunity or workplace harassment legislation, laws relating to defamation, libel, copyright (particularly useful in revenge porn cases), stalking, privacy, computer crime, or harassment must be invoked. Such legal remedies that focus on reputation may, however, do more damage than good: "If one of the significant harms of harassment is unwanted subjection to public scrutiny, litigation over defamation and invasions of privacy are almost certain to exacerbate this harm" (Franks 2011, 259). Harm can also be exacerbated by the act of litigation itself: seeking redress may, for example, offer more evidence that women are outsiders who simply cannot understand the humor and social norms of geeky cultures. A woman who fights back using formal mechanisms may reestablish herself as a threat, further perpetuating the cycles of hostility.

What is most troublesome, though, is that resorting to criminal or tort law individualizes the response and management of online harassment. Not only does this place the onus on individual victims to initiate legal remedies but it denies the systemic and structural role of harassment. As Franks (2011, 259–260) points out, "tort and criminal approaches treat cyber harassment principally as harm done to individuals, not groups." The same applies to all online harassment targeting minority individuals by virtue of their status. The necessity to resort to criminal or tort law indicates the devolution of responsibility to ensure a safe workplace from the employer to the individual worker. The onus to initiate proceedings and to manage the risks of litigation, including potentially significant financial costs, lies with the person experiencing harassment. In the event of a successful suit, liability is similarly devolved from the employer but this time to the individual harasser.

This is the context for the Data & Society best practices document for managing online harassment in academic research, discussed earlier in this chapter. It is focused on paid researchers or graduate students whose employment status is always unclear but who are typically covered by universities' policies relating to workplace safety, equal opportunity, and/or harassment (Marwick et al. 2016). The document outlines practical steps these institutions, senior faculty, and research supervisors can take to provide a safer workplace for researchers vulnerable to online harassment. The bulk of the document is nevertheless given over to describing what a researcher can do to protect himself or herself when undertaking the type of studies that engender harassment and noting useful resources to achieve that goal. Only a page and a half speak to institutions about their responsibilities and duty of care in relation to this unsafe work. Most of this information is repeated in a subsidiary two-page document that researchers are encouraged to give to university personnel to "educate them about the realities of online harassment and what administrators can do about it" (Marwick et al. 2016).

This protocol is particularly valuable, not least because its directions for institutions seek not only to create the kinds of protections that may prevent a hostile workplace for researchers but also to protect those researchers from incurring the reputational and economic costs that might otherwise be associated with online harassment. However, its framing as a document that the individual researcher must bring to the attention of managers, along with the extended focus on researchers' personal strategies for harm minimization, reiterates that this protection is not a right of the kind that may be expected in other workplaces. This critique is not to undermine or dismiss the importance of this resource and its practical value; rather, the protocol is to be commended as a good example of research-led activism and policy contribution. It is, though, to highlight the individualization of responsibility for safe work practices, with its echoes of victim blaming, that dominates contemporary precarious workplaces and, unfortunately, to which this protocol must speak.

We can also place here Ford's counterspeech against her harassers by retweeting or otherwise redistributing their messages and the often absurd outcomes of these actions. Ford has repeatedly been warned and banned from Facebook for "violating community standards" after republishing offensive messages she had received on the site. In one ironic instance, she was banned for reposting abuse received in response to a nude selfie that was itself a political critique. In an interview with BuzzFeed, Ford said the following about her banning: "It's not just inconvenient to me personally, it demonstrates exactly how backwards FB and its investigation processes are . . . I have reported numerous misogynistic posts in the past only to be told they were acceptable under FB's guidelines" (Sainty 2015). This example, which is one of many, involves the work of commercial content moderators addressed in the previous chapter, but also various kinds of devolution of responsibility that calls upon users to self-report abuse and offensive content (Gillespie 2010; Jarrett 2006; Light and McGrath 2010).

Capitalism as Geek Space

The individualization of risk management associated with online harassment at work is logical and perhaps even inevitable within the libertarianism that pervades the sites of geek masculinity that foster this kind of invective. When systemic privilege is unacknowledged and replaced by a firm belief that the cultural context is a meritocracy, individuals become responsible for their own status, standing, actions, and safety. Liberalism as a political philosophy and as a governance system problematizes external governance and privileges individual sovereignty. When this philosophy is further articulated as libertarianism, as it is in the dominant ideological frames of toxic geek spaces, there are only individuals left to take personal responsibility for what happens to them online or as consequence of their online activity. This responsibilization of the individual maintains the distribution of power and protects the privileged. There is also an economic dimension to these politics. While they are not the only governance systems that can sustain capitalism, liberal and libertarian principles enable the kinds of free market activities that both demand and exploit networked information systems, particularly for industries that move offshore. Victim blaming and free markets are not uncommonly colocated.

Individualizing responsibility through victim blaming also chimes with the logic of fragmented and precarious contemporary labor markets where individuals are increasingly burdened with managing economic risks (see Neff 2012). This context demands self-branding that exposes people to risks of reputational damage by online mobs and removes the protections provided by stable workplaces. It is also a context in which occupational and social privilege reside less in physical strength and more in cognition, communication, and the managing of affect. As the service sector has come to dominate economies in the global North, not least because physically demanding extractive and manufacturing work has been exported to cheaper labor markets in the developing world, labor practices have become associated with flexibility, mobility, and adaptability, rather than the rigidity and fixity of hegemonic masculinity and industrialized labor. This is part of the "feminization" of economic life as women's participation in the labor force has increased, but more importantly, as performances of normatively defined femininity—by people of all genders—have become important workplace resources (Adkins 2001, 2002; Gregg 2008; Morini 2007). Not only are the feminized attributes of caring, sociability, and communication valuable in corporate settings but so increasingly are "stylized presentations of self" (Adkins 2001, 674), such as those achieved in online self-branding. Such self-regulation, self-monitoring, and reflexivity, bolstered by constant employer feedback, feature widely in today's workplaces.

The term "feminization," and its affiliate "housewifisation" (Mies et al. 1988), is also used to describe how part-time, unstable, and precarious conditions mimicking the dominant modes of women's employment have come to dominate capitalism. It is equally used to capture the increasing incorporation of unpaid or undercompensated work into corporate life in ways that resemble the exploitation of domestic work in the capitalist mode of accumulation (Jarrett 2016). This is particularly true in white-collar and/ or creative work but also features in blue-collar industries such as manufacturing where computerization privileges particular immaterial labor activities, especially communication and cognition, and where instability of employment is rife through the twin dynamics of mechanization and utilization of offshore production. As we have already noted, geek masculinity excels in the kinds of communicative competences valorized in this feminized system, and it is its defense of that privilege that underscores a good deal of online harassment.

But geek masculinity is also under threat from the same capitalist system that grants it that privilege. The economic forces that generate precarity and insecurity impact white men in particular ways. While they are damaging for all, they entail a profound sense of loss for those who have historically occupied secure positions of superiority in the economy. For white men in the global North, for instance, the increasing impoverishment caused by downsizing, outsourcing, and labor market diversification has been experienced as a betrayal of the social and economic standing promised by capitalism; because white men assume entitlement to the agency that comes from economic power, its absence is infuriating (Faludi 1999). This has engendered angry laments for the loss of economic stability and status that is perceived to be the natural right of white men, manifesting in the kinds of angry invective, physical violence, and often contradictory resentments that typify online misogyny. Political movements like the Republican Tea Party, men's rights movements, and the alt-right emerge and flourish (Koulouris 2018; Lees 2016; Nagle 2015) in this context. But economic insecurity manifesting in symbolic violence is a widespread phenomenon. Emerging ethnonationalisms can be traced to similar changing socioeconomic dynamics across the globe, but particularly in (post)colonial settings, that have forced long-standing anger, anxieties, and forms of resistance to the surface (Mishra 2017). While we have been predominantly discussing here the aggrievement of white men in the geek spaces of the Anglophone Internet, the dynamics of online hate and harassment that make online work unsafe manifest in a variety of national, linguistic, and cultural contexts, traceable to similar, albeit particularly articulated, socioeconomic and cultural dispossessions (Han 2018; Jeong and Lee 2018; Philip 2018).

This sense of loss associated with these economic forces, no matter how illegitimate it may be, is the seat of the resentment and ressentiment from which online harassment stems. Drawing on Nietzsche's *Genealogy of Morals*, Martha C. Nussbaum (2010) describes the reactive emotion that is ressentiment. The goal is to gain power over people who have attributes valued by society. This involves creating a context in which the qualities of the weak are those that have value: "The weak need to affirm themselves, relieving the psychic distress that comes with subordination, by creating a virtual world, an expressive world, in which they hold sway" (Nussbaum 2010, 77). For geeks who both are dominated by hegemonic males and have their elevated status threatened by subaltern groups, this involves resentful punching up by asserting their superiority to "normies" but predominantly punching down to those most likely to articulate the skills, capabilities, and qualities from which they draw their status and who are thus the greatest threat to their economic and social standing.

To return to Skeggs's (2004, 182) distinction between ressentiment as an expression of powerlessness and resentment as an expression of the powerful, as discussed in chapter 4, geek masculinity can be seen as performing both simultaneously. The disparaging of women's capabilities by reducing them to merely bodies or shrill harpies, and the attempts to force them from online spaces and away from the economic and social privileges that accrue there, are articulations of such resentment but are often coded as ressentiment through (false) claims about the privileged status of minority groups. Viewed through this lens, online harassment is an attempt to shore up a masculinity made fragile through economic and (related) social change by forcefully retaining the privileges associated with both masculine and feminine workplace performances.

The Wrong Tag

Online harassment of the kind experienced by Clementine Ford and so many others has a disturbingly comfortable home within contemporary capitalism. It can be read as an effect of the privileging of digital, networked communications in labor relations; as a feature, rather than a bug, of capitalism's preferred governance systems; as a response to the anxieties capitalism produces; and as a means of reproducing the inequalities that ensure the stratified labor markets capitalism exploits. Considering work being made unsafe by online harassment as systemic to capitalism is not to dismiss the significant individual economic costs with which it is associated, nor to disregard the chilling effect it has on people's capacity for self-expression, autonomy, and agency. It is, however, to look for different avenues for redressing its inequities. This is both a civil rights issue (Citron 2009b, 2014; Franks 2012) and a matter of political economy. If we want to properly understand it, but also to propose remedies, we need to challenge or at the very least address how capitalist dynamics manifest. As demonstrated by the emergence of the alt-right in U.S. politics, further examining how the politics of white, male ressentiment/resentment articulated in geek cultures intersect with capitalist socioeconomics seems a matter of urgency. It certainly seems vital if we are to make online work safer.

We seem some way here from our initial discussion of how NSFW is mobilized as a hashtag on Twitter. However, our goal in this book was to consider not only what is included in its broad remit but what is excluded, as well as what might be gained by taking the notion literally as a framing device for addressing the risks involved in work as it intersects with, or is performed on, online platforms. Violence and hate speech are certainly elements of communication to be considered not safe for work, even as they consistently fall out of the general frame of what is understood as NSFW. The socioeconomics of such communication—the politics that also give rise to the encoding of certain bodies with risk and disgust and the normalization of others—equally drift out of such considerations. As this chapter documents, though, these conditions are what give shape to our intermeshing workplace and leisure communications and are hence integral to our understanding of what is not safe for work about social media.

Broadening the label NSFW to such a broad range of images, texts, and sentiments makes it evident that porn, dick pics, or the other sexualized media content associated with the tag are not among the primary factors rendering work unsafe. Rather, we need to address forms of hate, frustration, and misdirected anger. When these affects emerge on, and become amplified by, social media, the potential for harm and violence increases, especially given the ubiquity and necessity of such platforms in people's social and professional activities. To the degree that NSFW classification activities focus primarily on images of naked body parts deemed offensive by corporate community standards, the tag definitely falls short of indicating the urgent risks and harms posed to the safety of working lives online.

7 Conclusion: The Work of #NSFW

As a content classifier, the marker NSFW—together with its opposite, SFW—operates with a binary logic by more or less playfully drawing the boundaries of safe media consumption in spaces of work. As we have shown above, NSFW is far from being a singular, coherent practice or signifier. Its applications as a content category and a social media tag/hashtag involve convoluted negotiations concerning the definitions of humor, the politics of harassment, varying labor conditions and practices, and routines of platform governance, as well as the visibilities of different sexual imageries, attachments, and cultures. The work that NSFW performs as advertisement, warning, and filtering category is simultaneously straightforward and convoluted, and it is performed among and with human and nonhuman actors. Focusing on this singular tag, as has been the rationale of this book, makes it possible to unravel a variety of governance logics connected to sexuality in social media, as well as the various ways in which individual users, groups, and corporations apply, appropriate, play with, and resist them and, in doing so, each other.

Contra the notion of hashtag folksonomies emerging from the interactions between users in diverse group and communities, NSFW involves a firmly normative, taxonomical aspect similar to other media content classification mechanisms used for regulatory purposes. Its broad uses by bots promoting pay porn sites on Twitter further illustrate the ways in which folksonomies and taxonomies intermesh in tagging practices that are both automated and achieved with the human hand, and which circulate via engagement with a variety of economies. On Twitter, a key terrain of NSFW is comprised of images of naked female bodies linking to pay camera services and video tube sites which are broadly trafficked by bots. While sexual cultures of different shapes and sizes, bents, and palates thrive on Twitter because of its permissive content policies, they often do so without resorting to the general marker of NSFW.

While Twitter makes use of the somewhat euphemistic category of "sensitive" content as that which users may opt for either seeing or not, before banning adult content altogether, Tumblr deployed NSFW as a default category for marking out the genre of sexually explicit blogs, hence effecting their general searchability and accessibility. On Instagram and Pinterest, NSFW is connected to sexually suggestive, nonexplicit images and, on Facebook and current Tumblr, to virtually any posts dealing with sexuality, nudity, or embodiment, from photographs documenting childbirth to art projects and sex education resources. For their part, porn sites, which proudly advertise the unequivocally NSFW and XXX nature of their services, play with the boundaries of acceptability in their publicity stunts optimized for attention capture across mainstream social media outlets. As we have discussed throughout the book, NSFW content involves both potential risk of disapproval and considerable attraction in inviting curiosity, titillation, and shivers of excitement. Both of these affective dynamics work as attractors in the attention and sharing economy of social media.

Globally leading social media services originating from, and based in, the United States come ingrained with culturally specific sets of values that reverberate in, and are articulated as, community values regulating the visibility of sexual content in services, sites, and apps used daily by billions of people around the world. This is not to say that moral conservatism of the kind that we have identified in the applications of the content marker NSFW would be a property unique to U.S. culture. Chinese social media services are certainly strict in their censure of sexuality and nudity in accordance with national Internet content policies. For instance, in April 2018, the microblogging platform Sina Weibo jointly categorized pornography, bloody violence, and homosexuality and attempted to censor them within the service. It decoupled, and reinstated, content related to homosexuality after a public outcry days later (Kuo 2018). At the same time, the recent "gay propaganda laws" severely limit the sexual expression of Russian LGBTQI+ communities, both online and off, and VKontakte (a.k.a. "the Russian Facebook") has been broadly used to circulate homophobic, occasionally violent content. Although restrictions on sexual content are a regular feature of social media, these policies come from different cultural and political contexts and are built on distinct, albeit effectually similar, morally conservative rationales. Our decision to focus on U.S.-based services has centrally to do with these specificities and the importance of remaining sensitive toward them.

Following this line of thought, we suggest that the persistent associations of sex with the notions of risk and unsafety, as encapsulated in the community standards of a plethora of U.S.-based social media services—as well as those inherent in the very marker of NSFW—hark back not only to corporate conservatism but to a Puritan cultural legacy operating as a residual structure of feeling. Puritan conceptions of sexuality were marked by wariness, unease, and distaste toward sexual desires and acts deemed unclean and involving both the risk of punishment and the imperative for control (see Verduin 1983, 223–226). Sexuality was hence something to be feared, governed, and best avoided. Following Raymond Wiliams (1977), residual elements are on the one hand detached from dominant culture—as Puritanism, as a historical reformist ideology and practice, is from contemporary neoliberalism and entrepreneurial capitalism—yet ingrained in it as associations and norms. Conceptualized in this vein, Puritanism lingers on, tuning the affective dynamics of contemporary culture and becoming perceivable in social media platform governance.

The persistent, seemingly automatic association of unsafety with sex, and CCM with images of nudity rather than those of violence, that has concerned and perplexed us throughout this volume becomes understandable through both corporate conservatism and the residual Puritan structures of feeling that it taps into. Conceptualizing NSFW and social media content policies in this framework makes it possible to explain some of the logic encapsulated in the uses of the tag NSFW, where unsafety becomes an abstract, categorical, and inherent quality of media content, detached from the age of the people involved, their occupations, mutual relations, or the specific circumstances under, and the social spaces within which they encounter the said content.

The community standards and codes of conduct coined by social media services and tech companies articulate culturally specific attitudes toward sexuality and bodily display that become, because of their vast reach, opaque standards of communicative properness internationally. These norms are present in how Google fences off pornography from its advertisement policy while conditionally allowing promotional material for sex toys, affair and hookup apps, sex-related entertainment, and other content deemed "non–family safe." Google, similarly to Apple, excludes sexual explicitness from its app store, while Facebook engages in heavy content filtering of sexual content. In the course of writing this book, the tendency to fence off sexual content from social media has grown increasingly manifest, and aggressive, as witnessed in transformations in Tumblr and Facebook community standards banning adult content and sexual communication, respectively.

Dependent as they are on targeted advertising and optimized flow of data, social media services operate in an economy of peekaboo where sexual content is, on the one hand, accepted if moderately applied and followed by disclaimers about expected content. On the other hand, sexual content is weeded out from public view in its more explicit and straightforward manifestations in the name of unspecified, obscure safety. Given that the meanings attached to sexual media content are seldom straightforward, we argue for highlighting questions of consent involved in the production, use, and circulation of sexually explicit content, and for foregrounding the centrality of context over abstract classifications, if we are to understand something of the complexity involved.

To be clear, the argument of this book is not for doing away with content classifiers or contextual metadata as normative constructs, already given that this would render social media impossible to manage or operate. Nor is our argument one for lifting restrictions on the circulation of sexually explicit content within these platforms in the spirit of laissez-faire. Our point, and one developed throughout this volume, is simply that the subtle, yet tenacious, abstract conflation of sex with risk and harm is culturally specific as well as counterproductive in both limiting the exchanges that users may engage in and in effacing qualitative distinctions between them—such as those between a flirtatious exchange via naked selfies and a violent harassment campaign—while regulating the former rather than the latter.

Workplace social media, equal opportunity, and harassment policies, along with automated filtering and blocking practices, seek to govern that which may or may not circulate in occupational settings. Yet the ubiquitous presence of personal smart devices means that the spheres and spaces of work cannot be neatly pried apart from personal interests, dirty jokes, horseplay, hobbyist concerns, or sexual attachments. Meanwhile, workplace relations do not in all cases remain only such as they intermesh with wide-ranging dynamics of bullying, harassment, friendship, collective action, and sexual intimacy. These relations bleed into social media interactions, practical jokes, and coffee break discussion topics at the workplace. Since sex and sexuality are central features of individual and collective lives, in many instances the very forces propelling people toward various exchanges and encounters, they do not simply disappear during the hours of work. As constitutive elements of ways of being in the world, sex and sexuality are not inherently either safe or unsafe. They are, however, important, a fact efficiently downplayed in most social media community standards labeling them as both irrelevant and offensive.

In a context where work and other areas of life are not just blurred but quite explicitly part of one another, managing the risks of social media is typically individualized. It demands personal responses such as legal remedies, flagging of content, and self-policing, as much as it connects with institutional responses such as norms set by workplace policies, platform guidelines, and automated censoring systems. In this context, NSFW becomes an apparatus through which neoliberal ideals of self-sufficiency and personal autonomy may be perpetuated. These ideals equally feed the toxic technocultures associated with online hate, which underpin the neoliberal economic logic driving the same communicative excess that the marker NSFW seeks to manage. In effect, the marker fosters the increased absorption of risks from which it is ostensibly protecting us. The conservative qualities that we have ascribed to the notion of NSFW do not therefore concern only the nature of content but also the processes of sociality, economics, and socialization that the tag circulates within, from which it draws its meaning, and which it supports.

Working with NSFW

Framing the topic of NSFW in yet another way, and in a reflection of the process resulting in this book, scholarly work on a tag such as NSFW involves a different kind of blurring of professional boundaries of acceptability and individual responsibilization. In some university settings, access to materials tagged and flagged as unsafe, sensitive, and problematic is rendered impossible because of policies and technologies barring all adult content. Consequently, scholars need to conduct their research with their own personal devices and, possibly, in spaces beyond the office. In other academic contexts, access to such content requires specific permissions from and notifications for the IT departments purportedly efficiently and effectively screening the flows of traffic within the institution 24-7. In yet other sites of higher education, similar regulations simply do not exist.

This range of default positioning of scholars vis-à-vis NSFW social media content is tied in with the broader politics of doing research on sexually explicit materials, including in areas such as pornography, sexual harassment, and hooking up, as well as subject matter deemed risky and/or offensive more generally. Such work easily comes across as ethically and legally risky—if not necessarily directly NSFW—for institutions concerned with their public image or donation, sponsorship, and tuition fee revenues in cultural and national contexts where studies of sexuality and pornography, or even feminist and queer scholarship, are articulated in the public eye as trivial, politically fraught, or morally objectionable.

On an individual level, NSFW labels such as porn, hookup app, or meme researcher involve specific stickiness both in terms of temporality—for they do catch on and linger—and in terms of the professional encounters that they frame and facilitate. Depending on his or her age, gender, and sexual orientation, the scholar in question may come across as lacking in intellectual substance, as salaciously titillating, and/or as dubiously sleazy. The stakes involved in becoming thus labeled vary according to one's career stage, the institutional culture of one's place of employment, the views of colleagues at other higher education institutions, and even national sentiment given the increasing pressures on researchers to generate funding, public engagement, and impact. Entailing its own potential degree of riskiness, the sticky label of NSFW may, in some instances, render one less desirable a colleague and, hence, contribute to precarity in career building.

That watching and recording risky comedic, offensive, gross, and sexually explicit media content during office hours may qualify as scholarly work remains difficult for many to fathom. The dynamics involved are not altogether different from scholarship addressing other popular media genres such as romance or horror, yet NSFW content comes with a particular affective charge independent of the ways in which, or the purposes for which, it is being consumed: shivers of horror or ripples of amusement, while pleasurable as such, remain more in place in professional settings than the intensities connected to sexual arousal or the dynamics of a dirty joke. NSFW content remains, to use anthropologist Mary Douglas's (1991,

35) phrasing on dirt, "matter of out of place" in many spaces of work, academic offices included.

Scholarly work on NSFW content necessitates mundane vigilance in terms of what images or texts are visible on one's screen for others to see during transit or meetings with students and colleagues as the sight may cause offense or even be interpreted as a form of harassment. When presenting this research, it is often not possible to show the images or videos analyzed because of their explicit nature. Alternatively, if such content is presented, it may be necessary to frame it with content or trigger warnings that affectively attune and orient the audience to engage with the presentation in particular terms of potential risk, harm, and fascination: also here, NSFW functions as both warning and advertisement. Illustrating a book on the topic, such as this one, comes with its own balancing acts. Dick pics, for example, discussed above in terms of their ambiguity, sit uneasily within the genre of academic publishing as they have the power to transform the product in question into something NSFW in itself. Consequently, we have struggled to find appropriate solutions for illustrating the ubiquity and form of such content.

This difficulty was exacerbated by the importance of context to the understandings of the tag/hashtag NSFW and the broader question of how online communication becomes unsafe. It was challenging to find adequate illustrative examples that capture the contextual nuance associated with each articulation, not least since potential individual examples remained plentiful. Yet, as this study developed, the diverse ways in which the tag was applied and the concept mobilized across platforms, user groups, and legal and political geographies became not only an interesting point of data but an important methodological and analytical framework. In this sense, our study adds to an increasing body of work that offers multisited analysis—almost unavoidable with converged media—but that is attentive to specificity and difference that manifest across sites.

The stickiness that pertains to materials deemed NSFW, and that pursues scholars who research it, suggests that the notion retains some transcendent quality, particularly when the specific nature of that to which it refers becomes hollowed out. Returning to the semiotic terminology introduced at the end of chapter 4 in a discussion of dick pics, NSFW is not quite an empty signifier, for it always carries its connotations of risk, titillation, and impropriety, yet remains malleable in its denotations. Managing this plasticity in turn becomes part of the struggle for researchers of content labeled in this way. Writing this book has not been exempt from such ripples. In using multiple assemblages of social media, personal devices, and workplace technologies to share resources, information, and examples with each other, we have remained mindful of the public nature of these exchanges.

Indeed, it is not only the case that we have been mindful ourselves, as human and nonhuman actors alike have often reminded us of the NSFW quality of our investigation. In the course of working on this book we have, for example, received e-mails from colleagues asking us to give a warning when showing NSFW content in the future—even when the previous display had occurred in a seminar specifically focusing on the topic, and with a content disclaimer attached. Our e-mails to one another have been filtered off as spam and left undelivered by e-mail systems that have flagged the subject line, "dick pic chapter," as unsuitable. In more than one instance, links posted through private messaging were refused because of their unsafe qualities, and, in some instances, we were temporally banned from interacting on Facebook for violating their community standards. In other words, our communication practices in writing this book remained in constant, and highly concrete, interaction with NSFW content flagging, filtering, and blocking routines, making the endeavor meta at times.

Like the notion of work, that of safety underpinning all of these contortions remains elusive: it is connected to bodily integrity and violations thereof; to moral and symbolic breaches of proper demeanor; to the circulation and stickiness of online hate; and to risks and precarities connected to income, careers, and reputation. Meanwhile, the diverse applications and resonances of NSFW revolve around displays of sexuality and nudity, both within and outside the framing of humor. Sex ultimately remains the affective hub of NSFW because of the intensities, dangers, identifications, distinctions, and transgressions it offers. In order to sum this all up, we conclude with one final example to illustrate some of the multifaceted roles that the marker NSFW plays on current social media platforms.

The Attention Value of NSFW

In January 2017, Australian actor and musician Brendan Maclean released a music video to his electro-pop song "House of Air," only to have it soon banned from YouTube for violating their community guidelines forbidding sexually explicit content. This ban hardly came as a shock since the video involves a graphic visualization of Hal Fischer's 1977 *Gay Semiotics*, unpacking the semiotic codes of gay male fashion and accessories connected to sexual preferences in acts, positions, and roles. Directed by Brian Fairbairn and Karl Eccleston, the video dwells on 1970s retro aesthetics and specifies the individual characteristics of both the accessories used and the sexual acts they connect to within "gay semiotics." The video follows Fischer's visual style in which textual, laconic explainers came attached with still photographs. While Fischer's study was titled "A Photographic Study of Visual Coding among Homosexual Men," Maclean's video comes with the even more convoluted title "An Anthropological Study of Gay Semiotics, Taxonomies, and Sexual Behaviours." Beginning with a "casual homosexual encounter" between men coded as "street fashion leather" and "street fashion jock," the video continues to illustrate the hanky codes for fellatio, urophilia, anal sex, and fisting, as well as the acts themselves. Posing against a pale blue background, the performers equally engage in analingus and coprophilia: in the final shot, a piece of scat, followed by a stream of semen, hit Maclean on a cheek.

The video's NSFW markers seem warranted, to say the least. In his account of the YouTube controversy, journalist Ryan Kristobak (2017) defines "House of Air" as exceeding the generic attraction of the NSFW tag: "There are few greater tests of self-control than coming across something labeled NSFW during the work day. It's always a gamble what you will find on the other side of the jump, and while the rewards sometimes pose little risk to your state of occupation, Brendan Maclean's new music video for his song 'House of Air' is far from office-appropriate content—unless you work somewhere like an adult toy store." Unlike some content categorized as NSFW, this video is likely to be literally inappropriate for consumption in most spaces of work and, consequently, has a specific affective appeal. "House of Air" gained virality early with the help of YouTube star blogger and social media influencer PewDiePie's reaction video, and news of banning helped to further fuel interest in it (in much the same way as the 30-year-old, pre–social media video for Frankie Goes to Hollywood's debut single, "Relax," was promoted by its banning in 1984). By the time "House of Air" was awarded Most Trashy at the Berlin Music Video Festival in late May of the same year, it had some 1.4 million views on Vimeo, which has hosted the video since its banning from YouTube.

Many things central in terms of this book emerge from all this. *First*, and obviously, "House of Air" set out to knowingly test the boundaries of what constitutes acceptable social media content, even in combination with markers such as "NSFW," "explicit," "mature," and "adults only." Deemed inappropriate for one platform, it failed to be flagged on another, and links to the video continue to be shared across social media sites such as Facebook known for their strict content policies. *Second*, the video then exemplifies the affective stickiness of NSFW content as that which feeds social media's attention economy. While Maclean has defended his video as art, many others have defined it as pornography. Journalists have covered the incident in numerous click-worthy pieces, while user comments on Reddit and Vimeo remain divisive in their reactions of outrage, disgust, amusement, appreciation, and homophobic outpour. Such reactions feed the video's further circulation, continue to broaden its audience and reach, and generate value for the platforms in question.

Third, the work of the video itself illustrates not only the perpetually shifting boundaries of visibility involved in sexually graphic representation but those involved in the production of social media content. Analingus or urophilia practiced on camera may traditionally be considered the labor of porn—and, in fact, porn of the hardcore, extreme, kink, or even taboo kind. Here, they are integrated in a pop video designed for social media distribution and performed with a stylized detachment complete with textual markers such as "pleasure (homosexual)" in ways that disturb any preset categorizations of what may or may not be porn and, ultimately, render the whole question somewhat inconsequential.

Fourth, and finally, "House of Air" encapsulates the dynamic complexity involved in a marker as seemingly straightforward as NSFW in its combination of sexual explicitness, humor, visual experimentation, artistic expression, and promotional purpose. Both central in terms of the traffic flows of social media and partly grinding against their content policies, NSFW adds affective stickiness and aesthetic ambiguity to both. By doing so, NSFW continues to be used in mapping, tagging, hashtagging, and flagging out the leaky zones where sexually explicit, possibly offensive, disturbing, or arousing content threatens—and simultaneously promises—to ooze into the data streams of social media and to infect them with hues and flavors of their own.

References

Abidin, Crystal. 2015. "Communicative Intimacies: Influencers and Perceived Inter-connectedness." *Ada: A Journal of Gender, New Media, and Technology* 8. Accessed August 31, 2018. https://adanewmedia.org/2015/11/issue8-abidin.

Abidin, Crystal. 2016a. "'Aren't These Just Young, Rich Women Doing Vain Things Online?': Influencer Selfies as Subversive Frivolity." *Social Media + Society* 2 (2): 1–17.

Abidin, Crystal. 2016b. "Visibility Labour: Engaging with Influencers' Fashion Brands and #OOTD Advertorial Campaigns on Instagram." *Media International Australia* 161 (1): 86–100.

Abidin, Crystal, and Mart Ots. 2016. "Influencers Tell All? Unravelling Authenticity and Credibility in a Brand Scandal." In *Blurring the Lines: Market-Driven and Democracy-Driven Freedom of Expression*, edited by Maria Edström, Andrew T. Kenyon, and Eva-Maria Svensson, 153–162. Gothenburg, Sweden: Nordicom.

Abidin, Crystal, and Eric C. Thompson. 2012. "Buymylife.com: Cyber-Femininities and Commercial Intimacy in Blogshops." *Women's Studies International Forum* 35 (6): 467–477.

Adam, Alison. 2005. *Gender, Ethics and Information Technology*. Basingstoke, UK: Palgrave Macmillan.

Adam, Alison, and Eileen Green. 2005. *Virtual Gender: Technology, Consumption and Identity Matters*. London: Routledge.

Adkins, Lisa. 2001. "Cultural Feminization: 'Money, Sex and Power' for Women." *Signs: Journal of Women in Culture and Society* 26 (3): 669–695.

Adkins, Lisa. 2002. *Revisions: Gender and Sexuality in Late Modernity*. Buckingham, UK: Open University Press.

Ahmed, Sara. 2001. "The Organisation of Hate." *Law and Critique* 12 (3): 345–365.

Ahmed, Sara. 2004. *The Cultural Politics of Emotion*. New York: Routledge.

Albury, Kath. 2002. *Yes Means Yes: Getting Explicit about Heterosex*. Crows Nest, Australia: Allen & Unwin.

Albury, Kath. 2013. "Young People, Media and Sexual Learning: Rethinking Representation." *Sex Education* 13 (1): S32–S44.

Albury, Kath, and Kate Crawford. 2012. "Sexting, Consent and Young People's Ethics: Beyond Megan's Story." *Continuum* 26 (3): 463–473.

Alexander, Priscilla. 1998. "Sex Work and Health: A Question of Safety in the Workplace." *Journal of American Medical Women's Association* 53 (2): 77–82.

APAC (Adult Performer Advocacy Committee). 2017. "About." Accessed April 19, 2017. http://www.apac-usa.com/about.

Apple App Store. 2018. "App Store Review Guidelines: 1.1 Objectionable Content." Accessed September 1, 2018. https://developer.apple.com/app-store/review/guide lines/#objectionable-content.

Ashford, Chris. 2008. "Sex Work in Cyberspace: Who Pays the Price?" *Information & Communications Technology Law* 17 (1): 37–49.

Aswad, Evelyn. 2016. "The Role of US Technology Companies as Enforcers of Europe's New Internet Hate Speech Ban." *Columbian Human Rights Law Review* 1 (1): 2–14.

Attwood, Feona. 2009. "Introduction." In *Mainstreaming Sex: The Sexualization of Western Culture*, edited by Feona Attwood, xiii–xxiv. London: I.B. Tauris.

Auerbach, David. 2014. "Vampire Porn: MindGeek Is a Cautionary Tale of Consolidating Production and Distribution in a Single, Monopolistic Owner." *Slate*, October 23. Accessed May 21, 2017. http://www.slate.com/articles/technology/technology/ 2014/10/mindgeek_porn_monopoly_its_dominance_is_a_cautionary_tale_for_other _industries.html.

Barsoux, Jean-Louis. 1993. *Funny Business: Humour, Management and Business Culture*. London: Cassell.

Barzilai-Nahon, Karine. 2008. "Toward a Theory of Network Gatekeeping: A Framework for Exploring Information Control." *Journal of the American Society for Information Science and Technology* 59 (9): 1493–1512.

BBC. 2017. "Milo Yannipoulos: Who Is the Alt-Right Writer and Provocateur?" February 21. Accessed May 21, 2017. http://www.bbc.com/news/world-us-canada -39026870.

Bennett, David. 2001. "Pornography.Dot.Com: Eroticising Privacy on the Internet." *Review of Education, Pedagogy, and Cultural Studies* 23 (4): 381–391.

Berebitsky, Julie. 2012. *Sex and the Office: A History of Gender, Power, and Desire*. New Haven, CT: Yale University Press.

Berg, Heather. 2014. "Labouring Porn Studies." *Porn Studies* 1 (1–2): 75–79.

Berg, Heather. 2016. "'A Scene Is Just a Marketing Tool': Alternative Income Streams in Porn's Gig Economy." *Porn Studies* 3 (2): 160–174.

Bershidsky, Leonid. 2018. "Politicized Trolling is Worse Than Fake News." *Bloomberg*, July 24. Accessed February 3, 2019. https://www.bloomberg.com/opinion/articles/2018-07-24/politicized-trolling-on-line-is-more-destructive-than-fake-news.

Blackwell, Courtney, Jeremy Birnholtz, and Charles Abbott. 2015. "Seeing and Being Seen: Co-situation and Impression Formation Using Grindr, a Location-Aware Gay Dating App." *New Media & Society* 17 (7): 1117–1136.

Blum, Amanda. 2013. "Adria Richards, PyCon, and How We All Lost." *Amanda Blum* blog. March 21. Accessed May 21, 2017. https://amandablumwords.wordpress.com/2013/03/21/3.

Blunt, Carolyn, and Martin Hill-Wilson. 2013. *Delivering Effective Social Customer Service: How to Redefine the Way You Manage Customer Experience and Your Corporate Reputation*. Chichester, UK: John Wiley & Sons.

Bolding, G., M. Davis, L. Sherr, and G. Hart. 2004. "Use of Gay Internet Sites and Views about Online Health Promotion among Men Who Have Sex with Men." *AIDS Care* 16 (8): 993–1001.

Borra, Erik, and Bernhard Rieder. 2014. "Programmed Method: Developing a Toolset for Capturing and Analyzing Tweets." *Aslib Journal of Information Management* 66 (3): 262–278.

Bort, J. 2013. "I Spent a Month on Infidelity Dating Site Ashley Madison and Was Pleasantly Surprised by How Nice It Was." *Business Insider—Australia*. Accessed Jaunary 29, 2016. http://www.businessinsider.com.au/how-to-use-cheating-site-ashley-madison-2013-12.

Boyd, Colin. 2010. "The Debate over the Prohibition of Romance in the Workplace." *Journal of Business Ethics* 97 (2): 325–338.

Braithwaite, Andrea. 2016. "It's about Ethics in Games Journalism? Gamergaters and Geek Masculinity." *Social Media + Society* 2 (4): 1–10.

Bray, Abigail. 2011. "Capitalism and Pornography: The Internet as Global Prostitution Industry." In *Big Porn, Inc.: Exposing the Harms of the Global Porn Industry*, edited by Melinda Tankard Reist and Abigail Bray, 160–166. Melbourne: Spinifex.

Brazzers. 2016. "UPDATED: Brazzers Supports Nikki Benz." *Trendz*, December 21. Accessed May 21, 2017. http://www.trendzz.com/uncategorized/brazzers-supports -nikki.

Breslow, Jacob. 2018. "Moderating the 'Worst of Humanity': Sexuality, Witnessing, and the Digital Life of Coloniality." *Porn Studies*: Online First.

Bridges, Tristan, and Cheri J. Pascoe. 2014. "Hybrid Masculinities: New Directions in the Sociology of Men and Masculinities." *Sociology Compass* 8 (3): 246–258.

Browne, Jennifer. 2016. "This Woman's Response to Unwanted Dick Pic Has Won the Internet." *Unilad*. Accessed May 21, 2017. http://www.unilad.co.uk/viral/this -womans-response-to-unwanted-dick-pic-has-won-the-internet.

Bruns, Axel, and Jean Burgess. 2012. "Researching News Discussion on Twitter: New Methodologies." *Journalism Studies* 13 (5–6): 801–814.

Bruns, Axel, and Jean Burgess. 2015. "Twitter Hashtags from Ad Hoc to Calculated Publics." In *Hashtag Publics: The Power and Politics of Discursive Networks*, edited by Nathan Rambukkana, 13–28. New York: Peter Lang.

Bucher, Taina. 2014. "About a Bot: Hoax, Fake, Performance Art." *M/C Journal* 17 (3). http://journal.media-culture.org.au/index.php/mcjournal/article/view/814.

Buni, Catherine and Soraya Chemaly. 2016. "The Secret Rules of the Internet." *The Verge*, April 13. Accessed May 21, 2017. https://www.theverge.com/2016/4/13/ 11387934/internet-moderator-history-youtube-facebook-reddit-censorship-free -speech.

Burgess, Melinda C. R., Steven Paul Stermer, and Stephen R. Burgess. 2007. "Sex, Lies, and Video Games: The Portrayal of Male and Female Characters on Video Game Covers." *Sex Roles* 57 (5–6): 419–433.

Camp, L. Jean. 1996. "We Are Geeks, and We Are Not Guys: The Systers Mailing List." In *Wired_Women: Gender and New Realities in Cyberspace*, edited by Lynn Cherny and Reba Elizabeth Weise, 114–125. Seattle: Seal Press.

Campbell, John Edward. 2004. *Getting It On Online: Cyberspace, Gay Male Sexuality and Embodied Identity*. New York: Harrington Parker Press.

CareerBuilder. 2016. "Number of Employers Using Social Media to Screen Candidates Has Increased 500 Percent over the Last Decade." April 28. Accessed May 21, 2017. http://www.careerbuilder.co.uk/share/aboutus/pressreleasesdetail.aspx?sd=4% 2F28%2F2016&id=pr945&ed=12%2F31%2F2016.

Carroll, Rory. 2015. "Porn Industry Groups Cut Ties to Star James Deen amid Sexual Assault Claims." *Guardian*, November 3. Accessed May 21, 2017. https://www.the guardian.com/us-news/2015/nov/30/james-deen-sexual-assault-accusations-stoya -porn-industry.

Cassidy, Elija. 2013. "Gay Men, Social Media and Self-Presentation: Managing Identities in Gaydar, Facebook and Beyond." PhD diss., Queensland University of Technology, Brisbane, Australia.

Cassidy, Elija. 2016. "Social Networking Sites and Participatory Reluctance: A Case Study of Gaydar, User Resistance and Interface Rejection." *New Media & Society* 18 (11): 2613–2628.

Chaiyajit, Nada, and Christopher S. Walsh. 2012. "Sexperts! Disrupting Injustice with Digital Community-Led HIV Prevention and Legal Rights Education in Thailand." *Digital Culture & Education* 4 (1): 145–165.

Chandler, Adam. 2016. "Hotels: Pretty OK with Their Customers' Porn-Watching Habits." *The Atlantic*, July 21. Accessed May 21, 2017. https://www.theatlantic.com/business/archive/2016/07/hotel-wifi-porn/492290.

Chen, Adrian. 2012. "Inside Facebook's Outsourced Anti-Porn and Gore Brigade, Where 'Camel Toes' are More Offensive than 'Crushed Heads.'" *Gawker*, February 16. Accessed May 21, 2017. http://gawker.com/5885714/inside-facebooks-outsourced-anti-porn-and-gore-brigade-where-camel-toes-are-more-offensive-than-crushed-heads.

Chen, Adrian. 2014. "The Laborers Who Keep Dick Pics and Beheadings out of Your Facebook Feed." *Wired*, October 23. Accessed May 21, 2017. https://www.wired.com/2014/10/content-moderation.

Chen, Adrian. 2015. "When the Internet's Moderators Are Anything But." *New York Times*, July 21. Accessed May 21, 2017. https://www.nytimes.com/2015/07/26/magazine/when-the-internets-moderators-are-anything-but.html.

Chen, Adrian. 2017. "The Human Toll of Protecting the Internet from the Worst of Humanity." *The New Yorker*, January 28. Accessed May 21, 2017. http://www.newyorker.com/tech/elements/the-human-toll-of-protecting-the-internet-from-the-worst-of-humanity.

Chess, Shira, and Adrienne Shaw. 2015. "A Conspiracy of Fishes, or, How We Learned to Stop Worrying about #GamerGate and Embrace Hegemonic Masculinity." *Journal of Broadcasting & Electronic Media* 59 (1): 208–220.

Cho, Alexander. 2015. "Queer Reverb: Tumblr, Affect, Time." In *Networked Affect*, edited by Ken Hillis, Susanna Paasonen, and Michael Petit, 43–58. Cambridge, MA: MIT Press.

Chu, Arthur. 2014. "Your Princess Is in Another Castle: Misogyny, Entitlement and Nerds." *The Daily Beast*, May 27. Accessed May 21, 2017. http://www.thedailybeast.com/articles/2014/05/27/your-princess-is-in-another-castle-misogyny-entitlement-and-nerds.html.

Chun, Wendy Hui Kyong. 2006. *Control and Freedom*. Cambridge, MA: MIT Press.

Citron, Danielle Keats. 2009a. "Cyber Civil Rights." *Boston University Law Review* 89 (1): 61–125.

Citron, Danielle Keats. 2009b. "Law's Expressive Value in Combating Cyber Gender Harassment." *Michigan Law Review* 108 (3): 373–415.

Citron, Danielle Keats. 2014. *Hate Crimes in Cyberspace*. Cambridge, MA: Harvard University Press.

Clausner, Christian. 2017. "A Java Script for Post-Processing of T-CAT Data." Salford, UK: University of Salford.

Clerc, Susan. 1996. "Estrogen Brigades and 'Big Tits' Threads: Media Fandom Online and Off." In *Wired_Women: Gender and New Realities in Cyberspace*, edited by Lynn Cherny and Reba Elizabeth Weise, 73–92. Seattle: Seal Press.

Cohen, James, and Thomas Kenny. 2015. *Producing New and Digital Media: Your Guide to Savvy Use of the Web*. Burlington, MA: Focal Press.

Collins, Joshua C. 2013. "Stress and Safety for Gay Men at Work within Masculinized Industries." *Journal of Gay & Lesbian Social Services* 25 (3): 245–268.

Comella, Lynn. 2008. "It's Sexy. It's Big Business. And It's Not Just for Men." *Contexts* 7 (3): 61–63.

Connell, Robert W., and James W. Messerschmidt. 2005. "Hegemonic Masculinity: Rethinking the Concept." *Gender & Society* 19 (6): 829–859.

Consalvo, Mia. 2012. "Confronting Toxic Gamer Culture: A Challenge for Feminist Game Studies Scholars." *Ada: A Journal of Gender, New Media, and Technology* (1). Accessed August 31, 2018. https://adanewmedia.org/2012/11/issue1-consalvo.

Coser, Rose Laub. 1959. "Some Social Functions of Laughter: A Study of Humor in a Hospital Setting." *Human Relations* 12 (2): 171–182.

Cox, J. 2015. "Ashley Madison Hackers Speak Out: 'Nobody Was Watching.'" *Motherboard*. Accessed January 21, 2016. http://motherboard.vice.com/read/ashley-madison-hackers-speak-out-nobody-was-watching.

Crawford, Garry, Victoria K. Gosling, and Ben Light. 2011. "It's Not Just a Game: Contemporary Challenges for Games Research and the Internet." In *Online Gaming in Context: The Social and Cultural Significance of Online Games*, edited by Garry Crawford, Victoria K. Gosling, and Ben Light, 281–294. New York: Routledge.

Crawford, Kate. 2009. "Following You: Disciplines of Listening in Social Media." *Continuum: Journal of Media & Cultural Studies* 23 (4): 525–535.

Crawford, Kate, and Tarleton Gillespie. 2016. "What Is a Flag For? Social Media Reporting Tools and the Vocabulary of Complaint." *New Media & Society* 18 (3): 410–428.

Daily Mail. 2011. "Teacher Sacked for Posting Picture of Herself Holding Glass of Wine and Mug of Beer on Facebook." February 7. Accessed May 21, 2017. http://www .dailymail.co.uk/news/article-1354515/Teacher-sacked-posting-picture-holding-glass -wine-mug-beer-Facebook.html.

Dalla Costa, Mariarosa, and Selma James. 1973. *The Power of Women and the Subversion of the Community.* 3rd ed. Bristol, UK: Falling Wall Press.

Daniel, Kelly. 2011. *Yuck! The Nature and Moral Significance of Disgust.* Cambridge, MA: MIT Press.

Deal, Terence. E., and Allan A. Kennedy. 1982. *Corporate Cultures: The Rites and Rituals of Corporate Life.* Harmondsworth, UK: Penguin Books.

Dean, Jodi. 2009. *Democracy and Other Neoliberal Fantasies: Communicative Capitalism and Left Politics.* Durham, NC: Duke University Press.

Dean, Jodi. 2010. *Blog Theory: Feedback and Capture in the Circuits of Drive.* Cambridge, UK: Polity.

Dery, Mark. 2007. "Naked Lunch: Talking Realcore with Sergio Messina." In *C'Lick Me: A Netporn Studies Reader,* edited by Katrien Jacobs, Marije Janssen, and Matteo Pasquinelli, 17–30. Amsterdam: Institute of Network Cultures.

DiMicco, Joan M., and David R. Millen. 2007. "Identity Management: Multiple Presentations of Self in Facebook." The International ACM Conference on Supporting Group Work, Sanibel Island, FL.

Dottie Lux and Lil Miss Hot Mess. 2017. "Facebook's Hate-Speech Policies Censor Margnialized Users." *Wired.* Accessed August 31, 2018. https://www.wired.com/ story/facebooks-hate-speech-policies-censor-marginalized-users.

Douglas, Mary. 1991. *Purity and Danger: An Analysis of Concepts of Pollution and Taboo.* London: Routledge.

Duffy, Brooke Erin. 2017. *(Not) Getting Paid to Do What You Love: Gender, Social Media and Aspirational Work.* New Haven, CT: Yale University Press.

Duggan, Maeve. 2014. "Online Harassment." Pew Internet & American Life Project, October 22. Accessed October 31, 2016. http://www.pewinternet.org/2014/10/22/ online-harassment.

Duguay, Stefanie. 2016. "'He Has a Way Gayer Facebook than I Do': Investigating Sexual Identity Disclosure and Context Collapse on a Social Networking Site." *New Media & Society* 16 (6): 891–907.

Dwyer, Tom. 1991. "Humor, Power, and Change in Organizations." *Human Relations* 44 (1): 1–19.

Dyer-Witheford, Nick. 2015. *Cyber-Proletariat: Global Labour in the Digital Vortex.* London: Pluto Press.

eBay. 2017. Adult Items policy. Accessed April 19, 2017. http://pages.ebay.com/help/policies/adult-only.html.

Economist. 2013. "Peer-to-Peer Rental: The Rise of the Sharing Economy." *Economist,* March 9. Accessed September 15, 2015. http://www.economist.com/news/leaders/21 573104-internet-everything-hire-rise-sharing-economy.

Epstein, Cynthia Fuchs. 1992. "Tinkerbells and Pinups: The Construction and Reconstruction of Gender Boundaries at Work." In *Cultivating Differences: Symbolic Boundaries and the Making of Inequality,* edited by Michael Lamont and Marcel Fournier, 232–256. Chicago: University of Chicago Press.

European Union. 2016. Code of Conduct on Countering Illegal Hate Speech Online. Accessed May 21, 2017. http://ec.europa.eu/justice/fundamental-rights/files/hate _speech_code_of_conduct_en.pdf.

Evans, Sarah Beth, and Elyse Janish. 2015. "#INeedDiverseGames: How the Queer Backlash to GamerGate Enables Nonbinary Coalition." *QED: A Journal in GLBTQ Worldmaking* 2 (2): 125–150.

Facebook. 2017. "Community Standards." Accessed April 19, 2017. https://m.face book.com/communitystandards/?section=1.

Facebook. 2018a. "Adult Nudity and Sexual Activity." *Facebook.com.* Accessed August 31, 2018. https://www.facebook.com/communitystandards/adult_nudity _sexual_activity.

Facebook. 2018b. "Community Standards: Sexual Solicitation." *Facebook.com.* Accessed March 1, 2019. https://www.facebook.com/communitystandards/sexual _solicitation.

Falkenstein, Jun. 2011. "Machinima as a Viable Commercial Medium." *Journal of Visual Culture* 10 (1): 86–88.

Fallows, Deborah. 2005. "How Women and Men Use the Internet." Pew Internet & American Life Project, December 28. Accessed November 24, 2016. http://www .pewinternet.org/2005/12/28/how-women-and-men-use-the-internet.

Faludi, Susan. 1999. *Stiffed: The Betrayal of the American Man.* New York: HarperCollins.

Farley, Melissa. 2004. "'Bad for the Body, Bad for the Heart': Prostitution Harms Women Even if Legalized or Decriminalized." *Violence Against Women* 10 (10): 1087–1125.

Federici, Silvia. 2004. *Caliban and the Witch: Women, the Body and Primitive Accumulation*. New York: Automedia.

Feldman, Valerie. 2014. "Sex Work Politics and the Internet." In *Negotiating Sex Work: Unintended Consequences of Policy and Activism*, edited by Carisa R. Showden and Samantha Majic, 243–266. Minneapolis: University of Minnesota Press.

Ferrara, Emilio, Onur Varol, Clayton Davis, Filippo Menczer, and Alessandro Flammini. 2016. "The Rise of Social Bots." *Communciations of the Association for Computing Machinery* 59 (7): 96–104.

Filipovic, Jill. 2007. "Blogging while Female: How Internet Misogyny Parallels Real-World Harassment." *Yale Journal of Law and Feminism* 19 (1). http://digitalcommons.law.yale.edu/yjlf/vol19/iss1/10.

Fincham, Ben. 2016. *The Sociology of Fun*. Basingstoke, UK: Palgrave Macmillan.

Fink, Marty, and Quinn Miller. 2014. "Trans Media Moments: Tumblr, 2011–2013." *Television & New Media* 15 (7): 611–626.

Fisher, Kendall. 2017. "*Playboy* Is Bringing Naked Pictorials Back: 'Nudity Was Never the Problem Because Nudity Isn't a Problem.'" *E News*, February 13. Accessed May 21, 2017. http://www.eonline.com/news/829142/playboy-is-bringing-naked-pictorials-back-nudity-was-never-the-problem-because-nudity-isn-t-a-problem.

Fletcher, Gordon, and Ben Light. 2007. "Going Offline: An Exploratory Cultural Artifact Analysis of an Internet Dating Site's Development Trajectories." *International Journal of Information Management* 27 (6): 422–431.

Ford, Clementine. 2015. "Why I Reported Hotel Supervisor Michael Nolan's Abusive Comments to His Employer." *Sydney Morning Herald*, December 1. Accessed May 21, 2017. http://www.smh.com.au/lifestyle/news-and-views/opinion/clementine-ford-why-i-reported-hotel-supervisor-michael-nolans-abusive-comment-to-his-employer-20151201-glcf96.html.

Ford, Clementine. 2016. *Fight Like a Girl*. Crows Nest, Australia: Allen & Unwin.

Franke, Katherine M. 1997. "What's Wrong with Sexual Harassment?" *Stanford Law Review* 49 (4): 691–772.

Franks, Mary Anne. 2011. "Unwilling Avatars: Idealism and Discrimination in Cyberspace." *Columbia Journal on Gender and Law* 20 (2). https://cjgl.cdrs.columbia.edu/article/unwilling-avatars-idealism-and-discrimination-in-cyberspace.

Franks, Mary Anne. 2012. "Sexual Harassment 2.0." *Maryland Law Review* 71 (3): 655–704.

Friday, Nancy. 1973. *My Secret Garden: Women's Sexual Fantasies*. New York: Trident Press.

Friedman, Jane M. 1973. "The Motion Picture Rating System of 1968: A Constitutional Analysis of Self-Regulation by the Film Industry." *Columbia Law Review* 73 (2): 185–240.

Gandini, Alessandro. 2016. *The Reputation Economy: Knowledge Work in a Digital Society*. London: Palgrave Macmillan.

Gannes, Liz. 2010. "The Short and Illustrious History of Twitter #Hashtags." *Gigaom*, April 30. Accessed May 21, 2017. https://gigaom.com/2010/04/30/the-short-and-illustrious-history-of-twitter-hashtags.

Garland, Emma. 2018. "How FOSTA/SESTA Will Change the Future of Indie and Feminist Porn." *Vice*. Accessed August 31, 2018. https://www.vice.com/en_us/article/zmk89y/how-fostasesta-will-change-the-future-of-indie-and-feminist-porn.

Gaydar. 2014. "Frequently Asked Questions—Why Can't I See XXX Photos on the iPhone App?" Last modified February 10–2014. Accessed May 21, 2017. http://cpcconnectltd.kayako.com/Knowledgebase/Article/View/58/23/why-cant-i-see-xxx-photos-on-the-iphone-app.

Gehl, Robert W., Lucas Moyer-Horner, and Sara K. Yeo. 2017. "Training Computers to See Internet Pornography: Gender and Sexual Discrimination in Computer Vision Science." *Television & New Media* 18 (6): 529–547.

Gerberich, Susan G., Nancy M. Nachreiner, Andrew D. Ryan, Timothy R. Church, Patricia M. McGovern, Mindy S. Geisser, Steven J. Mongin, et al. 2011. "Violence against Educators: A Population-Based Study." *Journal of Occupational and Environmental Medicine* 53 (3): 294–302.

Gerlitz, Carolin, and Anne Helmond. 2013. "The Like Economy: Social Buttons and the Data-Intensive Web." *New Media & Society* 15 (8): 1348–1365.

Gilboa, Netta. 1996. "Elites, Lamers, Narcs and Whores: Exploring the Computer Underground." In *Wired_Women: Gender and New Realities in Cyberspace*, edited by Lynn Cherny and Reba Elizabeth Weise, 98–113. Seattle: Seal Press.

Gill, Rosalind. 2008. "Empowerment/Sexism: Figuring Female Sexual Agency in Contemporary Advertising." *Feminism & Psychology* 18 (1): 35–60.

Gill, Rosalind. 2011. "'Lift Is a Pitch': Managing Self in New Media Work." In *Managing Media Work*, edited by Mark Deuze, 249–262. London: Sage.

Gillespie, Tarleton. 2010. "The Politics of 'Platforms.'" *New Media & Society* 12 (3): 347–364.

Gillespie, Tarleton. 2013. "Tumblr, NSFW Porn Blogging, and the Challenge of Checkpoints." *Culture Digitally*, July 26. Accessed August 31, 2018. http://culturedigitally.org/2013/07/tumblr-nsfw-porn-blogging-and-the-challenge-of-checkpoints.

Ging, Debbie. 2017. "Alphas, Betas, and Incels: Theorizing the Masculinities of the Manosphere." *Men and Masculinities*: Online First. Accessed May 24, 2017. http://journals.sagepub.com/doi/10.1177/1097184X17706401.

Gladwell, Hattie. 2016. "Woman Receives Unsolicited D*ck Pic from a Total Stranger—Gives Him Taste of His Own Medicine." *Metro*, June 14. Accessed May 21, 2017. http://metro.co.uk/2016/06/14/woman-receives-unsolicited-dck-pic-from-a -total-stranger-gives-him-a-taste-of-his-own-medicine-5941696.

Goh, Gabriel. 2016. "Image Synthesis from Yahoo's open_nsfw." https://open_nsfw .gitlab.io.

Golder, Scott A., and Bernardo A. Huberman. 2006. "Usage Patterns of Collaborative Tagging Systems." *Journal of Information Science* 32 (2): 198–208.

Goode, Erich. 1999. "Sex with Informants as Deviant Behavior: An Account and Commentary." *Deviant Behavior* 20 (4): 301–324.

Google AdSense. 2014. "Advertising Policies Help—Adult Content." Last modified March 2014. Accessed May 21, 2017. https://support.google.com/adwordspolicy/ answer/4271759?hl=en&ref_topic=29265.

Google AdSense. 2018. "Advertising Policies Help—Adult Content." Accessed September 1, 2018. https://support.google.com/adspolicy/answer/6023699?hl=en&ref_topic =1626336.

Google Play. 2018. "Developer Policy Center: Restricted Content." Accessed September 1, 2018. https://play.google.com/about/restricted-content.

Google Search Help. 2018. "Autocomplete Policies". Accessed August 31, 2018. https://support.google.com/websearch/answer/7368877.

Grady, Constance. 2017. "Milo Yiannopoulos's Book Deal with Simon & Schuster, Explained." *Vox*, January 3. Accessed May 21, 2017. http://www.vox.com/culture/ 2017/1/3/14119080/milo-yiannopoulos-book-deal-simon-schuster-dangerous -boycott.

Greenfield, Patrick. 2016. "Artist Threatened with Lawsuits if She Sells Nude Donald Trump Painting." *Guardian*, April 17. Accessed May 21, 2017. https://www.theguardian .com/us-news/2016/apr/17/nude-donald-trump-painting-illma-gore-lawsuits.

Greenhouse, Steven. 2013. "Even if It Enrages Your Boss, Social Net Speech Is Protected." *New York Times*, January 21. Accessed May 21, 2017. http://www.nytimes .com/2013/01/22/technology/employers-social-media-policies-come-under -regulatory-scrutiny.html.

Gregg, Melissa. 2008. "The Normalisation of Flexible Female Labour in the Information Economy." *Feminist Media Studies* 8 (3): 285–299.

Gregg, Melissa. 2009. "Banal Bohemia Blogging from the Ivory Tower Hot-Desk." *Convergence: The International Journal of Research into New Media Technologies* 15 (4): 470–483.

Gregg, Melissa. 2011. *Work's Intimacy*. Cambridge, UK: Polity.

Griffiths, Lesley. 1998. "Humour as Resistance to Professional Dominance in Community Mental Health Teams." *Sociology of Health & Illness* 20 (6): 874–895.

Guardian. 2013. "Justine Sacco, Fired over Racist Tweet, 'Ashamed.'" December 22. Accessed May 21, 2017. https://www.theguardian.com/world/2013/dec/22/pr-exec -fired-racist-tweet-aids-africa-apology.

Gunelius, Susan. 2009. *Building Brand Value the Playboy Way*. Basingstoke, UK: Palgrave Macmillan.

Hamilton, Jill. 2015. "Meet the Woman Who Critiques Hundreds of Penises Every Day." Accessed May 21, 2017. http://www.alternet.org/meet-woman-who-critiques -hundreds-penises-every-day.

Han, Xiao. 2018. "Searching for an Online Space for Feminism? The Chinese Feminist Group Gender Watch Women's Voice and Its Changing Approaches to Online Misogyny." *Feminist Media Studies* 18 (4): 734–749.

Hardt, Michael, and Antonio Negri. 2005. *Multitude: War and Democracy in the Age of Empire*. London: Penguin.

Hardy, Simon. 2009. "The New Pornographies: Representation or Reality?" In *Mainstreaming Sex: The Sexualization of Western Culture*, edited by Feona Attwood, 3–18. London: I.B. Tauris.

Hatch, Mary Jo, and Sanford B. Ehrlich. 1993. "Spontaneous Humour as an Indicator of Paradox and Ambiguity in Organizations." *Organization Studies* 14 (4): 505–526.

Hawthorne, Susan, and Renate Klein. 1999. *Cyberfeminism: Connectivity, Culture and Critique*. Melbourne: Spinifex.

Hearn, Alison. 2010. "Structuring Feeling: Web 2.0, Online Ranking and Rating, and the Digital 'Reputation' Economy." *Ephemera: Theory & Politics in Organisation* 10 (3/4): 421–438.

Hearn, Jeff, and Wendy Parkin. 1987. *Sex at Work: The Power and Paradox of Organisation Sexuality*. New York: St. Martins Press.

Hemmasi, Masoud, Lee A. Graf, and Gail S. Russ. 1994. "Gender-Related Jokes in the Workplace: Sexual Humor or Sexual Harassment?" *Journal of Applied Social Psychology* 24 (12): 1114–1128.

Hefner, Cooper. 2017. "The New Playboy Philosophy: An Introduction." *Playboy*, February 13. Accessed May 21, 2017. http://www.playboy.com/articles/the-playboy -philosophy-2017.

Henry, Noah. 2016. "10 People Fired over Dick Pics." *Crave*, June 27. Accessed May 21, 2017. http://www.craveonline.com/mandatory/1109520-10-people-fired-over-dick -pics.

Henry, Nicola, and Anastasia Powell. 2015. "Beyond the 'Sext': Technology-Facilitated Sexual Violence and Harassment against Adult Women." *Australian & New Zealand Journal of Criminology* 48 (1): 104–118.

Hernandez, Patricia. 2015. "The People Who Make Brutal Video Porn." *Kotaku*, March 11. Accessed May 21, 2017. http://kotaku.com/the-people-who-make-brutal -video-game-porn-1690892332.

Hess, Amanda. 2014. "Why Women Aren't Welcome on the Internet." *Pacific Standard*, January 6. Accessed May 21, 2017. https://psmag.com/why-women-aren-t-welcome -on-the-internet-aa21fdbc8d6#.ni7j67azd.

Hester, Helen, Bethan Jones, and Sarah Taylor-Harman. 2015. "Giffing a Fuck: Non-narrative Pleasures in Participatory Porn Cultures and Female Fandom." *Porn Studies* 2 (4): 356–366.

Highfield, Tim. 2016. *Social Media and Everyday Politics*. Cambridge, UK: Polity.

Hochschild, Arlie R. 2003. *The Managed Heart*. Berkeley: University of California Press. Originally published 1983.

Hofer, Kristina Pia. 2014. "Pornographic Domesticity: Amateur Couple Porn, Straight Subjectivities, and Sexual Labour." *Porn Studies* 1 (4): 334–345.

Hoffman, Jenn. 2016. "The Artist behind 'Baby Dick' Trump Pic Is Now Banned from Facebook." *Motherboard*, March 8. Accessed May 21, 2017. http://motherboard.vice .com/read/the-artist-behind-baby-dick-trump-pic-is-now-banned-from-Facebook.

Holliday, Ruth, and Graham Thompson. 2001. "A Body of Work." In *Contested Bodies*, edited by John Hassard and Ruth Holliday, 117–133. London: Routledge.

Holmes, Janet, and Meredith Marra. 2002. "Having a Laugh at Work: How Humour Contributes to Workplace Culture." *Journal of Pragmatics* 34 (12): 1683–1710.

Huws, Ursula. 2014. *Labor in the Global Digital Economy: The Cybertariat Comes of Age*. New York: Monthly Review Press.

Ibrahim, Yasmin. 2012. "The Politics of Image: The Image Economy on Facebook." In *E-Politics and Organizational Implications of the Internet: Power, Influence, and Social Change*, edited by Celie Romm Livermore, 34–46. Hershey, PA: IGI Global.

Instagram. 2018. "Community Guidelines." Accessed September 1, 2018. https://help.instagram.com/477434105621119.

International Labour Office. 2012. *Improvement of National Reporting, Data Collection and Analysis of Occupational Accidents and Diseases*. Geneva: International Labour Office.

Iqbal, Mohammad, Hifshan Riesvicky, Hasma Rasjid, and Yulia Charli. 2016. "Multi Level Filtering to Classify and Block Undesirable Explicit Material in Website." Proceedings of Second International Conference on Electrical Systems, Technology and Information 2015 (ICESTI 2015).

Jane, Emma Alice. 2014a. "'Back to the Kitchen, Cunt': Speaking the Unspeakable about Online Misogyny." *Continuum* 28 (4): 558–570.

Jane, Emma A. 2014b. "'Your a Ugly, Whorish, Slut': Understanding E-Bile." *Feminist Media Studies* 14 (4): 531–546.

Jane, Emma A. 2015. "Flaming? What Flaming? The Pitfalls and Potentials of Researching Online Hostility." *Ethics and Information Technology* 17 (1): 65–87.

Jane, Emma. 2016. *Misogyny Online: A Short (and Brutish) History*. London: Sage.

Jane, Emma. 2018. "Gendered Cyberhate as Workplace Harassment and Economic Vandalism." *Feminist Media Studies* 18 (4): 575–591.

Jarrett, Kylie. 2006. "The Perfect Community: Disciplining the eBay User." In *Everyday Culture, Consumption and Collecting Online*, edited by Ken Hillis, Michael Petit, and Nathan Scott Epley, 107–121. New York: Routledge.

Jarrett, Kylie. 2014. "A Database of Intention?" In *Society of the Query Reader: Reflections on Web Search*, edited by Rene Konig and Miriam Rasch, 16–29. Amsterdam: Institute of Network Cultures.

Jarrett, Kylie. 2016. *Feminism, Labour and Digital Media: The Digital Housewife*. New York: Routledge.

Jeong, Euisol, and Jieun Lee. 2018. "We Take the Red Pill, We Confront the Dick-Trix: Online Feminist Activism and the Augmentation of Gendered Realities in South Korea." *Feminist Media Studies* 18 (4): 705–717.

JockBoy26. 2010. *The Big Book of Gaydar Uncut!* Brighton: Book Guild.

Johnson, Jennifer. 2010. "To Catch a Curious Clicker: A Social Analysis of the Online Pornography Industry." In *Everyday Pornography*, edited by Karen Boyle, 147–163. London: Routledge.

Jones, Angela. 2015. "For Black Models Scroll Down: Webcam Modeling and the Racialization of Erotic Labor." *Sexuality & Culture* 19 (4): 776–799.

Jones, Angela. 2016. "'I Get Paid to Have Orgasms': Adult Webcam Models' Negotiation of Pleasure and Danger." *Signs: Journal of Women in Culture and Society* 42 (1): 227–256.

Jones, Steven. 2010. "Horrorporn/Pornhorror: The Problematic Communities and Contexts of Online Shock Imagery." In *Porn.com: Making Sense of Online Pornography*, edited by Feona Attwood, 123–137. New York: Peter Lang.

Jonette. 2016. "Woman Brilliantly Makes Man Regret Sending Her Dick Pic." *Social News Daily*, June 15. Accessed May 21, 2017. http://socialnewsdaily.com/63590/woman-brilliantly-makes-man-regret-sending-her-dick-pics.

Kabeer, Naila, Ratna Sudarshan, and Kirsty Milward. 2013. "Introduction." In *Organizing Women Workers in the Informal Economy: Beyond the Weapons of the Weak*, edited by Naila Kabeer, Ratna Sudarshan, and Kirsty Milward, 1–48. London: Zed Books.

Karppi, Tero. 2011. "Digital Suicide and the Biopolitics of Leaving Facebook." *Transformations—Journal of Media and Culture* (20). Accessed March 19, 2014. http://www.transformationsjournal.org/journal/issue_20/article_02.shtml.

Karppi, Tero. 2014. "Disconnect.Me User Engagement and Facebook." Thesis Narrative for PhD by Publication, University of Turku.

Kaszubska, Gosia. 2016. "Not Just 'Revenge Porn'—Image-Based Abuse Hits 1 in 5 Australians." RMIT University, May 8. Accessed May 21, 2017. http://www.rmit.edu.au/news/all-news/2017/may/not-just-_revenge-porn--image-based-abuse-hits-1-in-5-australian.

Kendall, Lori. 2000. "Oh No! I'm a Nerd! Hegemonic Masculinity on an Online Forum." *Gender and Society* 14 (2): 256–274.

Kendall, Lori. 2002. *Hanging Out in the Virtual Pub: Masculinities and Relationships Online*. Berkeley: University of California Press.

Kendall, Lori. 2011. "'White and Nerdy': Computers, Race, and the Nerd Stereotype." *The Journal of Popular Culture* 44 (3): 505–524.

Kendrick, Walter M. 1996. *The Secret Museum: Pornography in Modern Culture*. 2nd ed. Berkeley: University of California Press.

Kerr, Aphra. 2017. *Global Games: Production, Circulation and Policy in the Networked Era*. New York: Routledge.

Kerr, Aphra, and John D. Kelleher. 2015. "The Recruitment of Passion and Community in the Service of Capital: Community Managers in the Digital Games Industry." *Critical Studies in Media Communication* 32 (3): 177–192.

Kipnis, Laura. 1996. *Bound and Gagged: Pornography and the Politics of Fantasy in America*. Durham, NC: Duke University Press.

Klotz, Laurence. 2005. "How (Not) to Communicate New Scientific Information: A Memoir of the Famous Brindley Lecture." *British Journal of Urology International* 96 (7): 956–957.

Know Your Meme. 2013. "NSFW." Last modified September 24. Accessed May 21, 2017. http://knowyourmeme.com/memes/nsfw.

Korn, Jenny Ungbha. 2015. "#FuckProp8: How Temporary Virtual Communities around Politics and Sexuality Pop Up, Come Out, Provide Support and Taper Off." In *Hashtag Publics: The Power and Politics of Discursive Networks*, edited by Nathan Rambukkana, 127–138. New York: Peter Lang.

Kotamraju, Nalini, and Laszio Bruszt. 2003. "Pushers, Plumbers, and Pediatricians: The Symbolism of the Pager in the United States—1975 to 1995." Paper presented at the annual meeting of the American Sociological Association, Atlanta, August 16.

Koulouris, Theodore. 2018. "Online Misogyny and the Alternative Right: Debating the Undebateable." *Feminist Media Studies* 18 (4): 750–761.

Krebs, Valdis. 2000. "Working in the Connected World." *IHRIM Journal* 4 (2): 89–91.

Kristobak, Ryan. 2017. "YouTube Really Hates Brendan Maclean's Extremely NSFW 'House of Air' Video." *Culture Trip,* February 27. Accessed September 1, 2018. https://the culturetrip.com/pacific/australia/articles/youtube-really-hates-brendan-macleans -extremely-nsfw-house-of-air-video.

Kuehn, Kathleen, and Thomas F. Corrigan. 2013. "Hope Labor: The Role of Employ-ment Prospects in Online Social Production." *The Political Economy of Communica-tion* 1 (1): 9–25.

Kuhn, Annette. 1994. *The Power of the Image: Essays on Representation and Sexuality*. London: Routledge.

Kuntsman, Adi. 2010. "Webs of Hate in Diasporic Cyberspaces: The Gaza War in the Russian-Language Blogosphere." *Media, War & Conflict* 3 (3): 299–313.

Kuo, Lily. 2018. "China's Weibo Reverses Ban on 'Homosexual' Content after Outcry." *Guardian.* Accessed August 24, 2018. https://www.theguardian.com/world/ 2018/apr/16/china-weibo-bans-homosexual-content-protest.

Lähdesmäki, Tuuli, and Tuija Saresma. 2014. "The Intersections of Sexuality and Religion in the Anti-Interculturalist Rhetoric in Finnish Internet Discussion on Muslim Homosexuals in Amsterdam." In *Building Barriers and Bridges: Interculturalism in the 21st Century*, edited by Jonathan Gourlay and Gabriele Strohschen, 35–48. Oxford: Inter-Disciplinary Press.

Lambert, Graham. 2008. "A Manual for (Im)politeness? The Impact of the FAQ in an Electronic Community of Practice." In *Impoliteness in Language: Studies on Its Interplay with Power in Theory and Practice*, edited by Derek Bousfield and Miriam A. Loucher, 281–304. New York: Mouton de Gruyter.

Landow, George P. 2006. *Hypertext 3.0: Critical Theory and New Media in an Era of Globalization*. Baltimore: Johns Hopkins University Press.

Lane, Frederick S. 2001. *Obscene Profits: Entrepreneurs of Pornography in the Cyber Age*. London: Routledge.

Laqueur, Thomas. 2003. *Solitary Sex: A Cultural History of Masturbation*. New York: Zone Books.

Lee, Murray, and Thomas Crofts. 2016. "Sexting and Young People: Surveillance and Childhood Sexuality." In *Surveillance Futures: Social and Ethical Implications of New Technologies for Children and Young People*, edited by Emmeline Taylor and Tonya Roomey, 81–92. New York: Routledge.

Lees, Matt. 2016. "What Gamergate Should Have Taught Us about the Alt-Right." *Guardian*, December 1. Accessed May 21, 2017. https://www.theguardian.com/technology/2016/dec/01/gamergate-alt-right-hate-trump.

Lenhart, Amanda, Michele Ybarra, and Myeshia Price-Feeney. 2016. "Nonconsensual Image Sharing: One in 25 Americans Has Been a Victim of 'Revenge Porn.'" Data & Society Research Institute and Centre for Innovative Public Health Research data memo, December 13. Accessed May 21, 2017. https://datasociety.net/pubs/oh/Nonconsensual_Image_Sharing_2016.pdf.

Levy, Ariel. 2006. *Female Chauvinist Pigs: Women and the Rise of Raunch Culture*. London: Simon & Schuster.

Levy, Megan. 2015. "Hotel Worker Michael Nolan Sacked over Facebook Post to Clementine Ford." *Sydney Morning Herald*, December 1. Accessed February 9, 2019. https://www.smh.com.au/national/hotel-worker-michael-nolan-sacked-over-facebook-post-to-clementine-ford-20151201-glc1y4.html.

Light, Ben. 2007. "Introducing Masculinity Studies to Information Systems Research: The Case of Gaydar." *European Journal of Information Systems* 16 (5): 658–665.

Light, Ben. 2014. *Disconnecting with Social Networking Sites*. Basingstoke, UK: Palgrave Macmillan.

Light, Ben. 2016a. "Producing Sexual Cultures and Pseudonymous Publics with Digital Networks." In *Race and Gender in Electronic Media: Challenges and Opportunities*, edited by Rebecca A. Lind, 231–246. London: Routledge.

Light, Ben. 2016b. "The Rise of Speculative Devices: Hooking Up with the Bots of Ashley Madison." *First Monday* 21 (6). Accessed September 30, 2016. https://first monday.org/ojs/index.php/fm/article/view/6426.

Light, Ben, and Elija Cassidy. 2014. "Strategies for the Suspension and Prevention of Disconnection: Rendering Disconnection as Socioeconomic Lubricant with Facebook." *New Media & Society* 16 (7): 1169–1184.

Light, Ben, Gordon Fletcher, and Alison Adam. 2008. "Gay Men, Gaydar and the Commodification of Difference." *Information Technology and People* 21 (3): 300–314.

Light, Ben, and Kathy McGrath. 2010. "Ethics and Social Networking Sites: A Disclosive Analysis of Facebook." *Information Technology and People* 23 (4): 290–311.

Light, Ben, Christian Clausner, Apostolos Antocopolous, Gordon Fletcher, and Cristina Vascilica. 2017. "The Big Content Machine—A Tool for Analysing Large Scale Qualitative and Quantitative Discussion Based Data." Salford, UK: University of Salford.

Light, Ben, Peta Mitchell, and Patrik Wikström. 2018. "Big Data, Method and the Ethics of Location: A Case Study of a Hookup App for Men Who Have Sex with Men." *Social Media + Society* 4 (2): 1–10.

Litt, Eden, and Eszter Hargittai. 2016. "The Imagined Audience on Social Network Sites." *Social Media + Society* 2 (1): 1–12.

Livia, Anna. 2002. "Public and Clandestine: Gay Men's Pseudonyms on the French Minitel." *Sexualities* 5 (2): 201–217.

Lynskey, Dorian. 2017. "The Rise and Fall of Milo Yiannopoulos: How a Shallow Actor Played the Bad Guy for Money." *Guardian*, February 21. Accessed May 21, 2017. https://www.theguardian.com/world/2017/feb/21/milo-yiannopoulos-rise-and -fall-shallow-actor-bad-guy-hate-speech.

Maddison, Stephen. 2015. "'Make Love Not Porn': Entrepreneurial Voyeurism, Agency, and Affect." In *Networked Affect*, edited by Ken Hillis, Susanna Paasonen, and Michael Petit, 151–167. Cambridge, MA: MIT Press.

Mahadeokar, Jay, and Gerry Pesavento. 2016. "Open Sourcing a Deep Learning Solution for Detecting NSFW Images." *Yahoo! Engineering*, September 30. Accessed May 21, 2017. https://yahooeng.tumblr.com/post/151148689421/open-sourcing-a -deep-learning-solution-for.

Mähönen, Erno. 2017. *Työolobarometri – Syksy 2016*. Helsinki: Työ- ja elinkeinoministeriön julkaisuja 34.

Mainiero, Lisa A. 1989. *Office Romance: Love, Power, and Sex in the Workplace*. New York: Macmillan.

Make Love Not Porn TV. 2017. Accessed April 19, 2017. https://talkabout.makelove notporn.tv.

Mäkinen, Katariina. 2016. "Uneasy Laughter: Encountering the Anti-Immigration Debate." *Qualitative Research* 16 (5): 541–556.

Manchester Evening News. 2005. "Firefighters Still Hot Stuff." April 10. Accessed May 21, 2017. http://www.manchestereveningnews.co.uk/news/local-news/firefighters-still -hot-stuff-1178578.

Mantilla, Karla. 2015. *Gendertrolling: How Misogyny Went Viral*. Westport, CT: Praeger.

Marcus, Stephen. 1964. *The Other Victorians: A Study of Sexuality and Pornography in Mid-Nineteenth-Century England*. New York: Basic Books.

Marlow, Cameron, Mor Naaman, danah boyd, and Marc Davis. 2006. "HT06, Tagging Paper, Taxonomy, Flickr, Academic Article, to Read." HYPERTEXT '06 Proceedings of the Seventeenth Conference on Hypertext and Hypermedia, Odense, August 22–25, 2006.

Martin, Phiona, and Antoni Barnard. 2013. "The Experience of Women in Male-Dominated Occupations: A Constructivist Grounded Theory Inquiry." *South African Journal of Industrial Psychology* 39 (2): 1–12.

Marwick, Alice. 2013a. "Donglegate: Why the Tech Community Hates Feminists." *Wired*, March 29. Accessed May 21, 2017. https://www.wired.com/2013/03/richards -affair-and-misogyny-in-tech.

Marwick, Alice E. 2013b. *Status Update: Celebrity, Publicity, and Branding in the Social Media Age*. New Haven, CT: Yale University Press.

Marwick, Alice E., Lindsay Blackwell, and Katherine Lo. 2016. "Best Practices for Conducting Risky Research and Protecting Yourself from Online Harassment." New York: Data & Society Research Institute. Accessed November 24, 2016. http://data society.net/output/best-practices-for-conducting-risky-research.

Marwick, Alice E., and danah boyd. 2011. "I Tweet Honestly, I Tweet Passionately: Twitter Users, Context Collapse, and the Imagined Audience." *New Media & Society* 13 (1): 114–133.

Maskeroni, Alfred. 2014. "Pornhub Erects Huge Billboard in Times Square after Long Search for a Great Non-Pornographic Ad." *Adweek*, October 2014. Accessed May 21, 2017. http://www.adweek.com/adfreak/pornhub-erects-huge-billboard-times-square -after-long-search-great-non-pornographic-ad-160632.

Massanari, Adrienne. 2017. "#Gamergate and The Fappening: How Reddit's Algorithm, Governance, and Culture Support Toxic Technocultures." *New Media & Society* 19 (3): 329–346.

Massanari, Adrienne L. 2015. *Participatory Culture, Community, and Play: Learning from Reddit*. New York: Peter Lang.

Mathes, Adam. 2004. "Folksonomies—Cooperative Classification and Communication through Shared Metadata." Accessed May 21, 2017. http://adammathes.com/academic/computer-mediated-communication/folksonomies.pdf.

Matulewicz, Kaitlyn. 2016. "Law's Gendered Subtext: The Gender Order of Restaurant Work and Making Sexual Harassment Normal." *Feminist Legal Studies* 24 (2): 127–145.

Mayer Brown. 2011. *Employee Privacy and Social Media in the Workplace—A Global Outlook*. Accessed May 21, 2017. http://www.lexology.com/library/detail.aspx?g=6d4e7f61-d797-4c36-950f-10cbb269f7d0.

McClean, Sara. 2013. "Let's Talk about Porn: An Interview." *Indypendent Reader*, July 8. Accessed May 21, 2017. https://indyreader.org/content/lets-talk-about-porn-interview.

McDonald, Paula, and Paul Thompson. 2016. "Social Media(tion) and the Reshaping of Public/Private Boundaries in Employment Relations." *International Journal of Management Reviews* 18 (1): 69-84.

McKee, Alan. 2016. "Pornography as a Creative Industry: Challenging the Exceptionalist Approach to Pornography." *Porn Studies* 3 (2): 107–119.

Messina, Chris. 2007. "Twitter Hashtags for Emergency Coordinator and Disaster Relief." *Factory Joe* blog, October 22. Accessed May 21, 2017. https://factoryjoe.com/2007/10/22/twitter-hashtags-for-emergency-coordination-and-disaster-relief.

Metz, Cade. 2015. "The Porn Business Isn't Anything Like You Think It Is." *Wired*, October 15. Accessed May 21, 2017. http://www.wired.com/2015/10/the-porn-business-isnt-anything-like-you-think-it-is/?mbid=social_fb.

Mies, Maria, Veronika Bennholdt-Thomsen, and Claudia Von Werlhof. 1988. *Women: The Last Colony*. London: Zed Books.

Miller, Brandon. 2015. "'Dude, Where's Your Face?' Self-presentation, Self-description, and Partner Preferences on a Social Networking Application for Men Who Have Sex with Men: A Content Analysis." *Sexuality & Culture* 19 (4): 637–658.

Miller-Young, Mireille. 2010. "Putting Hypersexuality to Work: Black Women and Illicit Eroticism in Pornography." *Sexualities* 13 (2): 219–235.

Milner, Ryan M. 2016. *The World Made Meme: Public Conversations and Participatory Media*. Cambridge, MA: MIT Press.

Milstein, Sarah. 2013. "I Have a Few Things to Say about Adria." *Dogs and Shoes* blog, March 24. Accessed May 21, 2017. http://www.dogsandshoes.com/2013/03/adria.html.

MindGeek. 2019. Accessed February 2, 2019. http://mindgeek.com.

Mishra, Pankaj. 2017. *The Age of Anger: A History of the Present*. New York: Picador.

misscheyenne. 2018. Misscheyenne Instagram account. Accessed September 2, 2018. https://www.instagram.com/misscheyenne.

Mnookin, Jennifer L. 1996. "Virtual(ly) Law: The Emergence of Law in LambdaMOO: Mnookin." *Journal of Computer-Mediated Communication* 2 (1). http://onlinelibrary .wiley.com/doi/10.1111/j.1083–6101.1996.tb00185.x/full.

Moloney, Mairead Eastin, and Tony P. Love. 2017. "#TheFappening: Virtual Manhood Acts in (Homo)Social Media." *Men and Masculinities*: Online First.

Montgomery, Alesia. 1999. "Everyday Use: Women, Work, and Online 'Play.'" In *Cyberfeminism: Connectivity, Critique and Creativity*, edited by Susan Hawthorne and Renate Klein, 98–118. Melbourne: Spinifex.

Monnlos, Kristina. 2014. "Inside Pornhub's Crusade to Tear Down the Taboos of Watching Sex Online: Can an Adult Site Become a Mainstream Brand?" *Adweek*, December 18. Accessed May 21, 2017. http://www.adweek.com/news/advertising -branding/inside-pornhubs-crusade-tear-down-taboos-watching-sex-online-161910.

Moore, Lane. 2015. "Why Twentysomething Women Are Obsessed with Tumblr Porn." *Cosmopolitan*, June 18. Accessed May 21, 2017. http://www.cosmopolitan .com/sex-love/news/a42078/why-twentysomething-women-are-obsessed-with -tumblr-porn.

Moore, Phoebe. 2017. *The Quantified Self in Precarity: Work, Technology and What Counts*. London: Routledge.

Moore, Phoebe, and Andrew Robinson. 2015. "The Quantified Self: What Counts in the Neoliberal Workplace." *New Media & Society* 18 (11): 2774–2792.

Morini, Cristina. 2007. "The Feminization of Labour in Cognitive Capitalism." *Feminist Review* 87 (1): 40–59.

Morris, Chris. 2012. "Meet the New King of Porn." *CNBC*, January 18. Accessed May 21, 2017. http://www.cnbc.com/id/45989405.

Moulier-Boutang, Yann. 2012. *Cognitive Capitalism*. Cambridge, UK: Polity.

Mowlabocus, Sharif. 2007. "Gay Men and the Pornification of Everyday Life." In *Pornification: Sex and Sexuality in Media Culture*, edited by Susanna Paasonen, Kaarina Nikunen, and Laura Saarenmaa, 61–71. Oxford: Berg.

Mowlabocus, Sharif. 2010a. *Gaydar Culture: Gay Men, Technology and Embodiment in the Digital Age*. Farnham, UK: Ashgate.

Mowlabocus, Sharif. 2010b. "Look at Me! Images, Validation and Cultural Currency on Gaydar." In *LGBT Identity and Online New Media*, edited by Christopher Pullen and Margaret Cooper, 201–214. London: Routledge.

Mulholland, Monique. 2013. *Young People and Pornography: Negotiating Pornification.* New York: Palgrave Macmillan.

Murphy, Dean, Patrick Rawstorne, Martin Holt, and Dermot Ryan. 2004. "Cruising and Connecting Online: The Use of Internet Chat Sites by Gay Men in Sydney and Melbourne." Sydney: National Centre in HIV Social Research, Faculty of Arts and Social Sciences, The University of New South Wales.

Murray, Susan. 2008. "Digital Images, Photo-Sharing, and Our Shifting Notions of Everyday Aesthetics." *Journal of Visual Culture* 7 (2): 147–163.

Murthy, Dhiraj. 2013. *Twitter: Social Communication in the Twitter Age*. Cambridge, UK: Polity.

Nafus, Dawn. 2012. "'Patches Don't Have Gender': What Is Not Open in Open Source Software." *New Media & Society* 14 (4): 669–683.

Nagle, Angela. 2013. "Not Quite Kicking Off Everywhere: Feminist Notes on Digital Liberation." In *Internet Research, Theory, and Practice: Perspectives from Ireland*, edited by Cathy Fowley, Claire English, and Sylvie Thouësny, 157–175. Dublin: Research-publishing.net.

Nagle, Angela. 2015. "An Investigation into Contemporary Online Anti-feminist Movements." PhD diss., Dublin City University.

Nakamura, Lisa. 2002. *Cybertypes: Race, Ethnicity, and Identity on the Internet.* London: Routledge.

Nakamura, Lisa. 2009. "Don't Hate the Player, Hate the Game: The Racialization of Labor in World of Warcraft." *Critical Studies in Media Communication* 26 (2): 128–144.

Nakamura, Lisa. 2015. "The Unwanted Labour of Social Media: Women of Colour Call Out Culture as Venture Community Management." *New Formations* 86 (86): 106–112.

Navani-Vazirani, Sonia, Davidson Solomon, Gopala Krishnan, Elsa Heylen, Aylur Kailasom Srikrishnan, Canjeevaram K. Vasudevan, and Maria L. Ekstrand. 2015. "Mobile Phones and Sex Work in South India: The Emerging Role of Mobile Phones in Condom Use by Female Sex Workers in Two Indian States." *Culture, Health & Sexuality* 17 (2): 252–265.

Neff, Gina. 2012. *Venture Labor: Work and the Burden of Risk in Innovative Industries.* Cambridge, MA: MIT Press.

Neff, Gina, Elizabeth Wissinger, and Sharon Zukin. 2005. "Entrepreneurial Labor among Cultural Producers: 'Cool' Jobs in 'Hot' Industries." *Social Semiotics* 15 (3): 307–334.

Neilson, Brett, and Ned Rossiter. 2008. "Precarity as a Political Concept, or, Fordism as Exception." *Theory, Culture & Society* 25 (7–8): 51–72.

Newitz, Annalee. 2015a. "Almost None of the Women in the Ashley Madison Database Ever Used the Site." *Gizmodo*. Accessed September 14, 2015. http://gizmodo.com/almost-none-of-the-women-in-the-ashley-madison-database-1725558944.

Newitz, Annalee. 2015b. "Ashley Madison Code Shows More Women, and More Bots." *Gizmodo*. Accessed January 20, 2016. http://gizmodo.com/ashley-madison-code-shows-more-women-and-more-bots-1727613924.

Newitz, Annalee. 2015c. "The Fembots of Ashley Madison." *Gizmodo*. Accessed January 20, 2016. http://gizmodo.com/the-fembots-of-ashley-madison-1726670394.

Newitz, Annalee. 2015d. "One Chart That Shows How Much Money Ashley Madison Made Using Bots." *Gizmodo*. Accessed January 25, 2016. http://gizmodo.com/one-chart-that-shows-how-much-money-ashley-madison-made-1727821132.

Nussbaum, Martha Craven. 2010. "Objectification and Internet Misogyny." In *The Offensive Internet*, edited by Saul Levermore and Martha Craven Nussbaum, 68–87. Cambridge, MA: Harvard University Press.

O'Riordan, Kate. 2005. "From Usenet to Gaydar: A Comment on Queer Online Community." *Siggroup Bulletin* 25 (2): 28–32.

Osgerby, Bill. 2001. *Playboys in Paradise: Masculinity, Youth and Leisure-Style in Modern America*. Oxford: Berg.

Paasonen, Susanna. 2005. *Figures of Fantasy: Internet, Women, and Cyberdiscourse*. Vol. 2. New York: Peter Lang.

Paasonen, Susanna. 2010. "Labors of Love: Netporn, Web 2.0 and the Meanings of Amateurism." *New Media & Society* 12 (8): 1297–1312.

Paasonen, Susanna. 2011. *Carnal Resonance: Affect and Online Pornography*. Cambridge, MA: MIT Press.

Paasonen, Susanna. 2015. "A Midsummer's Bonfire: Affective Intensitites of Online Debate." In *Networked Affect*, edited by Ken Hillis, Susanna Paasonen, and Michael Petit, 27–42. Cambridge, MA: MIT Press.

Paasonen, Susanna. 2016. "Fickle Focus: Distraction, Affect and the Production of Value in Social Media." *First Monday* 21 (10). https://firstmonday.org/ojs/index.php/fm/article/view/6949.

Paasonen, Susanna. 2017a. "The Collective Body of Colby Keller." *PHILE. The International Journal of Desire and Curiosity* 1: 72–78.

Paasonen, Susanna. 2017b. "Time to Celebrate the Most Disgusting Video Online." *Porn Studies* 4 (4): 463–467.

Paasonen, Susanna. 2018a. "Online Porn." In *The SAGE Handbook of Web History*, edited by Niels Brügger, Ian Milligan, and Megan Ankerson, 551–563. London: Sage.

Paasonen, Susanna. 2018b. "The Affective and Affectless Bodies of Monster Toon Porn." In *Sex in the Digital Age*, edited by Paul Nixon and Isabel Düsterhöft, 10–24. London: Routledge.

Paasonen, Susanna, Kaarina Nikunen, and Laura Saarenmaa. 2007. *Pornification: Sex and Sexuality in Media Culture*. Oxford: Berg.

Page, Allison. 2017. "'This Baby Sloth Will Inspire You to Keep Going': Capital, Labor, and the Affective Power of Cute Animal Videos." In *The Aesthetics and Affects of Cuteness*, edited by Joshua Paul Dale, Joyce Goggin, Julia Leyda, Anthony P. McIntyre, and Diane Negra, 75–94. New York: Routledge.

Palson, Charles, and Rebecca Palson. 1972. "Swinging in Wedlock." *Society* 9 (4): 28–37.

Paul, Pamela. 2005. *Pornified: How Pornography Is Transforming Our Lives, Our Relationships, and Our Families*. New York: Owl Books.

Payne, Robert. 2014. *The Promiscuity of Network Culture: Queer Theory and Digital Media*. London: Routledge.

Pfaffenberger, Bryan. 1996. "'If I Want It, It's OK': Usenet and the (Outer) Limits of Free Speech." *The Information Society* 12 (4): 365–386.

Philip, Shannon. 2018. "Youth and ICTs in a 'New' India: Exploring Changing Gendered Online Relationships among Young Urban Men and Women." *Gender & Development* 26 (2): 313–324.

Phillips, Whitney. 2015. *This Is Why We Can't Have Nice Things: Mapping the Relationship between Online Trolling and Mainstream Culture*. Cambridge, MA: MIT Press.

Pierce, Charles A., Donn Byrne, and Herman Aguinis. 1996. "Attraction in Organizations: A Model of Workplace Romance." *Journal of Organizational Behavior* 17 (1): 5–32.

Pinterest. 2018a. "Community Guidelines." Accessed September 1, 2018. https://policy.pinterest.com/en/community-guidelines.

Pinterest. 2018b. "Terms of Service." Accessed September 1, 2018. https://policy.pinterest.com/en-gb/terms-of-service.

Plant, Sadie. 1995. "The Future Looms: Weaving Women and Cybernetics." In *Cyberspace/Cyberbodies/Cyberpunk: Cultures of Technological Embodiment*, edited by Mike Featherstone and Roger Burrows, 45–64. London: Sage.

Pollert, Anna. 1981. *Girls, Wives, Factory Lives*. London: Macmillan.

Politi, Daniel. 2017. "Milo Yiannopoulos Loses CPAC Invite, Book Deal after Pedophilia Defense." *Slate*, February 20. Accessed May 21, 2017. http://www.slate.com/blogs/the_slatest/2017/02/20/cpac_under_pressure_to_cancel_milo_speech_after_pedophilia_defense.html?wpsrc=sh_all_dt_fb_top.

Pornhub. 2015. "Wankband." Accessed April 19, 2017. http://www.pornhub.com/devices/wankband.

Postigo, Hector. 2003. "Emerging Sources of Labor on the Internet: The Case of America Online Volunteers." *International Review of Social History* 48 (S11): 205–223.

Postigo, Hector. 2009. "America Online Volunteers: Lessons from an Early Coproduction Community." *International Journal of Cultural Studies* 12 (5): 451–469.

Potter, Claire. 2016. "Not Safe for Work: Why Feminist Pornography Matters." *Dissent* 63 (2): 104–114.

Powell, Chris. 1988. "A Phenomenological Analysis of Humour in Society." In *Humour in Society: Resistance and Control*, edited by Chris Powell and George E. Panton, 86–105. London: Macmillan.

Poynor, Rick. 2006. *Designing Pornotopia: Travels in Visual Culture*. New York: Princeton Architectural Press.

Preece, Jenny, Blair Nonnecke, and Dorine Andrews. 2004. "The Top Five Reasons for Lurking: Improving Community Experiences for Everyone." *Computers in Human Behavior* 20 (2): 201–223.

Preston, Jennifer. 2011. "Social Media History Becomes a New Hurdle." *New York Times*, July 20. Accessed May 21, 2017. http://www.nytimes.com/2011/07/21/technology/social-media-history-becomes-a-new-job-hurdle.html.

Race, Kane. 2015. "Speculative Pragmatism and Intimate Arrangements: Online Hook-up Devices in Gay Life." *Culture, Health & Sexuality: An International Journal for Research, Intervention and Care* 17 (4): 496–511.

Rambukkana, Nathan. 2015a. "From #RaceFail to #Ferguson: The Digital Intimacies of Race-Activist Hashtag Publics." In *Hashtag Publics: The Power and Politics of Discursive Networks*, edited by Nathan Rambukkana, 29–46. New York: Peter Lang.

Rambukkana, Nathan. 2015b. "#Introduction: Hashtags as Technosocial Events." In *Hashtag Publics: The Power and Politics of Discursive Networks*, edited by Nathan Rambukkana, 1–12. New York: Peter Lang.

Rawlinson, Kevin. 2016. "Private Messages at Work Can Be Read By European Employers." *BBC News*, January 14. Accessed May 21, 2017. http://www.bbc.com/news/technology-35301148.

Ray, Audacia. 2007. "Sex on the Open Market: Sex Workers Harness the Power of the Internet." *C'Lick Me: A Netporn Studies Reader*, edited by Katrien Jacobs, Marije Janssen, and Matteo Pasquinelli, 45–68. Amsterdam: Institute of Network Cultures.

Reagle, Joseph. 2013. "'Free as in Sexist?' Free Culture and the Gender Gap." *First Monday* 18 (1). Accessed May 24, 2017. http://firstmonday.org/ojs/index.php/fm/article/view/4291.

Reece, Robert L. 2015. "The Plight of the Black Belle Knox: Race and Webcam Modelling." *Porn Studies* 2 (2–3): 269–271.

Reddit. 2017. "Reddit Content Policy." Accessed April 19, 2017. https://www.reddit.com/help/contentpolicy.

Reid, Rebecca. 2015. "Why Women Are Turning to Tumblr for Their Secret Porn Fix." *The Telegraph*, August 13. Accessed May 21, 2017. http://www.telegraph.co.uk/women/sex/11800746/Tumblr-Gif-porn-Young-women-are-loving-it-heres-why.html.

Reist, Melinda Tankard, and Abigail Bray. 2011. *Big Porn Inc: Exposing the Harms of the Global Pornography Industry*. North Melbourne: Spinifex.

Rekart, Michael L. 2006. "Sex-Work Harm Reduction." *The Lancet* 366 (9503): 2123–2134.

Renninger, Bryce J. 2015. "'Where I Can Be Myself . . . Where I Can Speak My Mind': Networked Counterpublics in a Polymedia Environment." *New Media & Society* 17 (9): 1513–1529.

Rheingold, Howard. 1994. *The Virtual Community: Homesteading on the Electronic Frontier*. New York: HarperCollins. Originally published 1983.

Ries, Christian X., and Rainer Lienhart. 2014. "A Survey on Visual Adult Image Recognition." *Multimedia Tools and Applications* 69 (3): 661–688.

Ringrose, Jessica, and Laura Harvey. 2015. "Boobs, Back-Off, Six Packs and Bits: Mediated Body Parts, Gendered Reward, and Sexual Shame in Teens' Sexting Images." *Continuum* 29 (2): 205–217.

Ringrose, Jessica, and Emilie Lawrence. 2018. "Remixing Misandry, Manspreading, and Dick Pics: Networked Feminist Humour on Tumblr." *Feminist Media Studies* 18 (4): 686–704.

Rippin, Ann. 2011. "Ritualized Christmas Headgear or 'Pass Me the Tinsel, Mother: It's the Office Party Tonight.'" *Organization* 18 (6): 823–832.

Ritzer, George. 1993. *The McDonaldization of Society*. Thousand Oaks, CA: Pine Forge Press.

Robert Walters. 2017. "Using Social Media in the Recruitment Process." Robert Walters whitepaper. Accessed May 21, 2017. https://www.robertwalters.co.uk/hiring/hiring-advice/robert-walters-recruitment-whitepapers/using-social-media-in-the-recruitment-process.html.

Roberts, Sarah T. 2016. "Commercial Content Moderation: Digital Laborers' Dirty Work." In *The Intersectional Internet: Race, Sex, Class and Culture Online*, edited by Saifiya Umoja Noble and Brendesha M. Tynes, 147–160. New York: Peter Lang.

Rodrigues, Suzana B., and David L. Collinson. 1995. "'Having Fun'? Humour as Resistance in Brazil." *Organization Studies* 16 (5): 739–768.

Ronson, Jon. 2015. "How One Stupid Tweet Blew Up Justine Sacco's Life." *New York Times Magazine*, February 12. Accessed May 21, 2017. https://www.nytimes.com/2015/02/15/magazine/how-one-stupid-tweet-ruined-justine-saccos-life.html?_r=0.

Rose, Almie. 2016. "How One Woman Got Justice When Unsolicited Dick Pics Went Too Far." *Attn*, June 17. Accessed May 21, 2017. http://www.attn.com/stories/9269/woman-responds-to-unsolicited-dick-pics.

Rosenblat, Alex, and Luke Stark. 2016. "Algorithmic Labor and Information Asymmetries: A Case Study of Uber's Drivers." *International Journal of Communication* 10: 3758–3784.

Ross, Michael W., Beth R. Crisp, Sven-Axel Månsson, and Sarah Hawkes. 2012. "Occupational Health and Safety among Commercial Sex Workers." *Scandinavian Journal of Work, Environment and Health* 38 (2): 105–119.

Roth, Yoel. 2015. "'No Overly Suggestive Photos of Any Kind': Content Management and the Policing of Self in Gay Digital Communities." *Communication, Culture & Critique* 8 (3): 414–432.

Ryan, Paul. 2016. "# Follow: Exploring the Role of Social Media in the Online Construction of Male Sex Worker Lives in Dublin, Ireland." *Gender, Place & Culture* 23 (12): 1713–1724.

Sainty, Lane. 2015. "A Woman Has Been Banned from Facebook after Sharing the Abusive Messages She Was Sent by Men." *BuzzFeed*, June 21. Accessed May 21, 2017. https://www.buzzfeed.com/lanesainty/a-woman-has-been-banned-from-facebook-after-sharing-the-abus?utm_term=.oeaWJ3zXO#.gdm5bYXeJ.

Salmon, Felix. 2015. "How MindGeek Transformed the Economics of Porn." *Fusion*, October 10. Accessed May 21, 2017. http://fusion.net/story/212078/how-mindgeek-transformed-the-economics-of-porn.

Salter, Michael. 2016. "Privates in the Online Public: Sex(ting) and Reputation on Social Media." *New Media & Society* 18 (11): 2723–2739.

Sanders, Teela, and Rosie Campbell. 2007. "Designing Out Vulnerability, Building in Respect: Violence, Safety and Sex Work Policy." *The British Journal of Sociology* 58 (1): 1–19.

Sanders, Teela, Jane Scoular, Rosie Campbell, Jane Pitcher, and Stewart Cunningham. 2018. *Internet Sex-Work*. Basingstoke, UK: Palgrave Macmillan.

Sandoval, Greg. 2013. "The End of Kindness: Weev and the Cult of the Angry Young Man." *The Verge*, September 12. Accessed May 21, 2017. http://www.theverge.com/2013/9/12/4693710/the-end-of-kindness-weev-and-the-cult-of-the-angry-young-man.

Sara, Meghan. n.d. "'Critique My Dick Pic' Is a Body-Positive Approach to Sexting: BUST Interview (NSFW)." Accessed May 21, 2017. http://bust.com/sex/16085-critique-my-dick-pic-interview.html.

Sarracino, Carmine, and Kevin M. Scott. 2008. *The Porning of America: The Rise of Porn Culture, What It Means, and Where We Go from Here*. Boston: Beacon Press.

Scholz, Trebor. 2016. *Uberworked and Underpaid: How Workers Are Disrupting the Digital Economy*. New York: John Wiley & Sons.

Schultz, Vicki. 2003. "The Sanitized Workplace." *Yale Law Journal* 112 (87): 2061–2193.

Senft, Theresa M. 2008. *Camgirls: Celebrity and Community in the Age of Social Networks*. New York: Peter Lang.

Senft, Theresa M. 2015. "Microcelebrity and the Branded Self." In *A Companion to New Media Dynamics*, edited by John Hartley, Axel Bruns, and Jean Burgess, 346–354. Oxford: Wiley-Blackwell.

Shaw, Adrienne. 2014. "The Internet Is Full of Jerks, because the World Is Full of Jerks: What Feminist Theory Teaches Us about the Internet." *Communication and Critical/Cultural Studies* 11 (3): 273–277.

Shaw, David F. 1997. "Gay Men and Computer Communication: A Discourse of Sex and Identity in Cyberspace." In *Virtual Culture: Identity and Communication in Cybersociety*, edited by Steven G. Jones, 133–146. London: Sage.

Shaw, Frances. 2016. "'Bitch I Said Hi': The Bye Felipe Campaign and Discursive Activism in Mobile Dating Apps." *Social Media + Society* 2 (4): 1–10.

Shepherd, Tamara, Alison Harvey, Tim Jordan, Sam Srauy, and Kate Miltner. 2015. "Histories of Hating." *Social Media + Society* 1 (2): 1–10.

Shifman, Limor. 2013. *Memes in Digital Culture*. Cambridge, MA: MIT Press.

Shifman, Limor, and Menahem Blondheim. 2010. "The Medium Is the Joke: Online Humor about and by Networked Computers." *New Media & Society* 12 (8): 1348–1367.

Skeggs, Beverley. 1997. *Formations of Class and Gender: Becoming Respectable.* London: Sage.

Skeggs, Beverley. 2004. *Class, Self, Culture.* London: Routledge.

Smith, Clarissa. 2010. "Pornographication: A Discourse for All Seasons." *International Journal of Media & Cultural Politics* 6 (1): 103–108.

Smythe, Dallas. 2014. "Communications: Blindspot of Western Marxism." In *The Audience Commodity in a Digital Age*, edited by Lee McGuigan and Vincent Manzerolle, 29–53. New York: Peter Lang. Originally published 1977.

Solon, Olivia. 2017. "Facebook Is Hiring Moderators: But Is the Job Too Gruesome to Handle?" *Guardian*, May 4. Accessed May 21, 2017. https://www.theguardian.com/technology/2017/may/04/facebook-content-moderators-ptsd-psychological-dangers.

Spender, Dale. 1995. *Nattering on the Net: Women, Power and Cyberspace.* Melbourne: Spinifex.

Spišák, Sanna, and Susanna Paasonen. 2017. "Bad Education? Childhood Recollections of Pornography, Sexual Exploration, Learning and Agency in Finland." *Childhood* 24 (1): 99–112.

Squirt. 2016. "FAQ: Using Squirt with Mobile Devices." Accessed April 19, 2017. http://www.squirt.org/about/faq/mobile.

Stermer, Paul, and Melissa Burkley. 2012. "Xbox or SeXbox? An Examination of Sexualized Content in Video Games." *Social and Personality Psychology Compass* 6 (7): 525–535.

Stevenson, Alison. 2016. "This Woman Turned Her Collection of Unsolicited Dick Pics into an Art Show." *Vice*, April 15. Accessed May 21, 2017. https://www.vice.com/en_us/article/this-woman-turned-her-collection-of-unsolicited-dick-pics-into-an-art-show.

Stewart, George Lee. 1972. "On First Being a John." *Urban Life and Culture* 1 (3): 255–274.

Stone, Allucquere Rosanne. 2000. "Will the Real Body Please Stand Up?" In *The Cybercultures Reader*, edited by David Bell and Barbara M. Kennedy, 504–528. London: Routledge.

Streeter, Thomas. 2011. *The Net Effect: Romanticism, Capitalism, and the Internet.* New York: NYU Press.

Stroud, Scott R. 2014. "The Dark Side of the Online Self: A Pragmatist Critique of the Growing Plague of Revenge Porn." *Journal of Mass Media Ethics* 29 (3): 168–183.

Stuart, Hunter. 2013. "Pornhub Super Bowl Commercial Rejected by CBS, Won't Air Despite SWF Content." *Huffington Post*, January 30. Accessed May 21, 2017. http://www.huffingtonpost.com/2013/01/30/pornhub-super-bowl-commercial-rejected _n_2577912.html.

Studio FOW. 2014. "Lara in Trouble." Last modified February 6, 2013. Accessed May 21, 2017. http://www.studiofow.com/movie/2.

Summers, Nick. 2009. "Facebook's 'Porn Cops' Are Key to Its Growth." *Newsweek*, April 30. Accessed May 21, 2017. http://www.newsweek.com/facebooks-porn-cops -are-key-its-growth-77055.

Sundén, Jenny, and Susanna Paasonen. 2018. "Shameless Hags and Tolerance Whores: Intersectionality and Affective Circuits of Online Hate." *Feminist Media Studies* 18 (4): 643–656.

Sutton, Laurel A. 1996. "Cocktails and Thumbtacks in the Old West: What Would Emily Post Say?" In *Wired_Women: Gender and New Realities in Cyberspace*, edited by Lynn Cherny and Reba Elizabeth Weise, 169–187. Seattle: Seal Press

Tarrant, Shira. 2016. *The Pornography Industry: What Everyone Needs to Know*. Oxford: Oxford University Press.

Terranova, Tiziana. 2000. "Free Labor: Producing Culture for the Digital Economy." *Social Text* 18 (2): 33–58.

Terranova, Tiziana. 2004. *Network Culture: Politics for the Information Age*. London: Pluto Press.

Thomae, Manuela, and Afroditi Pina. 2015. "Sexist Humor and Social Identity: The Role of Sexist Humor in Men's In-group Cohesion, Sexual Harassment, Rape Proclivity, and Victim Blame." *Humor* 28 (2): 187–204.

Tiidenberg, Katrin. 2014. "Bringing Sexy Back: Reclaiming the Body Aesthetic via Self-shooting." *Cyberpsychology: Journal of Psychosocial Research on Cyberspace* 8 (1). http://www.cyberpsychology.eu/view.php?cisloclanku=2014021701.

Tiidenberg, Katrin. 2016. "Boundaries and Conflict in a NSFW Community on Tumblr: The Meanings and Uses of Selfies." *New Media & Society* 18 (8): 1563–1578.

Tiidenberg, Katrin. n.d. "NSFW as Method." *Future Making*. Accessed August 31, 2018. https://futuremaking.space/skagen-institute/nsfw-as-method.

Tiidenberg, Katrin, and Edgar Gómez Cruz. 2015. "Selfies, Image and the Re-making of the Body." *Body & Society* 21 (4): 77–102.

Till, Chris. 2014. "Exercise as Labour: Quantified Self and the Transformation of Exercise into Labour." *Societies* 4 (3): 446–462.

Titley, Gavan. 2014. "No Apologies for Cross-posting: European Trans-media Space and the Digital Circuitries of Racism." *Crossings: Journal of Migration & Culture* 5 (1): 41–55.

Truong, Alice. 2013. "Advertising on Porn Sites Works, Just Ask Eat24." *Fast Company*, December 9. Accessed May 21, 2017. https://www.fastcompany.com/3017329/advertising-on-porn-sites-works-just-ask-eat24.

Trustify. 2017. Accessed May 11, 2017. https://www.trustify.info/landing/catch-a-cheating-spouse-ashley-madison.

Tufecki, Zeynep. 2014. "No, Nate, Brogrammers May Not Be Macho, but That's Not All There Is to It." *The Message*, March 18. Accessed May 21, 2017. https://medium.com/message/no-nate-brogrammers-may-not-be-macho-but-thats-not-all-there-is-to-it-2f1fe84c5c9b#.9hhs9m5dm.

Tumblr. 2018. "Adult Content." Accessed March 1, 2019. https://tumblr.zendesk.com/hc/en-us/articles/231885248-Adult-content.

Turkle, Sherry. 1995. *Life on the Screen*: London: Weidenfeld & Nicolson.

Tyler, Imogen. 2006. "Chav Scum: The Filthy Politics of Social Class." *M/C Journal* 9 (5). http://www.journal.media-culture.org.au/0610/09-tyler.php.

van der Nagel, Emily. 2016. "Harassment and High Fives: The Many Victims of Shaming Culture." *Medium*, October 10. Accessed May 25, 2017. https://medium.com/@emily.vdn/harassment-and-high-fives-the-many-victims-of-shaming-culture-c83437eed7f2#.4vvhgial4.

van Dijck, José. 2009. "Users Like You? Theorizing Agency in User-Generated Content." *Media, Culture and Society* 31 (1): 41–58.

van Dijck, José. 2013. *The Culture of Connectivity: A Critical History of Social Media*. Oxford: Oxford University Press.

van Doorn, Niels. 2010. "Keeping It Real: User-Generated Pornography, Gender Reification, and Visual Pleasure." *Convergence: The International Journal of Research into New Media Technologies* 16 (4): 411–430.

van House, Nancy A. 2009. "Collocated Photo Sharing, Story-Telling, and the Performance of Self." *International Journal of Human-Computer Studies* 67 (12): 1073–1086.

van Hoye, Greet, Edwin A. J. van Hooft, and Filip Lievens. 2009. "Networking as a Job Search Behaviour: A Social Network Perspective." *Journal of Occupational & Organizational Psychology* 82 (3): 661–682.

van Maanen, John. 1991. "The Smile Factory: Work at Disneyland." In *Reframing Organizational Culture*, edited by Peter J. Frost, Larry F. Moore, Meryl R. Louis, Craig C. Lunberg, and Joanne Martin, 58–76. Newbury Park, CA: Sage.

Verduin, Kathleen. 1983. "Our Cursed Natures: Sexuality and the Puritan Conscience." *The New England Quarterly* 56 (2): 220–237.

Vitis, Laura, and Fairleigh Gilmour. 2016. "Dick Pics on Blast: A Woman's Resistance to Online Sexual Harassment Using Humour, Art and Instagram." *Crime, Media, Culture*: Online First. http://journals.sagepub.com/doi/abs/10.1177/1741659016652445.

Voon, Clare (2016). "Drawing of Donald Trump with a Micropenis Might Get Artist Banned for Life from Facebook #NSFW." *Hyperallergic*, March 11. Accessed May 21, 2017. http://hyperallergic.com/282740/drawing-of-donald-trump-with-a-micropenis-might-get-artist-banned-for-life-from-facebook-nsfw.

Wajcman, Judy. 1991. *Feminism Confronts Technology*. Oxford: Polity Press.

Wakeford, Nina. 2000. "Networking Women and Grrrls with Information/Communication Technology: Surfing Tales of the World Wide Web." In *The Cybercultures Reader*, edited by David Bell and Barbara M. Kennedy, 350–359. London: Routledge. Originally published 1997.

Waling, Andrea, and Tinonee Pym. 2019. "'C'mon, No One Wants a Dick Pic': Exploring the Cultural Framings of the 'Dick Pic' in Contemporary Online Publics." *Journal of Gender Studies* 28 (1): 70–85.

Walker, Jill. 2005. "Feral Hypertext: When Hypertext Literature Escapes Control." Proceedings of the Sixteenth ACM Conference on Hypertext and Hypermedia.

Ward, Jane. 2015. *Not Gay: Sex between Straight White Men*. New York: NYU Press.

Warner, Michael. 2000. *The Trouble with Normal Sex: Sex, Politics, and the Ethics of Queer Life*. Cambridge, MA: Harvard University Press.

Waterloo, Lucy. 2015. "'I Lost My Job, My Reputation and I'm Not Able to Date Anymore': Former PR Worker Reveals How She Destroyed Her Life One Year after Sending 'Racist' Tweet before Trip to Africa." *Mail Online*, February 16. Accessed May 21, 2017. http://www.dailymail.co.uk/femail/article-2955322/Justine-Sacco-reveals-destroyed-life-racist-tweet-trip-Africa.html.

Watson, Tony. 1994. *In Search of Management: Culture, Chaos and Control in Management Work*. London: Routledge.

Watts, Jacqueline. 2007. "Can't Take a Joke? Humour as Resistance, Refuge and Exclusion in a Highly Gendered Workplace." *Feminism & Psychology* 17 (2): 259–266.

Webster, Juliet. 1996. *Shaping Women's Work: Gender, Employment and Information Technology*. London: Routledge.

Wei, Chia, Susan G. Gerberich, Bruce H. Alexander, Andy D. Ryan, Nancy M. Nachreiner, and Steve J. Mongin. 2013. "Work-Related Violence against Educators in

Minnesota: Rates and Risks Based on Hours Exposed." *Journal of Safety Research* 44: 73–85.

Weitzer, Ronald. 2009. "Sociology of Sex Work." *Annual Review of Sociology* 35: 213–234.

Westwood, Sallie. 1984. *All Day, Every Day*. London: Pluto Press.

Wichowski, Alexis. 2009. "Survival of the Fittest Tag: Folksonomies, Findability, and the Evolution of Information Organization." *First Monday* 14 (5). http://firstmonday .org/article/viewArticle/2447/2175.

Williams, Christine L., Patti A. Giuffre, and Kirsten Dellinger. 1999. "Sexuality in the Workplace: Organizational Control, Sexual Harassment, and the Pursuit of Pleasure." *Annual Review of Sociology* 25 (1): 73–93.

Williams, Linda. 2004. "Porn Studies: Proliferating Pornographies On/Scene: An Introduction." In *Porn Studies*, edited by Linda Williams, 1–23. Durham, NC: Duke University Press.

Williams, Raymond. 1977. *Marxism and Literature*. Oxford: Oxford University Press.

Wittel, Andreas. 2001. "Toward a Network Sociality." *Theory, Culture and Society* 18 (6): 51–76.

Worth of the Web. 2018. "How Much Is Pornhub.com Worth?" https://www.worth ofweb.com/website-value/pornhub.com.

Yang, Ni, and Daniel Linz. 1990. "Movie Ratings and the Content of Adult Videos: The Sex–Violence Ratio." *Journal of Communication* 40 (2): 28–42.

Zandt, Deanna. 2013. "Why Asking What Adria Richards Could Have Done Differently Is the Wrong Question." *Forbes*, March 22. Accessed May 21, 2017. http:// www.forbes.com/sites/deannazandt/2013/03/22/why-asking-what-adria-richards -could-have-done-differently-is-the-wrong-question/#1fcdf7403768.

Zappavigna, Michele. 2011. "Ambient Affiliation: A Linguistic Perspective on Twitter." *New Media & Society* 13 (5): 788–806.

Zetter, K. 2015. "Hackers Finally Post Stolen Ashley Madison Data." *Wired.com*. Accessed January 25, 2016. http://www.wired.com/2015/08/happened-hackers -posted-stolen-ashley-madison-data.

Zijderveld, Anton C. 1968. "Jokes and Their Relation to Social Reality." *Social Research* 35: 286–311.

Index